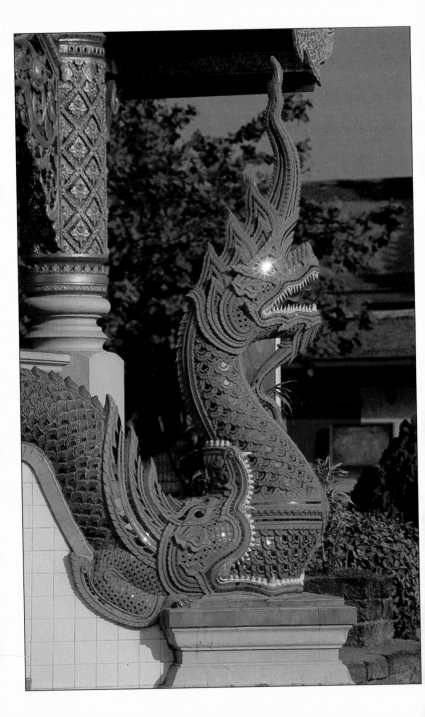

THAILAND

First Edition
1991

TABLE OF CONTENTS

INTO THE DEEP SOUTH

SPECIAL INTERESTS

FEATURES

GUIDELINES

LIST OF MAPS

Please note: in some cases the spelling of the names on the maps is not the same as in the text, because the spelling on the maps is according to UN guidelines, whereas the usual English spelling is used in the text.

THAILAND
©Nelles Verlag GmbH, München 45
  All rights reserved
  ISBN 3-88618-364-5

First Edition 1991
Co-publisher for U.K.:
Robertson McCarta, London
ISBN 1-85365-183-4 (for U.K.)

Publisher:	Günter Nelles	**DTP-Exposure:**	Printshop Schimann,
Chief Editor:	Dr. Heinz Vestner		Pfaffenhofen
Project Editor:	Hardy Stockmann	**Color**	
Cartography:	Nelles Verlag GmbH,	**Separation:**	Priegnitz, München
(in charge)	Dipl.Ing. C. Heydeck	**Printed by:**	Gorenjski Tisk, Kranj,
	Dipl.Ing. C.P. Waider		Yugoslavia

                                                                              - 01 -

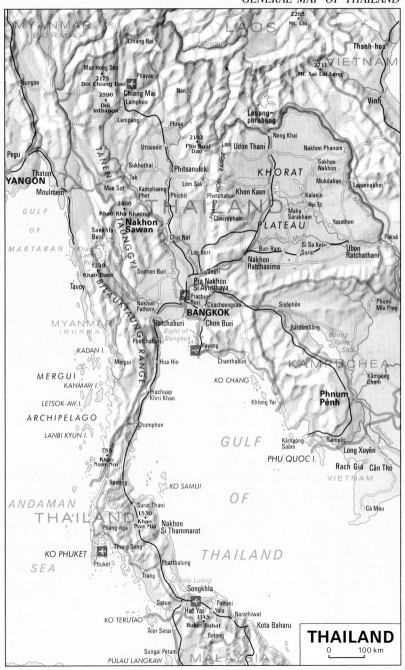

PORTRAIT
OF A FABLED LAND

Several million dollars' worth of sophisticated aviation engineering, sporting the THAI logo, sits on the tarmac at Bangkok airport. Raised on a platform, an elderly, saffron-robed Buddhist monk stands nose to nose with this latest jumbo from Boeing as he performs a ritual as old as the aircraft is young.

It's an odd, arresting scene that takes place every time Thailand's national carrier inaugurates a new aircraft. Only few people witness it, if only because it usually takes place early in the morning at a time officially pronounced auspicious. Yet this remarkable ceremony encapsulates the country's quintessential attraction.

Thailand is a glorious paradox. It is a fabled land where an ancient culture is preserved to a remarkable degree. At the same time, it enthusiastically embraces the dynamic development of the modern world.

Known as Siam until 1939, the kingdom was founded in the thirteenth century and the pattern of its cultural fabric has remained constant through 700 years of independence. The strongest threads in that fabric are Buddhism, the national religion, and the monarchy. The spirit of the religion is almost tangible as Buddhism is practiced as well as professed by 94 per cent of the 50-million population, while the monarchy, constitutional since 1932, is as deeply revered today as it was in the past when kings were literally "Lords of Life".

Previous pages: Buddha in Sukhothai style. Naga the Snake King. The Wat Haripoonchai in Lamphun. The Jungle in the Khao Yai National Park. Painting on parasols. Left: Napping in the cool shadow of a temple.

The lasting impact of these two cohesive forces is readily apparent and pervades the entire nation to produce an indelible stamp of "Thainess". Cityscapes are characterized by the gilded spires of awe-inspiring Buddhist temples, while pageantry and royal ceremonial touch the lives of the people.

The present monarch, His Majesty King Bhumibol Adulyadej, Rama IX, maintains a high profile. He continues to preside over ancient rites, like the annual Ploughing Ceremony, as well as overseeing rural development projects to display the relevance and effectiveness of enlightened modern kingship.

Buddhism and the monarchy are but the more obvious manifestations of continuing traditions and traditional values which in myriad ways distinguish daily life to give the impression of an ancient land that is different.

Together with this, the Thais miraculously combine resilience with adaptability and flexibility to plant themselves firmly in the twentieth century, blending a respect for the old with a zest for the new.

Paradoxical Bangkok

Bangkok, established as the capital in 1782, is the epitome of Thailand's remarkable paradox. More than anywhere else in the country it expresses that adherence to tradition coupled with a vibrant involvement with progress.

It stands on the Chao Phraya river, a few kilometers upstream from its outflow into the Gulf of Thailand, and sprawls monstrously across a flat alluvial plain. It is the capital in every sense of the word. It is where the Royal Family resides, it is the seat of government and administration, and it is the focal point for all major industrial, commercial and financial activity. It is the country's principal gateway, main port and home to one tenth of the kingdom's population.

15

Such an all-important role is reflected in the name which is not, strictly speaking, Bangkok. Translating as "Village of the Wild Plum", this was the title before capital status was conferred, and is today used only by foreigners. When it became the Kingdom's power center it was renamed Krung Thep, "City of Angels". Actually this is only the first of a whole string of illustrious titles which earns the capital a mention in the *Guinness Book of Records* as the world's longest place name. You will never hear Thais call their capital "Bangkok". To them it is always Krung Thep, the spiritual and symbolic, as well as physical heart of the nation.

At first glance Bangkok is an unprepossessing city. The skyline is dominated by the thrusting highrise blocks of offices, condominiums, luxury hotels and tinselled department stores. In between are rows of drab shophouses, while the streets are clogged with unbelievable

Above: Bangkok, where skyscrapers cast their long shadows on an ancient city.

traffic jams. You would scarcely credit that it was once a waterborne city – the "Venice of the East" – and formerly canals were the main highways. The first roads date from the 1860s and since then the waterways have nearly all been filled in to make way for wheeled traffic. Only a few canals still exist to remind you of a more leisurely – and quieter – era.

Air pollution and the constant heat – in the 90s in the summer and not appreciably less in the inappropriately titled cool season – combines with the monstrous traffic to produce an air of impending chaos. None of this helps the first-time visitor's confusion at the lack of a definable downtown area.

It takes only a short while, however, to become captivated by the spell the city casts. There is an uncanny charm about the place that wins the heart and draws you irresistibly to an appreciation of what is the Orient's most exotic capital.

Joyfully exuberant, the city embraces latter-day and largely Western-inspired development. Hence the profusion of shining new office towers and apartment blocks. Yet, incredibly, the schizophrenic post-modern architecture does not obliterate monuments to traditional glories. In the soaring roofs and tapering spires of the Grand Palace (the official royal residence until the present reign), the Temple of the Emerald Buddha, the Temple of Dawn and the rest of the city's more than 400 Buddhist temples, you are presented with images of medieval Oriental wonder, the very stuff of Eastern fairytales. And contained within Bangkok's monuments are masterpieces of sculpture, mural painting and decorative art inspired by religious devotion.

Nor is the influence of the past limited to static sights. It pervades daily life. Files of saffron-robed monks making their early morning alms round, for example, present an image unaltered in essentials by the passing of time. Today's backdrop of highrise buildings only adds wonder to the timeless scene, while the city draws definition from it.

Through Bangkok the Chao Phraya snakes its way in a series of broad curves. It was once the nation's main artery and strings of heavy-laden barges still ply this historic waterway. The city originally rose up on its banks but expansion prompted by the forging of international trade links in the mid-19th century led inevitably away from the river. Now there is a trend to return to that original focal point and several modern hotels have chosen riverfront locations to become neighbors of the world-famous Oriental Hotel where Joseph Conrad once dined.

Gradually the city reveals itself to the visitor not as the monotonous urban pancake it first appears, but as an intriguing amalgam of distinct quarters characterized by scene and mood. The old royal city, centered on the Grand Palace, presents a very different aspect to what can be termed the new royal city in the Dusit area. Here the Marble Temple, a superb example of turn-of-the-century religious architecture, and Chitralada Palace, the modern royal residence, display a fresh direction in Thai styles.

Dusit, uncluttered and with tree-lined streets, is comparatively untouched by the recent building boom and as such presents a further contrast when compared to the built-up business and tourist areas around Silom and Sukhumvit roads. The bustle of these quarters is different again from the air of commercial frenzy found in Chinatown centered on Yawaraj and Charoenkrung (New) roads. Famous for its gold merchants and sellers of Chinese medicines, among other ethnic commodities, the district has changed little over the years other than somehow managing to cram in more shops and stalls.

The Chinese have, in fact, contributed enormously to Bangkok's development, firstly as immigrant labor in the early 19th century and then, as the city became a center of international trade, as middlemen and entrepreneurs. Unlike in many other cities, however, the Chinese are totally integrated, their cultural influence adding diversity but not social division.

As culturally and historically fascinating as Bangkok is, it cannot be denied that it is also a sybaritic city. Food is abundant and available from kerbside noodle stalls and up through the whole dining gamut to posh expensive restaurants. One place even chalks up another *Guinness Book of Records* entry, the world's largest open air dining area, 2.5 hectares and space for 3,000 diners. The deliciously varied spicy Thai cooking is a gourmet's discovery, though virtually every other national cuisine worthy of the name is to be found in the city.

Shopping is a further city delight and in recent years smart plazas, malls and department stores have mushroomed to augment the facilities provided by markets and street stalls. Best buys include silks, gems and jewelry (Bangkok is a world center for colored gemstones), tailor-made clothing, leathergoods, an-

tiques and an enormous array of handicrafts in teakwood, ceramic, bronze and other traditional materials.

The dedicated bargain-hunter should not be blinded to the fact that old Bangkok markets are sightseeing attractions in their own right. At fresh produce centers, like Bangrak Market or Pak Klong Talaat, Bangkok's answer to London's now vanished Covent Garden, you can see the colorful and fragrant abundance of fresh fruit, vegetables and flowers, including fabulous orchids, that the fertile land produces.

For entertainment, Bangkok has a nightlife scene that has achieved near legendary fame. There are massage parlors with literally hundreds of gorgeous masseuses arrayed behind one-way glass walls for the customers' selection. Just as salacious are the go-go bars of the renowned Patpong area where scantily-clad girls dance to the latest pop sounds.

Above: Even a Buddhist novice has to use the telephone now and then.

The bawdy side of Bangkok tends to get a bad press, though, surprisingly, what it offers is essentially good-natured fun, lacking in that sense of pathos and the sordid which typifies the red light districts of Western cities.

Though its reputation may lead you to think otherwise, the city does not cater exclusively to the single male. Entertainment possibilities are more varied than one imagines, and range from displays of the classical masked *khon* dance to the excitement of gigantic discos equipped with the latest light and sound systems.

Especially popular sporting entertainment is provided by Thai kick-boxing. This traditional sport, once a martial art, is a thrilling affair in which the protagonists fight with feet, knees and elbows as well as gloved fists. A good deal of amusement is also generated by the crowd of local aficionados who yell impassioned advice mixed with screams of abuse. It is said that Thai-style boxing is becoming commercialized, but there are still hundreds of authentic matches.

18

Whatever changes Bangkok is undergoing (and in physical terms they are enormous), one thing never changes – the essential "Thainess" of the place. It is this which ultimately makes sense of the paradox, the juxtaposition of old and new, of classical forms and Western façades, of the noodle vendor standing in the shadow of Big Mac. As Alec Waugh has written: "Bangkok has been loved because it is an expression of the Thais themselves, of their lightheartedness, their love of beauty, their reverence for tradition, their sense of freedom, their extravagance, their devotion to their creed – to characteristics that are constant and continuing in themselves."

This is true and ultimately Bangkok derives its unique ambience from the people. Their fun-loving nature and propensity for *sanuk* – having a good time – is contagious. Above all else they possess a rare tolerance and there is a very real sense of freedom about life in the capital. It may appear at times hectic, chaotic, even downright frustrating, yet what finally comes across is the city's good natured acceptance of life with all its idiosyncrasies.

Natural Variety

Like other capital cities Bangkok is an exaggeration, a larger-than-life manifestation of a nation's traits. Yet there is a cohesiveness through continuity which indelibly stamps the nation as a whole to impart that crucial element of "Thainess" and a sense of freedom.

The exotic character of Thailand which springs from the preservation of its cultural heritage is complemented and enhanced by natural attributes. There is an amazing topographical variety and nature had been generous with her gifts.

Roughly the size of France, Thailand covers an area of 514,000 sq km and is bordered by Burma on the west, Laos in the north and northeast, Cambodia in the east and Malaysia in the south. The climate is tropical with three seasons: hot from March to May, rainy from June to

19

October, and cool from November through February.

Watered by the annual rains, the land in most parts of the country is extremely fertile and, despite modern developments, Thailand is still largely an agricultural nation. It is the world's fifth largest food exporter and some 75 per cent of the 50-plus million population derives its livelihood from the land in one way or another. The staple crop is rice which is a major export item along with tapioca, pineapples and other produce.

Lush vegetation abounds and there are many species of trees, shrubs and flowers, perhaps most notable among the latter being the nearly 1,000 different varieties of orchids. Thailand's fauna includes elephants, tigers, leopards, snakes, monkeys and several hundreds of species of birds and butterflies. Sadly, as in many other places, the numbers of the larger

Above: Landscape near the Burmese border. Right: An Akha woman in the north.

wild animals, elephants and tigers in particular, have declined drastically in recent decades.

An alarming percentage of forest cover has also been destroyed and there is now a rather belated ban on logging. This scenario is sadly only too common in the world today, although there is increasing concern about the environment and the need for conservation. Much has been lost, but Thailand nonetheless remains a place of considerable and varied scenic beauty.

Topographically the country divides into four distinct areas, each with an individual charm and interest. Stretching north of Bangkok are the Central Plains, a flat patchwork of emerald green paddies watered by the Chao Phraya river, Thailand's Nile. It is here that much of the nation's early history and culture evolved. Nakhon Pathom, 56 km west of the capital, is widely believed to have been the earliest center of Buddhist learning in the area. The ruins of Ayutthaya, Bangkok's predecessor, stand on the

banks of the river, while the site of the nation's first capital, Sukhothai, is on the northern edge of the plains.

Beyond Sukhothai lies Thailand's northern region, an area of forest-clad mountains, distant offshoots of the Himalayas among which is the country's highest peak, Doi Inthanon, which rises to 2,565 m. Suddenly the flat plains give way to breathtaking landscapes, rolling hills hiding valleys within their folds that could be contenders for Shangri-La. There are rivers, caves and waterfalls, but above all the north is colored by various distinct groups of hilltribes.

These are people of separate ethnic origin who maintain independent lifestyles, cut off from mainstream society. They are semi-nomadic, surviving by slash-and-burn agriculture and, for some of them, by the cultivation of the opium poppy, for this is the "Golden Triangle", source of much of the world's heroin. The tribespeople have traditionally used opium as a general cure-all medicine, though they are poor and it is the wily

drug traffickers, the opium warlords, who reap the profits of their labor.

There are an estimated 250,000 to 500,000 tribespeople living in the north, split amongst seven major groups: Karen, Akha, Lahu, Lawa, Lisu, Meo and Yao. All have distinct cultures, languages and religious beliefs (mostly animistic). Their most obvious distinction, however, is their dress, each tribe having its own traditional style of colorful costume, commonly adorned by hand-crafted chunky silver jewelry. They are hospitable people and trekking to their villages has become a popular tourist activity. Inevitably such contact is diluting their culture and their lifestyles are changing, as they must. Moreover various government and royal projects are being carried out to raise their living standards and, through the introduction of substitute cash crops, to eradicate poppy cultivation. Success in the latter has been considerable in some areas.

The north is also teak country, or rather was as today most of the forests have been destroyed through over-exploitation, illegal logging and the slash-and-burn techniques of the hilltribes. Nonetheless, that loveable creature the elephant, for long man's most efficient aid in the extraction of teak, remains a typical figure in the landscape.

The capital of the north is Chiang Mai. It is Thailand's second city, though considerably smaller than Bangkok. Charmingly located on the banks of the Ping river, it is an historic city, founded in the late 13th century. Accordingly it presents a very different picture from the much younger Bangkok. Many of its ancient temples, all of distinct northern architecture, are several hundred years old. Typical landmarks such as Wat Chiang Man, Wat Phra Singh and Wat Chedi Luang, were first built in the 13th, 14th and early 15th centuries respectively. The atmosphere of the place also has its own charm. The people are easygoing and display a quiet pride in their separate heritage. They are also fun-loving and, for example, the Songkran New Year celebrations, a one-day affair in Bangkok, last nearly a week in Chiang Mai.

The capital of the north is also famous as a handicraft center and is arguably the world's largest center for cottage industries. Craftsmen, using skills that have been passed down from generation to generation, produce silverware, woodcarving, celadon pottery, lacquerware, paper umbrellas and other attractive artifacts that are popular buys. This makes Chiang Mai a shopper's paradise, though it is intriguing to simply visit the workshops and see the crafts in the making.

The northeast region – Isarn, as the Thais call it – is a vast semi-arid plateau bordering on Laos and Cambodia. It is the poorest part of the country and in many ways the most traditional. Besides a few large towns, the area is intensely rural and the agricultural communities struggle to make a living from the low-yielding soil.

In spite of, or perhaps because of, a relatively low living standard, manifestations of a timeless culture – music, folk dances, legends, local dialects and, above all, festivals – are better preserved in the northeast than elsewhere in the country. Annual celebrations, like the rain-invoking Rocket Festival at Yasothon or the Candle Festival at Ubon Ratchathani, are genuine expressions of folk culture, occasions for enormous fun and a welcome break from the toil of tending the land. The visitor may join in but the events are not maintained as mere tourist attractions.

Thailand's fourth topographical area, comprising the east coast and southern peninsula, affords very different attractions from the rest of the country. The 2480 km of coastline are generously provided with superb sandy beaches, sheltered bays and idyllic offshore islands. In the hinterland are hills, rain forests and rubber plantations, and the culture of the deep south is noticeably influenced by the proximity of Muslim Malaysia.

For the visitor the lure of the east coast and the south is the promise of sun, sea and sand at a tropical resort. As with everything else in Thailand, variety is the spice of life and while all the beach resorts offer the classic ingredients for a fun-filled vacation by the sea, no two places are quite the same.

Pattaya on the east coast of the Gulf of Thailand, a two-hour drive from Bangkok, is the most developed of the resort areas. It has a sheltered bay and a majestically curving beach and just a couple of decades ago was an insignificant fishing village. Then came a building boom of mounting frenzy which saw the sprouting of luxury resort hotels and all the amenities to turn the place into an international playground. Brash, bawdy, bold and alive with activity, it now has no parallel.

Right: Life goes easy on the beach at Jomthien.

With remarkable self-assurance it presents a kaleidoscope of not only every conceivable activity to get you on, in, above and below the water, but also of land-based sports, go-go bars, massage parlors, restaurants, nightclubs, discos and shops to ensure there is never a dull moment day or night. It is not to everyone's taste, though it is most certainly a phenomenon that needs be seen to be believed.

Across the Gulf on the west shore, Hua Hin stands in marked contrast to its shameless sister over the water. It is Thailand's oldest resort, first coming to prominence in the 1920s when King Rama VI established a summer palace there. A vogue was created and the seaside town became the resort for Bangkok society. The summer palace remains and the present Royal Family continues to reside there for a spell every year, King Bhumibol being an amazingly keen and accomplished yachtsman.

In the last few years foreigners have been rediscovering Hua Hin and new deluxe hotels, as well as a faithfully restored property dating from the 1920s, offer modern amenities. Unlike Pattaya, however, the town is proud of its royal associations and prefers to maintain a traditional ambience, rather than attempt any imitation of the international scene. If offers watersports, though the main accent is decidedly on peace, recreation and relaxation.

Among the many beaches and islands of the deep south, Phuket island, an hour's flight from Bangkok, is the pearl of Thailand's tropical resorts. Attached to the mainland only by a causeway, Phuket is roughly the same size as Singapore, though there the comparison ends. By contrast, the population is small, the landscape is one of low hills in varied hues of green, coconut groves, rubber plantations and a coastline dotted with a dozen spectacular beaches.

Traditional occupations are tin mining and, more recently, the cultivation of pearls. Today, however, the boom is in the tourism industry as sun-worshipping

23

visitors flock to escape a cold and grey winter at home.

They are not disappointed. Bathed in year-round sunshine there are uncluttered beaches of fine white sand, each one with a charm and character of its own and separated from its neighbors by attractive headlands and backdrops of wooded hills. Lapping the shore are the sparkling turquoise waters of the Andaman Sea. To these gifts of nature man has added luxury resort hotels.

Spectacular though Phuket is, it is not alone in vying for attention. Nearby is Phang Nga Bay which presents a seascape of fantastic limestone outcrops rising from the water. Some are sheer, others are humped or jagged, and all are strange and hauntingly beautiful. Such is the exotic picture they present that one island was used as a location for the 007-movie, *The Man with the Golden Gun.*

Above: A Thai speciality – the all-duty long-tail boat. Right: One of the "many smiles" on the face of a young Thai.

Another boat excursion leads to the twin Phi Phi islands of pristine beauty where the attraction of a lovely beach is dramatized by sheer 300-m cliffs. It is here that intrepid climbers risk life and limb to collect birds' nests used in the soup so highly prized by Chinese gourmets. Beyond are more dreamlike tropical islands, most uninhabited.

These islands are part of Krabi province and the mainland is no less scenic with similar high limestone cliffs and long stretches of beach. For the moment tourism development is slight and the coastline here is perhaps the finest in the whole country.

Up and coming in Thailand's world of beach resorts is Samui, off the southeast coast. One of a group of islands, Samui is smaller than Phuket though equal in natural beauty. First put on the map by budget travelers, and still a backpackers paradise, Phuket is nevertheless now being groomed for more upmarket tourists.

It must be admitted that infrastructure development to accommodate ever-in-

creasing numbers of tourists is having a detrimental effect on the environment at Samui as well as at other, better established beauty spots like Phuket. Created without the benefit of coordinated planning and, in many cases, by man's downright greed, the problem is of growing concern. In certain places the state of the natural environment is extremely precarious and one of today's greatest challenges is how to preserve the essence of Thailand's natural beauty that has traditionally charmed the visitor.

Historical Independence

The word "Thai" means "free" and the country is the "Land of the Free". This sounds suspiciously trite, and yet there has been historical freedom that has permitted remarkable consistency. National values and special character traits which underpin the Thai culture have evolved through a rare continuity of development.

As a sovereign nation, the Thais were first united in the thirteenth century with the founding of the kingdom of Sukhothai. The history of the land now defined by the borders of Thailand, however, stretches much further back and includes various civilizations of which the Thais eventually became cultural heirs.

Situated almost equidistant between India and China, the region of Thailand occupies the central and western parts of the Indochina peninsula, together with its own narrow southern peninsula. Its original inhabitants were probably non-Mongoloid peoples, perhaps Negritos or Polynesians. While little is known about these earliest settlers, excavations in the 1970s at Ban Chiang in northeastern Thailand indicate an advanced culture flourishing in the area as far back as 3600 BC. This predates sites in China and Mesopotamia as the earliest known evidence of an agrarian, bronze-making culture, and suggests that the Khorat plateau may be one of the "cradles of civilization".

Most remarkable of the Ban Chiang finds are examples of distinctly and finely patterned pottery which are today

25

on display at museums in Bangkok and Khon Kaen. For anyone interested in archaeological digs, one of the excavation pits at the village of Ban Chiang has been left open as an exhibit displaying various objects in situ.

Our knowledge of the pre-history of the area is still hazy, though it appears that the first inhabitants were displaced by diverse waves of immigration until, ultimately, the Thais, originally from what is now part of southern China, became dominant. Prior to their ascendancy, however, various influences were at work.

Fundamental to the cultural development of the entire Indochina peninsula was the impact of ancient India. Social, religious and artistic roots can all be traced back to this shaping force.

In the first centuries AD, Indian traders were crossing the Bay of Bengal and ven-

Above: The restored temple complex Prasat Hin Phimai, a beautiful Khmer remain. Right: Buddha statues in Sukhothai style.

turing into the Far East. Because of the types of ships they sailed and the prevailing seasonal monsoons, their journeys east and south required stops at ports along the Indochina peninsula. Here they would wait for the change in the winds that would allow them to continue their voyage.

During the course of these sojourns a process of Indianization very gradually took place through various means. The merchants themselves probably had little lasting impact on the indigenous cultures and it was more likely that Indian princes set themselves up to rule over petty states, probably marrying into the local population to legitimize their authority. It is also possible that Indian Brahmins and scholars were invited to settle and serve as administrators, advisors and astrologers at local courts. Brahmanism, the ancient form of Hinduism, was especially attractive as it lent support to the idea of a god-king, a concept that was to be most spectacularly developed by the Khmer of Angkor.

India was also the birthplace of Buddhism and this, too, was eventually to take hold in the region, though it arrived by a more indirect route. Theravada Buddhism was ultimately adopted by the Thai as their national religion, but the earlier impact of Brahmanism was to persist, as it does to this day in royal rites and ceremonies.

The process of Indianization formed a cultural base out of which gradually developed a number of independent kingdoms in the centuries before the rise of the Thais. Three, in particular, were especially influential on what would later become Thailand.

The first of these, Dvaravati, was a vaguely united group of Mon people who settled in a collection of city states with, most likely, a power base at what is now Nakhon Pathom, west of Bangkok. The Dvaravati kingdom flourished in the Chao Phraya river basin from the sixth or seventh to the eleventh century. It embraced Theravada Buddhism and it is generally assumed that the Thais were initially converted to the faith through contact with the Mon. Other major influences were in sculpture and temple architecture. Examples of the latter are best seen today in the *chedis* (reliquary towers) of the oldest temples of Lamphun, the former capital of an offshoot Mon kingdom known as Haripunchai.

The second formative kingdom was that of Srivijaya, an approximate contemporary of Dvaravati which held sway in the Malay peninsula and Indonesian archipelago from the eighth to the late thirteenth centuries. This civilization molded the early culture of southern Thailand, notably in sculpture.

The third and most influential of the pre-Thai kingdoms was that of the Khmer whose vast empire was centered on Angkor. By the eleventh century the Khmer dominated not only what is now Cambodia, but also large tracts of eastern and central present-day Thailand.

The Khmer were master builders and traces of their architectural achievement are still readily discernable in Lopburi

27

and various sites in the northeast, such as Phimai and Phanom Rung, where extensive ruins of Khmer temples survive.

Birth of a Nation

By the early thirteenth century the power of the Khmer was waning while the Thais, who had been migrating steadily southwards from Nan Chao in southwestern China and setting up tiny independent settlements, were gaining strength. In circa 1238 the chieftains of two such Thai groups united their forces and succeeded pushing back the western borders of the Khmer empire to establish the first Thai capital at Sukhothai.

One of the chieftains, Phor Khun Bang Klang Thao, was proclaimed king, taking the title Sri Intradit and establishing the first Thai dynasty, Phra Ruang.

This was the first unification of the Thai people under a single monarch and a

cohesive national religion. Appropriately, the name Sukhothai translates as "Dawn of Happiness".

As the undisputed center of this new Thai nation, Sukhothai reigned supreme for only 140 years. In 1378 it became a vassal of up-and-coming Ayutthaya to the south, and 60 years later it was totally absorbed by the younger Thai kingdom. Yet in that brief time it established religious, cultural and political patterns that have never been completely obliterated.

The history of the pre-Khmer and Khmer periods of Sukhothai is still not fully understood. Khmer architectural influences are readily discernible in the ruins of a few temples, notably the earliest parts of Wat Si Sawai and Wat Phra Phai Luang, but it is unclear whether the site was a fully-fledged Khmer settlement or merely a military stronghold. Whatever they inherited from the Khmers, it is obvious that the Thais wasted little time in constructing their own capital on a scale and in a style befitting the birth of a nation.

Above: Old and new in today's Thailand.

In the first two reigns – those of King Sri Intratit and his son, King Ban Muang (died c.1279) – nothing disturbed the peace of the young kingdom which at the time extended little beyond the capital and the second city of Si Satchanalai some 70 km to the north. It was in the reign of King Ramkamhaeng (c.1279-1299) that Sukhothai experienced its golden age. Under his masterful leadership the kingdom was consolidated, politically through territorial gains and culturally through the adoption of Theravada Buddhism.

It was this religion that came not only to serve as the major cohesive force of the Thai people, but also to motivate and distinguish Sukhothai's great achievements in art and architecture. Its influence is seen most graphically in the Buddha image, in line engraving, in decorative stucco work and, most importantly, in the bell-shaped *chedi*.

Although Sukhothai's political and social organization was perfected under King Ramkamhaeng, its art and architecture did not reach their apogee until around the mid-fourteenth century. At that time, during the reign of King Lithai (1347-c.1368), a man noted for his religious conviction and scholarship, Theravada Buddhism was much strengthened through direct links with Sri Lanka. The faith had arrived earlier indirectly via monks from Nakhon Sri Thammarat in southern Thailand. In consequence the building of *chedis* and other religious structures was accelerated.

It was now that the so-called lotus-bud *chedi*, characterized by a bulbous dome at the top of the spire and unique to Sukhothai architecture, made its appearance. The construction of Sri Lankan bell-shaped *chedis* also became more widespread, replacing the pyramid and *prang* (round tower) of the old Khmer style, while Singhalese stylistic influences in stucco decoration and line engraving were incorporated. It is generally agreed

that the art of sculpting Buddha images reached perfection during the reign of King Lithai.

As a city influencing the devlopment of a nation's art and culture, Sukhothai thrived only briefly. Like one of its festive candles, it burned bright, then flickered and was finally extinguished. In 1438 the Phra Ruang dynasty came to an end and Sukhothai was ruled by an Ayutthaya prince. Then, probably around the end of the 15th century or the start of the 16th, the city was finally abandoned.

This brief passage of 140 years of independence does not truly reflect Sukhothai's enormous contribution to the nationhood of the Thais. In virtually all fields of human activity – political, religious, civic and cultural – it established traditions that, despite adaptation and development to various degrees, are still discernible in present-day society. The system of monarchy set by Sukhothai, albeit undergoing dynastic changes and shifts in character, has continued to serve the nation throughout its history.

On the popular level, the persistence of Sukhothai can be found in the Loy Krathong festival, held annually on the night of the November full moon in honor of the "Mother of Waters". This festival evolved in its present form at Sukhothai and even today, while celebrated throughout the country, it is still best seen in the ruins of the first capital.

Although Sukhothai under King Ramkamhaeng cast at least a degree of influence over most of present-day Thai territory, its sphere of influence was curtailed in later reigns and the kingdom disintegrated geographically. Hence the rise of the rival Thai state, Ayutthaya.

Founded by King U Thong (later crowned Ramathibodi) in 1368, Ayutthaya rapidly gained power and, after absorbing Sukhothai, remained the heart of the Thai state for the next 350 years. Situated at the junction of the Chao Phraya, Lopburi and Pa Sak rivers, it was created

as an island city and its network of communication canals set the pattern of riverine settlement that typifies Thai communities.

Indeed, until the 20th century, foreign travelers frequently remarked on the waterborne nature of Thai settlements. "The existence of the people of Bangkok may be called amphibious," wrote Queen Victoria's envoy Sir John Bowring in the 1850s. "The children pass much of their time in the water, paddling and diving and swimming, as if it were their native element." Although roads and the motor car have well and truly taken over communications today, traces of the traditional riverine lifestyle remain. This is especially true in the provinces, though even modern Bangkok has managed to keep a few of its old canals.

Inheriting much from Sukhothai, Ayutthaya quickly came to take over the role

Above: Temple in Prang style. Right: Reliquary shrines known as Chedis in Ayutthaya.

of religious, cultural and commercial capital of the Thais and was later to be the model for Bangkok. At the height of power in the 17th century, Ayutthaya, exercising control over nearly all of Thailand except the north, was one of the biggest and most magnificent cities in the Orient. It is claimed to have had a population of one million. The city walls enclosed palaces, hundreds of temples and quarters for the military, scholars, artists, artisans and so forth. Outside the walls were the settlements, or "factories" as they were called, of various foreign communities, European such as French, Dutch and British, as well as Asian.

The kingdom went from strength to strength and, in addition to what is now Thai territory, Ayutthaya ruled over parts of Laos and Cambodia (Angkor, a shadow of its former self, was defeated by the Thais in 1431). Its might was not unchallenged, however, and Burma was a constantly threatening presence in the west. Steady, if periodic, warfare with Burma dominated Ayutthaya's foreign affairs throughout most of its history.

The full flowering of Ayutthaya's glory, its cultural achievements and its wealth, came in the 17th century and was based on trade. The Thais themselves were not great merchants – the common people were farmers, the nobles were administrators–but they permitted others to carry on trade under a royal monopoly.

With China and Japan effectively closed to outsiders, Ayutthaya became a major entrepot for the expanding East-West trade. First, in 1511, came the Portuguese, then the Dutch in 1605, the English in 1612 and the Danes in 1621. The French, eventually to have great, albeit ill-fated and short-lived, influence at court, arrived in 1662.

Seventeenth-Century Intrigue

As a center of international interest, Ayutthaya came into its own during the

reign of King Narai (1656-88). It and the city of Lopburi, which Narai used as a second capital, were where one of the most thrilling episodes in Thai history was played out.

King Narai ranks as one of the greatest Thai monarchs and his long reign presents a fine record of achievements, though he is most noted for an ambitious policy that ultimately failed. He was the first Thai king to recognize the value and need for development and progress through international relations. His rule coincided with the culmination of the first big wave of European interest in Southeast Asia, and he was determined to reap benefits while safeguarding his nation's sovereignty.

In this he was 200 years ahead of his time and it was not until the mid-19th century that King Mongkut succeeded in establishing international trade along mutually beneficial lines. King Narai was finally defeated by conservative elements at court which compounded international intrigues of Byzantine complexity.

Yet failure does not diminish Narai's stature as a monarch of intelligence, understanding, foresight and great personal dignity. And for a while his policies seemed as if they would meet with success. He attracted Westerners to come and trade with Siam and he fitted out his own ships, usually with foreign crews, to trade with India, Persia, China and Japan. He became in effect the country's main import-export company and temporarily boosted royal revenues.

The treasury should actually have benefited more, though many *farangs* (Westerners) taken into royal service were adventurers, like the swashbuckling Englishman, Samuel White, one-time Narai's harbor master at Mergui, whose main concern was that of lining their own pockets.

The one *farang* who played a leading role at this moment of Ayutthaya's history was, however, a more complex character. Phaulkon, as he was known, was a Greek born with the family name Gerakis ("falcon") Constantine who ran away to

31

sea as a boy and worked as a sailor mostly on British ships. He eventually came to the Orient on a vessel of the East India Company and with the help of British friends set himself up as a trader at Ayutthaya, though not before some adventures in the East Indies.

An amazingly resourceful man, driven by powerful ambition, he soon attracted the attention of King Narai. He entered government service in 1680 and from 1683 until his death five years later he was the king's first minister and the principal go-between during the first diplomatic exchanges between France and Siam. In effect he was the second most important man in the land and never before nor ever again did a foreigner hold such a dominant position in Thailand.

During the height of his career Phaulkon wielded incredible power and influence, in the process amassing enor-

Above: The Chakri Maha Prasat, with its marble façade and siamese style roof. Right: Statue of King Mengrai.

mous wealth and living in great opulence. The ruins of his house at Lopburi serve to illustrate his status, both in size and in the fact that few buildings of the period, except temples, were constructed in stone. Let it be said, however, there is a case to be made for arguing that Phaulkon, unlike most other *farangs* in Siamese service, did genuinely dedicate his undeniable talents to the service of his adopted king and country.

The mainspring of events focusing on Phaulkon was King Narai's fear of Dutch commercial and colonial intentions in the region and his desire to balance their power by courting another European faction. At first Phaulkon, as the king's chief minister, turned to his old employers, the British East India Company, but they, through a mix of vacillation and the bunglings of some most inept officials, lost the initiative. This left France which was at the time the all-powerful nation in Europe.

Although lacking the commercial setup of the Dutch and the English, the

French were building influence in Siam through the presence of Jesuit missionaries who were befriended by Phaulkon, himself a Catholic convert after his marriage to a lady of Japanese and Portuguese extract.

In favoring the French, Phaulkon was initially simply pursuing earlier policies as, in 1680, Narai had already sent a first Siamese mission to Paris, though it never arrived and was presumed lost at sea. He then urged the dispatch of a second mission in 1685, and this prompted the French to return the compliment in the form of their own ambassador, Chevalier de Chaumont, who arrived in Siam in September 1685. Narai received de Chaumont in October when a curious scene took place. The Frenchman had a letter for the Siamese monarch from Louis XIV, but he refused to present it in customary style by kneeling. A compromise was reached; Narai appeared on a small balcony and de Chaumont stood holding the letter on a plate, thus remaining below the head of the king, as strict custom demanded, while not having to kneel. He failed to hold the plate high enough for Narai to reach, despite promptings from the prostrate Phaulkon. To avoid an embarrassing confrontation with Gallic pride, the king reached down for the letter. At least this is how the scene was recorded in an engraving from which a much later painting was made, now on display at Lopburi museum.

De Chaumont returned to France in 1686, accompanied by a third Siamese embassy to the court of Louis XIV. The success of the latter is reflected in the fact that France dispatched a second diplomatic group to Siam in 1687.

Yet despite these exchanges a Franco-Siamese relationship did not prosper. In simple terms Narai wanted military aid as a deterrent to whatever designs the Dutch might have, and the French desired trade concessions. In addition to port facilities and favorable commercial terms, the latter were also motivated by an absurd desire to convert Narai to Catholicism. This provided the excuse for dissatisfied figures at the Siamese court to attack both the French and Phaulkon.

Phaulkon was condemned for conniving with the French in their totally unrealistic religious aim. Certainly he championed their interests, though arguably only for political expediency as he would have known better than any other foreigner that Buddhism was not just a matter of personal faith because it was a unifying thread running through the very cultural fabric.

Nevertheless, Phaulkon, perhaps over confident, attempted to walk an impossible diplomatic tightrope. What he may have achieved in terms of international relations will never be known; he was overtaken by events. On his way to the second most powerful position in the land he had made numerous enemies, partly through his own arrogance and partly through others' envy of his wealth and status. He had no greater enemies

than General Phetracha and his son Luang Surasak, who had long been vicious personal antagonists.

In 1688 King Narai was dying at Lopburi; Phetracha, seeing his opportunity, led a palace revolt, murdered Narai's possible successors and took control of the nation even while Narai lingered on his death bed.

Called to the palace at Lopburi, Phaulkon was captured by the rebels. He was imprisoned and tortured for several days before being beheaded in a squalid nightime execution. He met his end bravely, denying to his last breath that he had betrayed his king.

The French were subsequently unceremoniously expelled from the country and Phetracha became king on the death of Narai a few weeks after Phaulkon's execution. The dynastic change effectively closed Thailand to any significant foreign relations until the mid-19th century. The

Above: Deforested hills in northern Thailand.

nation once again became introspective and was weakened by internal squabbles. In 1767 that perennial enemy, Burma, made an all-out attack and after a lengthy siege captured Ayutthaya, systematically looted it, killed or took off into slavery all but 10,000 inhabitants and razed the city. It was the end of an era.

Ferocious though the Burmese attack was, the invaders were unable to consolidate territorial gains. The Thais, showing characteristic resilience, quickly rallied under General Taksin, who had established a resistance base at Thonburi on the opposite bank of the Chao Phraya river from Bangkok. Before the close of the year that had witnessed the wholesale destruction of Ayutthaya, he had established a new capital, had been crowned king and had begun to reunite the people.

The Kingdom of the North

Thailand was shortly to be launched into the modern era, but it is necessary to pause here and look at a parallel Thai

34

kingdom, Lanna, that was a contemporary of Sukhothai and held out against the power of Ayutthaya.

Northern Thailand today is a popular tourist destination and draws at least part of its charm from a distinct character of its own. It is Thai, yet its separate historical development has left many distinguishing traits which indelibly mark the area, its people, towns and art.

Northern Thailand is topographically different from the Central Plains and the Chao Phraya basin, where Sukhothai and Ayutthaya rose to power. It is an area of high hills cut through by river valleys running north to south. This distinction of geography, readily seen today in the changing landscape as you travel across the Central Plains and into the northern region, is important.

It meant that Sukhothai could be absorbed comparatively easily by the more powerful Ayutthaya in the fifteenth century, while Lanna, protected by physical barriers, could defend its autonomy and resist integration into the Thai nation proper until much later.

The earliest inhabitants of the north were probably the Lawa who lived for centuries in the valleys until they were forced up into the highlands where, in greatly reduced numbers, they continue to survive as one of the major hilltribes. As you travel in the north today, it is easy to see that whoever controlled the valleys, much more suitable for cultivation than the rugged hills and offering easier communication, would hold sway over the area.

Supplanting the Lawa was a group of Mons, an offshoot of the Mon kingdom of Dvaravati centered in the Chao Phraya river basin near what is now Bangkok. They were led by a legendary queen, Chama Devi, who founded her capital in 660 AD at Haripunchai, present-day Lamphun, located 25 km south of Chiang Mai. Today she is remembered in the two ancient *chedis* at Lamphun's temple of

Wat Chama Devi, reputedly constructed on her death by her son.

The Mon were of great importance as they had the foremost civilization at that time and place. They were Theravada Buddhists rather than animists as were most other peoples of the region, and they were accomplished in the arts and architecture. The largest *chedi* at Wat Chama Devi, for example, is a fine example of their distinctive architectural forms.

Controlling the Chiang Mai valley and the Ping river, respectively the most fertile land in the area and the major communication link, Haripunchai long dominated the area. But they were not alone. Gradually some of the Thais who migrated south from China began to settle in the area and set up petty city states. By the thirteenth century the most powerful of these was Chiang Saen, on the banks of the Mekong river, across the mountains northwest of the Chiang Mai valley.

In 1259, King Mengrai succeeded his father as the ruler of Chiang Saen. A man of ambition and determination, he saw that neighboring Thai principalities were frequently in conflict with one another, and decided to impose his authority over the entire region. Descent from a legitimate royal house would be the justification for his actions.

Setting out from Chiang Saen, he acted swiftly and, in quick succession, took nearby states before driving south to set up a temporary capital at Chiang Rai in 1262. This initial triumph is honored today in the town's statue of Mengrai, while his ashes are enshrined in Chiang Rai's Wat Ngam Muang.

Mengrai had done well, but when you travel to Chiang Rai you'll see that he had not achieved a good strategic base. The terrain is extremely rugged and hampers easy territorial expansion. Mengrai had yet to conquer natural barriers. In 1274 he made a major breakthrough and crossed westwards over the moun-

tains to settle in Fang, due north of Chiang Mai. This still didn't give him control of the Chiang Mai Valley and the plum of his conquests, Haripunchai, remained to be picked.

This was a different proposition from the weak little principalities he had so far conquered. It was extremely powerful and not easy to lead a large army against as the surrounding countryside must have been densely forested. Just notice the huge old trees that still line the road between Chiang Mai and Lamphun. So Mengrai's advisors warned him that the Mon kingdom could not be taken by force and would fall only to guile.

After seizing the throne of Haripunchai, Mengrai was de facto ruler of a state he was to call Lanna, meaning the kingdom of "a million rice fields". Seeing the fertile Chiang Mai valley today, which yields nearly half a million tonnes of rice

Above: A rice paddy in the north during the harvest season. Right: Rice planting in the plains of Chiang Mai.

a year, it is still easy to imagine how appropriate the old name was and still is.

In 1287 Mengrai consolidated his position by agreeing to a pact of friendship between his two most powerful neighbors; King Ngam Muang of Phayao, a state occupying the next valley east of Chiang Mai, and King Ramkamhaeng who ruled Sukhothai which at the time controlled most of the rest of what is now Thailand south of the highlands. Phayao was later absorbed by Lanna, though Sukhothai remained a stalwart ally throughout its brief history.

For some reason Mengrai decided not to install himself at Haripunchai, certainly then the finest settlement in the territories of Lanna. Instead he set up yet another temporary base, this time at Kum Kam, not far from the site of Chiang Mai. The question of a capital worthy of his kingdom, however, could not be postponed indefinitely.

It was in 1291, so legend has it, that Mengrai was out hunting one day and passed by the banks of the Ping River. At one spot he sighted a pair of white sambar deer, a pair of white barking deer and a white mouse with five young. The appearance of such a notable collection of creatures was deemed auspicious. Mengrai immediately halted his caravan and decided that here, a short distance west of the river, he would build his capital.

Anxious to construct a city that would reflect the glory of the Lanna kingdom, Mengrai consulted his allies, the kings of Phayao and Sukhothai, over the design. The three of them worked out plans for a rectangular walled settlement measuring 2 km by 1.6 km. It was to be called Nopphaburi Si Nakhonping Chiangmai which, in its use of both Sanskrit and Thai words, is an oddly repetitive name that translates roughly as "new city, city of the Ping, new city".

Construction was delayed until 1296, probably because Mengrai was forced to contend with threats from the Mongols

who, under the famed Kublai Khan, had conquered Pagan (Burma) in 1287 and were contemplating expansion eastward into Lanna. As it turned out hostilities were avoided, but their warlike posturing was tantamount to recognition of Lanna's new-found power and influence.

When building was begun, it is believed that more than 90,000 workers were involved. The city was originally centered on Wat Chiang Man, a temple that can still be seen today, though the focus was shifted at various times in subsequent eras, and the plan indicated by the existing fortified gates and moat probably dates from the early nineteenth century.

Mengrai was not just a conqueror, he was also a civilizing force and had a well-tuned respect for culture. He evidently admired the accomplishments of Haripunchai and one of the Buddha images enshrined in Wat Chiang Man, the temple where he once resided, possibly originally belonged to Queen Chama Devi and was brought to Chiang Mai after the

fall of Haripunchai. Moreover artists were taken from the Mon city and were put by force to work embellishing the Lanna capital.

Mengrai was further an upholder of Theravada Buddhism which became Lanna's single most cohesive force, as it was for Sukhothai and later Thai kingdoms. Adherence to the faith is reflected in Chiang Mai's many temples and in the sculpture, mural painting, woodcarving and other decorative arts.

Mengrai died in 1317, reputedly struck by lightning. Thus ended a remarkable reign that had spanned nearly 60 years and had brought much of what is now northern Thailand into one fold, Lanna, with Chiang Mai as its power base.

Immediate successors were kings of lesser stature and there were some troubled times as the state was weakened by internal squabbles. Nevertheless, a vital boost to political and cultural identity was achieved in the reign of King Ku Na (1355-85). He was a man of learning as well as an accomplished administrator

and he invited a much respected monk from Sukhothai, the Venerable Sumana, to establish his order of Singhalese Buddhism in Chiang Mai. The temple built for him, Wat Suan Dork, still stands albeit in greatly restored form.

The importance of Sumana and his sect of Theravada Buddhism on the evolution of Lanna was crucial. As one historian has remarked: "Coupled with the slowly increasing preponderance of Chiang Mai, the cultural leadership exerted by the Singhalese sect encouraged the centralization of the kingdom and the development of a regional sense of identity as Tai Yuan (Northern Thai) among its population."

While Chiang Mai continued to grow, the power of Lanna became such as to attract the hostile interest of Ayutthaya. Although centered on the southern edge of the Central Plains, this Thai kingdom was

Above: Murals have survived the centuries in many ancient temples. Right: A mural depicting Rama, accompanied by monkeys.

expanding fast in the late 14th century. Its primary target was Sukhothai, which, as Lanna's ally, received assistance from Chiang Mai.

Once Sukhothai had been taken, Ayutthaya turned its attention towards Lanna. However, partly because the northern terrain inhibited military expeditions, Chiang Mai was never permanently defeated. It lost battles with Ayutthaya, but didn't lose the war.

A conflict with fleeting triumphs by either side but never a conclusive victory, became the established pattern in relations between Lanna and Ayutthaya from the mid-fifteenth century onwards.

None of this prevented Chiang Mai from experiencing its golden age during the reign of King Tilokaraja (1442-87). A formidable warrior, he was a worthy opponent of Ayutthaya's equally forceful King Trailok.

The history of the period is a thrilling one and the tales of successive military campaigns in which each king tried to outwit the other make exciting reading.

For both of them, despite their valor and guile, any advantage remained elusive.

King Tilokaraja was, however, more successful in battle elsewhere. In 1449 he took the state of Nan, lying in the eastern-most valley of the north, and brought it under the sway of Lanna. A reminder of this victory can be seen today in the 4-meter high bronze Buddha image of Phra Chao Thong Tip, enshrined in Nan's Wat Suan Tan. It was made to commemorate Lanna's triumph and, so legend has it, Tilokaraja gave the people of Nan just seven days to find sufficient metal and set a 100-day time limit for it to be cast.

In between military campaigns, Tilo-karaja showed himself to be a stalwart upholder of Buddhism and a patron of the arts. Several notable Chiang Mai temples and Buddha sculptures date from his reign – the 86 m *chedi* at Wat Chedi Luang, now partially ruined, was raised to its full height at this time – and generally the period was one of renewed cultural endeavor. Most importantly Chiang Mai's prestige was enhanced when the eighth World Buddhist Synod was convened at the city's Wat Chet Yot in 1477.

Nonetheless, these were belligerent times. Warfare between Chiang Mai and Ayutthaya was never concluded, though by the sixteenth century it was over-shadowed by a much greater threat from Burma. Lanna was conquered by the Burmese in 1557 and for the next two centuries Chiang Mai was subjugated.

The form of the eclipse was erratic; sometimes there were puppet Lanna kings, at other times there was direct rule from Burma: occasionally various princi-palities made a bid for independence, while Ayutthaya was never totally out of the picture. This state of affairs persisted until the late 18th century when Taksin forced the Burmese out of the north and the rest of the country. Reconstruction of the north now began although the region, while part of the Thai fold, retained a cer-tain autonomy under a line of hereditary rulers until the early twentieth century when there was direct rule in all spheres from the central government.

Emergence of the Modern State

While King Taksin, from his capital at Thonburi, had led the Thais to a remarkably recovery from the Burmese invasion and largely reunified the nation, including, for the first time, the northern regions, his reign was short-lived. By 1782 he was showing increasing signs of megalomania and became alienated from the people who, faced with a deteriorating situation, called on army commander General Chakri to solve the problem.

By the time Chakri returned from a military expedition in Laos, King Taksin had reputedly become insane and was executed. The army commander was popularly proclaimed king, being crowned Rama I and thus founding the Chakri dynasty which reigns to this day.

The year 1782 was a momentous one, for not only was a new dynasty created but also a new capital was established.

Above: Buddhas in the assembly line in a manufacture near Chiang Mai.

One of the first acts of King Rama I was to transfer his power base across the Chao Phraya from Thonburi to Bangkok, at the time little more than a customs post and a huddle of Chinese traders' huts. The reason for the move was partly strategic (a broad bend in the river made Bangkok easier to defend), and partly symbolic as Rama I wished to restore national pride by constructing a city that would recreate the lost glory of Ayutthaya.

Accordingly throughout Rama I's reign and that of his two successors, Bangkok was, step by step, transformed from a sleepy riverside village into a metropolis that replicated Ayutthaya as faithfully as possible. The construction of canals effectively turned it into an island city, while the building of the Grand Palace, the Temple of the Emerald Buddha and the other classical monuments that today constitute Bangkok's major sights successfully reflected a material and spiritual wealth worthy of the capital's status.

With the succession of King Mongkut, Rama IV, in 1851, there was a radical shift of emphasis. The idea of recreating Ayutthaya, which had well served the first three monarchs of the Chakri dynasty well, was abandoned along with the nation's introspective stance. Now Thailand began to look towards the outside world, especially the West, for ways in which to modernize.

King Mongkut, contrary to the portrait painted in the musical *The King and I* (incidentally the film is banned in Thailand), was an enlightened monarch possessed of an intelligent and inquiring mind. During the 27 years he spent in the monkhood prior to ascending the throne he had proved himself a scholar of considerable attainment. As king he was to set the country on the path to modernization by opening the door to Western influence.

Not since the ill-fated French embassies of the late 1680s had Thailand made overtures to the outside world and encouraged foreign interests. That was to change in 1855 when King Mongkut signed a mutually favorable trade agreement with Sir John Bowring, envoy of Queen Victoria. Similar accords with other European countries and with the United States followed soon after. The way was thus cleared for the nation's modern development while, at the same time, any colonial territorial designs Western powers may have been harboring were cleverly side-stepped.

International trade grew steadily from the mid nineteenth century onwards and, in conjunction with an outward looking stance in relation to commerce, the country embarked upon a programme of modernization of far-reaching proportions. Infrastructure was expanded and developed to meet new needs (notably roads for wheeled traffic began to replace canals), and the machinery of state was overhauled with ministries organized more along European lines. Art and architecture also began to reflect an interest in things Western, a fact perhaps most obviously witnessed today in the Italianate design of the old National Assembly building.

An increase in foreign trade and the attendant proliferation of jobs gave rise to a more prominent role for the Chinese immigrants, who for long had made up a sizeable proportion of the population. The Thais historically had no inclination for trade and hence the Chinese, with their natural flair for business, found in the 19th century fresh opportunities as clerks, wholesalers and the whole army of middlemen who keep the wheels of trade turning.

The contribution of Thai Chinese to the development of modern Thailand is considerable yet they have been well assimilated into the society and, while contributing enormously, their impact has scarcely altered the nation's quintessential "Thainess". American academic Charles F. Keyes has described the phenomenon: "Although Siamese society, with its large Chinese migrant population, was in some ways similar to the societies of other Southeast Asian nations because of its incorporation into an international economic system, in other fundamental ways it evolved differently because, unlike those other societies, it was transformed politically by an indigenous elite rather than by Western colonial rulers."

King Chulalongkorn (1868-1910), Mongkut's successor, vastly furthered the policies of modernization. He successfully introduced various sweeping reforms, the abolition of slavery among them, and broadly adopted European concepts of administration, justice, education and public welfare. The pattern persisted in the following reign of King Vajiravudh (1910-25) who established compulsory education and, on the international scene, brought Thailand into World War I on the side of the Allies.

41

In the wake of economic change and material development it was almost inevitable that traditional concepts of power would be questioned. For centuries Thai kings had been literally "Lords of Life", but by the 1920s Vajiravudh's successor, King Prajadhipok (1925-35), was considering ways to liberalize the whole system.

Events, however, influenced considerably by shocks in the world economy, overtook him. In 1932 a bloodless revolution changed the system of government to a constitutional monarchy. Prajadhipok accepted a fait accompli though he abdicated in 1935 and lived until his death six years later as a self-imposed exile in England. His nephew, King Ananda, then ascended the throne.

During World War II the Thai government acquiesced in the Japanese occupation of the country, although the Thai

Above: In the Wat Doi Suthep near Chiang Mai. Right: A monk meditating in the stillness of ancient ruins.

minister in Washington refused to deliver his country's declaration of war on the US and instead set about organizing a Free Thai Movement.

In the post-war years Thailand has moved slowly and at times with difficulty towards establishing an effective democracy. Since 1932 there have been 23 prime ministers and the constitution has been changed a number of times. The role of the military has been strong and some 16 coups, successful and abortive, have to varying degrees disturbed the peaceful evolution of government, but have scarcely had any fundamental effect on economic progress.

Throughout, the monarchy, albeit constitutional, has had a valuable stabilizing effect.The young King Ananda was tragically killed in 1946 under circumstances that have never been made fully clear and was succeeded by his brother, the present monarch, King Bhumibol Adulyadej, Rama IX.

A man of considerable personal accomplishment, King Bhumibol has

shown himself to be the model of a modern constitutional monarch, both preserving regal traditions and taking an active part in working towards the greater social and economic well-being of his people. The people's respect and love for the monarchy is as great today as it has ever been. Continuity in today's Thailand persists in the face of change.

Art, Society and Religion

Thailand's major achievements in sculpture, painting and architecture are inextricably bound up with the national religion, Theravada Buddhism. Both are expressed in the nation's most dominant social or socio-religious institution – and, incidentally, a major tourism attraction – the Thai temple.

Somerset Maugham, on a visit to Bangkok in the 1920s, was struck by this singular sight: "They are unlike anything in the world, so that you are taken aback, and you cannot fit them into a scheme of the things you know. It makes you laugh

with delight to think that anything so fantastic could exist on this sombre earth. They are gorgeous; they glitter with gold and whitewash, yet are not garish; against that vivid sky, in that dazzling sunlight, they hold their own, defying the brilliancy of nature and supplementing it with the ingenuity and playful boldness of man."

Maugham thus captures the delight that nearly all visitors to Bangkok find in the city's temples. They are rightly at the top of anyone's sightseeing list. The immediate attraction lies, as Maugham so vividly portrays, in their fabulous appearance, their exotic architecture and their wealth of decorative detail.

Yet there is more than just the initial visual impact, and a closer look at Buddhist temples opens up a whole world of understanding about Thai society and its art and culture.

Buddhism runs as a constant thread through the nation's entire cultural and social fabric. It was the religion under which the people (originally animists)

43

were first united, it remained a visible and binding force in daily life throughout more than 700 years, and is today as vital as ever.

Buddhism, established in India around 500 BC, was initially an oral tradition, founded on the teachings of an Indian prince, Siddhartha Gautama, who renounced the world and sought a path of salvation. After achieving ultimate insight into reality he was given the title Buddha, "The Enlightened One".

Buddhism was eventually expelled from India but not before it had taken a hold in South and Southeast Asia. In the process of its spread it split into two schools. Hinayana (known as Theravada in Thailand) or the "Lesser Vehicle" which first took root in Sri Lanka, and Mahayana, or the "Greater Vehicle" which developed in India. The former claims a closer adherence to the original

Above: Buddhist novices carrying food offerings. Right: A school for young monks in the Wat Po in Bangkok.

teachings, while the latter was devised to have more popular appeal.

Hinayana, spreading out from Sri Lanka, took root in Burma, Thailand, Laos and Cambodia, while Mahayana was adopted by Tibet, Nepal, Vietnam, China, Korea and Japan.

The essence of all Buddhist teaching is in the four Noble Truths: *dukkha* (suffering and its inevitability), *samudaya* (the cause of suffering which is desire), *nirodha* (the cessation of suffering through the extinction of desire) and *magga* (the way to the cessation of suffering, i.e. the Noble Eightfold Path, namely: right understanding, right intention, right speech, right action, right livelihood, right effort, right mindfulness and right concentration).

The ultimate goal of the religion is *nirvana*, the extinction of suffering, which is reached through gaining merit in a long cycle of death and rebirth, the nature of the latter being dictated by karma or action. In practice most people aim simply for rebirth into a better existence, the

state of *nirvana* being literally incomprehensible.

Before the division of the two basic Buddhist sects, the religion first came to what is now Thailand in third century BC when, according to tradition, the Indian emperor Ashoka sent two missionaries to the "Land of Gold". This has been tentatively identified as the Mon kingdom of Dvaravati centered on the town of Nakhon Pathom.

The country of this time was not yet dominated by the Thais, though those who had begun to migrate from southern China would have received their first contact with Buddhism through mingling with the Mon. While the seeds of the religion were sown early and had come directly from India, the form of Buddhism eventually adopted by the Thais as their national religion was developed later from the Sri Lankan school.

By the time of the founding of the first Thai sovereign state at Sukhothai in the early thirteenth century, Buddhist monks in the southern part of the country had made contact with Sri Lanka and with its doctrine of Hinayana or Theravada Buddhism based on Pali texts. Sukhothai's greatest monarch, King Ramkamhaeng, reputedly met these southern monks and invited them back to his capital to establish the religion according to the Sri Lankan school. With both royal patronage and subsequent direct contact with Sri Lanka, Theravada Buddhism was embraced by the Thai nation.

Quintessential to the religion is the monkhood. Central to Buddhist practice is the concept of making merit and the supreme form of merit, for men at least, is to become, even temporarily, a monk. In modern Thailand most young men will still comply with this custom, becoming ordained and entering a monastery for a period of perhaps one, two or three months.

Women and the population at large make important merit by giving daily food offerings to monks. At any one time, present-day Thailand supports a religious community of some 250,000 monks who reside at an estimated 27,000 temples throughout the country.

A detailed appreciation of the meaning and practice of Buddhism is not possible here, and the ways of making merit are varied. However, an understanding of the importance of the religious community is crucial to an appreciation of Buddhist temples.

The word "temple" is largely unsatisfactory as a translation of the Thai word *wat*. It implies a single structure, as is the case with a Christian church, but this is not so with a Buddhist *wat*. Besides monks' residential quarters which are commonly, though not always, found at a *wat*, a Thai temple complex comprises several distinct religious buildings.

The principal structure is the *bot*, the most sacred part of the temple and the place where ordination ceremonies are conducted. The building is identified by eight boundary stones, called *sima*, placed outside at the four corners and four cardinal points.

A temple will also probably have one or more *viharns*, a hall virtually identical to a bot but without the *sima*. This building is used as a sermon hall for monks and lay worshipers. Both the *viharn* and the *bot* enshrine Buddha statues, a presiding image and commonly several smaller statues.

Both *bot* and *viharn* follow identical architectural styles, being rectangular buildings with sweeping multi-tiered roofs covered with glazed brown and green or blue tiles. Each end of the roof's peak terminates in a gilded finial known as a *cho fa*, or "sky tassel". A gracefully curved ornamentation, it looks like a a slender bird's neck and head, and is generally believed to represent the mythical Garuda, half-bird, half-man.

Along with the *bot* and *viharn*, the most characteristic of temple structures is

Right: Mortal hands fashioning the eternal Buddha in a factory.

the *chedi* or *stupa*. Dominating the compound of a *wat*, this is a tall decorative spire constructed over relics of the Buddha, sacred texts or an image. Essentially there are two basic forms: bell-shaped and raised on square or round terraces of diminishing size, and tapering to a thin spire, or a round, finger-like tower. The latter, derived from Khmer architecture and symbolic of the mythical mountain abode of the gods, is known as a *prang*.

Other buildings in a temple compound can include a library for sacred texts, and a *mondop*. Traditionally the former was built on stilts over a pond to protect the fragile manuscripts from ants. The *mondop* is a square-shaped building with tapering roof enshrining some relic, often a Buddha footprint.

Some larger *wats* may also have cloisters, open-sided galleries perhaps displaying rows of Buddha images, while bell towers and various pavilions can be additional features.

Some *wats* also have a crematorium, identified by its needle-like chimney and, usually, a school for monks and perhaps also for lay children. These buildings are indicative of the traditional functions of a temple which extend beyond those of a place of worship and home to a religious community.

Rather like a medieval Christian church, the Thai temple was the focal point of every village. Unlike the church, however, it served far more than the community's spiritual needs. In the past, and still today in some rural areas, cultural life revolved around the *wat*, which stood as a social services center, school, hospital, dispensary, hostelry and village news, employment and information agency.

The most vivid illustration of the *wat's* community role these days is seen at annual temple fairs. Most *wats* continue the tradition of these fund-raising events when the normally serene temple compound becomes filled with swings and

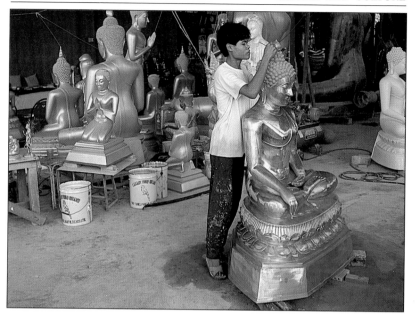

roundabouts, sideshows, *likay* (traditional folk opera) theatre shows and all the other typical fun-of-the-fair amusements, while the otherwise serene air is rent by loudspeakers blaring out raucous Thai music. In Bangkok, Wat Saket has the biggest of these affairs.

In a more serious vein, the temple has also been the storehouse of knowledge, sacred and profane (as with herbal medicine, for example) while monks, as one commentator has put it, "provided the vast majority of the inhabitants of premodern Siam with the ultimate basis for making sense of the world."

Thailand's high literacy rate, both now and in the past, owes much to temple schools where youngsters were and still are taught to read the sacred texts. On the day-to-day practical level, abbots will also often take the lead in instigating community projects such as digging a village well.

Most fascinating from the visitor's point of view is the temple as art center. Unlike its other functions, this role was unwittingly assumed by the *wat*. Until the modern period all Thai art was religious art, it had no conscious aesthetic function and served purely didactic and devotional aims. Thus sculpture, painting and the minor arts, such as gilt on lacquer, mother-of-pearl inlay and woodcarving, found expression almost exclusively in temple decoration.

Sculpture was largely limited to images of the Buddha. These are not idols but rather reminders of the teachings and, in theory at least, are all modelled on the same attributes of the Enlightened One. In practice, of course, sculpture did evolve different styles during various art periods and Buddha statues do vary considerably in form and expression.

Statues were executed in one of four basic postures – standing, sitting, walking and reclining – and, in addition, individual images display different *mudras*, or hand gestures. For example, both hands placed in the lap of the sitting Buddha indicate the meditation pose, whereas if the fingers of the right hand

47

are pointing to the ground, the statue indicates the Buddha's subduing of *mara* (forces of evil). In the standing image, the right hand raised signifies the *mudra* of "Dispelling Fear".

These and other *mudras*, as well as the four postures, remain constant throughout Thailand's art history, though at different periods schools of sculpture developed distinctive styles. These evolved from early Indian influences through the pre-Thai art of the Mon and the Khmer, and on to the Thai schools proper. The latter display considerable stylistic differences and vary from the serene and poetic images of the Sukhothai period to the crowned and highly ornamental statues of Ayutthaya times.

The major Thai schools of sculpture and their accepted dates are: Dvaravati, seventh-eighth century; Lopburi, thirteenth century; Haripunchai, thirteenth century; Chiang Saen, thirteenth-fourteenth century; Sukhothai, fourteenth century; U-Thong, thirteenth-fifteenth century; Ayutthaya, seventeenth-eighteenth century; and Rattanakosin, late eighteenth century to the present.

While there is a certain overlapping of periods and, in some cases, a fusion of styles – and the subject is rather complex – the interested visitor can nevertheless appreciate the stylistic variations to be seen in numerous Buddha images at different temples.

The *wat* is also a showcase of Thai classical painting, the art form achieving its finest expression in murals. Typically these were painted on all four walls of *bots* and *viharns*, though due to the fragile nature of the medium and the ravages of the climate, few surviving examples pre-date the eighteenth century.

All murals were purely didactic in purpose and the classic formula was to decorate the side walls with episodes from the life of the Buddha or his previous incarnations, individual scenes being sepa-

Above: Lavish costumes and intricate masks are used in dance performances. Right: Garuda, the mythical bird-king.

rated by registers of praying celestial beings. The back wall generally showed a graphic interpretation of the Buddhist cosmology, and the front wall was covered with the scene of Buddha's victory over *Mara*.

Typically, murals lack any attempt at perspective and figures tend to be small, while the entire picture area is "busy" and filled with detail. Because of the latter convention, artists often completed backgrounds with genre scenes of Thai daily life. These are fascinating both for their content and as areas where the painters display greater self-expression.

Doors and window shutters also sometimes have painted scenes, while all flat surfaces are commonly brilliantly adorned. Especially notable among the decorative arts are mother-of-pearl inlay and gilt-on lacquer works, which frequently have a high pictorial quality. Colored glass mosaic is also quite often used and does add to a temple's lavish overall decoration, brilliant and kaleidoscopic in effect yet managing to avoid the garish.

Not all travelers, however, have been enamored with Thai decoration. "The principle of Siamese architecture is the same as Cambodian, but with knobs on — lots of knobs. Wherever a bit of decoration or twirly-whirly can be fixed with some possibility of its staying put, it is stuck on," wrote Geoffrey Gorer in 1936. He was far too harsh in his judgement, though it is true that the Thais have a passion for decoration which is perhaps an expression of their natural exuberance. The point that Gorer couldn't or wouldn't admit and which Somerset Maugham picked up on, is that the mass of decorative detail is completely successful in its overall effect.

Finally, in wandering around a temple compound you can come across a number of mythological beings. As mentioned, high-art sculpture was limited to images of the Buddha, but there is some

statuary of creatures that play major roles in Thai myths and legends.

Among those most commonly seen are the half-man, half-bird Garuda, the mount of the god Vishnu; the Naga, king of serpents, frequently made in the form of balustrades flanking stairways at temple entrances; Yakshas, guardian giants; Kinnaris, half-woman, half-bird; and Apsaras or celestial nymphs who dance for the gods.

Only one major classical art form, the dance drama, springs not from Buddhism but from court entertainment. It does nonetheless have a clear moral content and themes are taken almost exclusively from classic epic tales.

The most distinctive form of dance drama is the *khon* in which performers wear lavish costumes and elaborate masks depicting the various characters. The plot is taken from the *Ramakien*, the Thai version of the Indian classic *Ramayana*, recounting the story of Prince Rama and the struggle of good over evil. Performed to music, *khon* is a highly stylized form of dance in which slow graceful body and hand movements express emotion as well as action.

While Buddhism unquestionably dominates Thai art and culture, there are other influences which color Thai society. Although the national religion is devoutly followed and unifies the people, beliefs which can be traced back to both Brahmanism and early animism not only persist but provide a ritualistic and existential basis for virtually all Thai customs.

Elements of Brahmanism, the ancient Indian religion and forerunner of both Hinduism and Buddhism, were inherited by the Thai from the Khmer. Specifically they relate to royal ritual and ceremonial. Today, Brahmanism in Thailand has made certain adaptations to become fully compatible with Buddhism and a small number of Brahman priests, recognizable by their white robes and long hair worn in a chignon, continue to preside over the major royal ceremonies.

Whereas Brahmanism has a court function, animism has a strong grassroots appeal. It scarcely conflicts with Buddhism, a tolerant faith which does not exclude belief in phenomena outside its basic tenets.

Animistic Heritage

Moreover, in placing ultimate responsibility firmly on each individual, the religion does not address in any practical way people's fears and hopes as encountered in daily life. Accordingly, traditional customs designed to cope with the spirit world, to placate evil forces and to seek good fortune from benevolent spirits, are still practised.

The most readily seen manifestations of such customs are spirit houses. Found in the compounds of virtually every house, business premises, government office and public building, these are small – and often not so small – ornate model dwellings, designed in the form of temples or traditional-style Thai houses. Commonly raised on a short column, they are usually garlanded with flowers and often provided with food offerings.

Their ubiquitous presence stems from the old belief that spirits inhabited the site before humans settled in and, lest they should become angered and bring misfortune, they must be placated by the provision of a home of their own. Much ceremony surrounds the positioning of a spirit house, which should then be constantly tended to ensure that its inhabitants remain contented.

Other shrines, similarly erected to ward off misfortune, can earn a reputation as being especially potent. The most famous example in Bangkok is the Erawan Shrine, which honors the Hindu god Brahma and was originally erected in the 1950s to end a string of misfortunes that had plagued the construction of the now demolished Erawan Hotel.

Shortly after it was erected the Erawan Shrine became widely regarded as possessing powers to grant all kinds of wishes. Its reputation has grown with the years, and it is visited daily by hundreds of supplicants seeking good fortune for all manner of things, from an easy childbirth to winning the lottery.

It is a reciprocal business and once a wish has been answered the supplicant will return to the shrine to make an offering of thanks – often lavishly prepared food or flowers and incense. Traditional dancers can also be hired to perform as an offering to the shrine and the daily scene is like something out of an Oriental fairytale.

Another common manifestation of belief in the supernatural is the wearing of amulets to provide protection for all manner of things, from snake bites to bullet wounds. Usually, but not always, they take the form of miniature Buddha im-

Right: The spirit's house, built to accommodate the spirit of the compound.

ages, though they must be ritualistically blessed to be potent. Amulets are more favored by men than women and it is not unusual to see someone with a string of a dozen or so hung around his neck.

While not all Thais have faith in amulets, most certainly have a great belief in astrologers and other types of fortune tellers. Rarely will someone embark on any major undertaking without first consulting an expert – sometimes a monk – about the most auspicious times.

Belief in superstitions, spirits and sources of good fortune are indeed widespread, and if not everyone admits to implicit belief, there is a general feeling that there is no harm in hedging one's bets. The Thais have a strong practical streak. The rain-invoking Rocket Festival held in northeast Thailand in May, for example, is firmly rooted in animism. To what extent people taking part in it today actually believe that it will bring rain is arguable, but all hold to the tradition if for no other reason than that the celebrations are good fun.

The pervading lifestyle is in fact strongly influenced by the concept of fun, having a good time – *sanuk*, as it is called in Thai.

Co-existing with religious faith and spiritual beliefs is a conviction that life is to be enjoyed, and *sanuk* is found in all things from organized entertainment to eating or simply taking a walk. Combine an easy-going, hospitable and fun-loving nature with a deep-rooted pride, sense of national identity and adherence to traditions, such as respect for parents, teachers and elders, and you have the quintessential Thai character.

Thailand Today

As Thailand enters the 1990s it is passing through a period of unprecedented change. Bangkok's skyline, bristling with highrise towers, the product of a mere decade, is but the most obvious outward sign of an economic boom that is not just altering the face of the capital, but also affecting the lifestyles of all Thais.

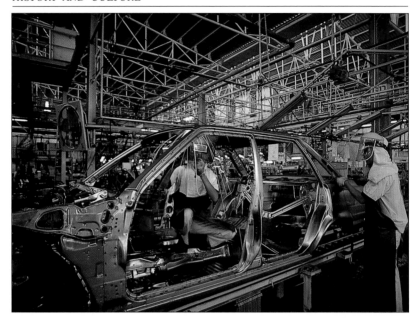

The annual economic growth rate has averaged just over seven per cent since 1986, a performance unrivaled by Thailand's neighbors, and the nation is now poised to assume NIC (Newly Industrialized Country) status. After Japan and the so-called "Little Dragons" of Taiwan, South Korea, Singapore and Hong Kong, the phrase-makers are now talking about Asia's "third wave" of NICs, and Thailand is currently riding the crest of the wave.

The boom has been gathering momentum over the past several years and has been spearheaded by a dynamic export drive. Exports have performed consistently well since the middle of the decade, and the net figure for 1988 was around 500 billion baht, a 24 per cent increase over the previous year and well ahead of the usually reliable Bank of Thailand projections.

Above: Even some of the Japanese Toyotas are "Made in Thailand".

Diversification has been the key to success. Agriculture, the traditional source of income, remains strong enough to ensure Thailand's ranking as the world's fifth largest food exporter. Its performance, however, has now been outstripped by manufacturing. Today, not only does the world buy most of its rice, tapioca and tinned pineapples from the kingdom; it is also increasingly shopping for "Made in Thailand" shoes and other leatherware, garments, jewelry and other manufactured items. Overall, manufactured goods account for 60 per cent of Thailand's exports. In 1960 the figure stood at a minute 2.4 per cent.

The third leg of the country's sturdy economic stool is the service industry and nothing quite matches the success of tourism, today's largest money-spinner. A "Visit Thailand Year" promotion brought in a then record of 3.5 million visitors to the kingdom in 1987, and its ongoing impact boosted 1988 arrivals to exceed the four-million mark; and still the boom has yet to peak.

Increased exports and an enhanced international profile combined with a pool of inexpensive labor and other incentives, have further served to promote the kingdom as an investment center. With rising costs hitting manufacturers in Japan, Taiwan, Korea and countries further afield, Thailand has come to be seen as an attractive production base and is drawing more and more overseas investment. In the first ten months of 1988, the Board of Investment (BoI), which oversees permits for investment projects, received 1,755 applications for promotional privileges with a combined investment value of 408,653.63 million baht, an all-time record.

A crucial factor in Thailand's recent success has been stability. The economy enjoys stability through being resilient, broad-based and diversified; political stability was an underpinning characteristic of government under former prime minister Prem Tinsulanonda, who held the top post from 1980 to 1988; and, finally, social stability springs from what is probably the region's most homogeneous society, molded by enduring traditions and long-held values.

Thailand is not, of course, problem-free and in particular communications and business infrastructure are overburdened and proving increasingly unable to cope with soaring demand. Telephones, electricity supply and other utilities, port facilities, road transport, airline capacity and hotel accommodation are all being stretched to the limit.

Infrastructure bottlenecks are not new – Bangkok's traffic congestion, for one, is legendary. The difference now is that rapid economic growth is pushing the problems to a critical point.

Presently such difficulties do affect mostly Bangkok, though that in itself is indicative of another problem – decentralization, or rather the lack of it. Historically the capital has always been the center of all major activity, but the current pace of growth means that what is almost a city-state concept must change. Moreover, a greater proportion of the increasing wealth needs to be channeled to the country's poorer rural areas. At present annual per-capita income in Bangkok is nearly three times greater than the national average.

Certain provincial districts, however, have not escaped latter-day difficulties. Tourism development has been rapid, too rapid in some places, and while it has brought great benefits to the traveler in terms of both access and facilities, largely unplanned development is having a detrimental effect on the environment.

A sense of euphoria typifies the boom times and this is quintessentially Thai. Unfortunately, in some quarters it goes beyond that to become greed, which is not a traditional Thai trait. Yet even without the baser human urges, the national catch-phrase *mai pen rai*, meaning "never mind", while endearing in many respects, needs to be held in check when, for example, environmental pollution threatens. Fortunately, there are signs of a growing awareness of the need to balance the pursuit of material prosperity with consideration for conservation and similar issues.

Challenges there certainly are. They are bigger and are happening more rapidly than ever before. Yet throughout their history the Thais have been well served by the near-opposite qualities of resilience and adaptability.

Today the country takes something of a Janus stance, it looks to the past with pride and to the future with confidence. The balance in outlook is not perfect, but it is steadied by a unique sense of "Thainess". The younger generation is grasping Western ways with both hands, yet it continues to echo that musical refrain, "We are Siamese if you please. We are Siamese if you don't please." So come to meet both – the traditional and the modern Thailand.

BANGKOK
A CAPITAL OF
CONTRADICTIONS

THE CITY OF ANGELS
GLITTERING TEMPLES
EXOTIC NIGHTLIFE

THE CITY OF ANGELS

Introducing a city invites superlatives, especially when that city is **Bangkok**. It seems that every travel guide must impress its readers with the most grandiose and arcane aspects of the metropolis into which they are about to dive. But chances are that, for most, Bangkok's reputation has preceded its reality. So it would be wise of those reading these words, who are about to plunge into the maze of Bangkok's whirl, to review their preconceptions.

Bangkok is undoubtedly a famous place on the global map, a place of intrigue, mystique and even notoriety. And yet interwoven into the intricate tapestry of this bustling, booming metropolis and international transportation hub, is the humility that Buddhism teaches, the splendor of one of the few remaining monarchies in Asia and the simplicity of the rural Thais, many of whom are drawn to this mecca of opportunity to seek their fortunes.

Bangkok of yesterday was invariably approached by either ship or rail and the

Preceding pages: Bananas for sale. It's gold and glitters – the Wat Phra Kaew temple in Bangkok. Left: Advertising billboard.

words of travelers taking those more leisurely forms of transport are accordingly more romantic. For example, envisage the approach of Anna Leonowens, the famous "Anna" in the popular film *The King and I*. She came by sailing ship and disembarked at the mouth of the Chao Phraya River, which was at that time the main access route to the city. And what did she see? "... every curve of the river is beautiful, with an unexpectedness of its own. Plantations spreading on either hand as far as the eye could reach, and level fields of living green, billowy with crops of rice, maize and sugar cane..."

Alas, today's traveler will be immediately confronted by the modernity of it all. The newly enlarged and renovated Bangkok International Airport serves most major airlines and makes Bangkok an important stop on international air routes. As his taxi carries him into the anarchy of Bangkok's traffic, the traveler may wonder where all the boats and buffalo carts have gone. By the time the city's outskirts are reached with their glistening skyscrapers and modern shopping plazas, the hapless voyager will realize one salient detail that might have been forgotten in the hurried weeks before departure. Bangkok is the nerve center of one of the fastest growing economies in the world. Romance in the

59

fabled East may still be found, but the boomtown bustle makes it certainly more elusive than in the days when Anna sailed up the River of Kings.

The Village of the Wild Plums

Bangkok is not an ancient city. It was chosen as the site for the capital of Siam by the first king of the present Chakri dynasty in 1782, a mere fifteen years after Siam's former capital, Ayutthaya, had been ransacked and totally destroyed by the Burmese in 1767.

At the time of its founding, it was a small river port with a name meaning "Village of the Wild Plums". To a foreign ear, the Thai name sounded like "Bangkok" and so for foreigners that name has stuck. But the Thais still call their capital "Krung Thep", a short form of a much longer, more auspicious name chosen by

Above: View across the Chao Phraya river.
Right: The Emerald Buddha is a mere 75 cm tall and sits in the Wat Phra Kaew.

the first king, Rama I. "Krung Thep" means simply "City of Angels".

Bangkok's history as the capital of Siam began in 1782 when King Rama I began the task of converting the village into a city. Construction of palaces and temples with fortifications was begun in a river bend, the site which the **Grand Palace** still occupies today. This area is crescent-shaped and bounded on the west by the river and on the east by a canal called Klong Krung Kasem, initially built as a protective moat. Two other canals, Klong Banglampu and Klong Lord were also excavated to provide waterways across the new capital.

The visitor may best understand this period by touring the area around the **Pramane Grounds**, an open field ringed by tamarind trees and bordered by Wat Phra Kaew to the south and Klong Lord/Rajdamnoen Avenue to the north. This area, also called *Sanam Luang*, was the heart of the old capital. It is still regarded by Thais as the symbolic center of the Kingdom and was the site for many

elaborate celebrations when the reigning monarch, King Bhumibol Adulyadej, celebrated his sixtieth birthday, and on the occasion of his becoming the longest reigning monarch in Thai history. In addition to royal events, the open space is used by vendors, kite-flyers and families on weekend picnics.

This area is one of the few a visitor can realistically visit on foot, although even here distances are long. Within the district can be found the Grand Palace complex and the **Temple of the Emerald Buddha** (*Wat Phra Kaew*). This compound, with its massive whitewashed, castellated walls, is open to the public every day for an admission fee, which includes the entrance ticket to **Vimanmek Palace**, located some distance away (to be mentioned later).

King Rama I founded the Grand Palace after seeing that the site was the least vulnerable to attack. But his contribution was merely the laying of foundations. Each of his successors built upon the earlier beginnings so that the buildings in the complex date from different periods. The main palace, **Chakri Maha Prasad**, was constructed in 1867 by Rama IV, or King Mongkut, who had invited Anna Leonowens to come to Siam to tutor his children. Guidebooks, available at the palace, explain the history and architectural features in detail. The compound is large and, together with the Temple of the Emerald Buddha, can easily require a half-day tour to do it justice.

Continuing around Sanam Luang, one can see, facing north, the **Ministry of Defense** with its collection of canons on the lawn, and across the street, in a marble pavilion, the shrine housing the **Rak Muang** or **City Pillar**, placed there by King Rama I. This is regarded as Bangkok's symbolic foundation stone, with the power to grant wishes.

On the other side of Sanam Luang, still facing north but on the left, can be seen **Wat Mahathat** and **Silpakorn University**. Further on are the buildings of the **National Museum**, **National Theatre** and behind, on the river, the buildings of

61

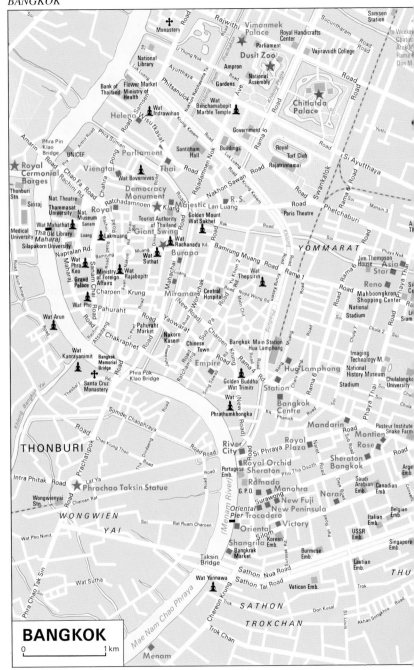

BANGKOK

0   1 km

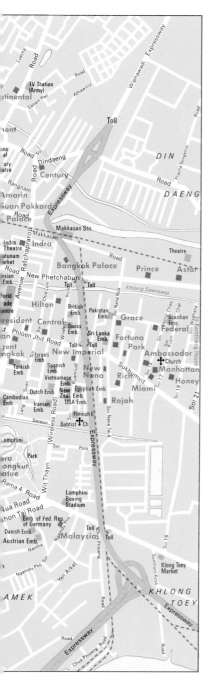

Thammasat University. This center of learning, called the University of Morals and Politics before World War II, was an internment camp for citizens of the Allied countries, some five hundred of whom stayed there throughout the war.

Tours of the National Museum are conducted in many languages by volunteers, starting in the mornings on weekdays. The **Tourism Authority of Thailand (TAT)** office, located on Rajdamnoen Nok Avenue, will have the exact times and days for these tours. A tour of Sanam Luang can easily consume a day if a visit to the Grand Palace and the National Museum are combined. But to understand Thailand's historical and cultural roots, there is no better place to start. The Palace gives you a glimpse of the court life of the Chakri kings and through its extensive collection, the museum depicts the art history of the country going back to its prehistoric beginnings.

Bangkok Moves into the Modern Era

At the turn of the century, Bangkok remained a sleepy backwater, especially if compared to the burgeoning ports of Singapore to the south and Rangoon to the west. But the monarch of the time, the much-revered King Chulalongkorn (Rama V), was a man of vision and education. He made a number of trips abroad, and what he saw in Europe impressed him. Thus began a series of projects to modernize Bangkok, the results of which can still be seen to this day.

The cramped area around the Grand Palace and the congested warrens of Chinatown close by were no longer to the king's taste. His majesty had seen grand boulevards, gaslit streets, electric trams and even motorcars plying the streets of Europe. Not content with the Bangkok he returned to, King Chulalongkorn began to construct streets and canals. He built a throne hall in marble and a large teak palace which he called the **Palace in the**

Clouds or **Vimanmek**. Nearby, he had a Royal Garden laid out which is now **Dusit Zoo**.

The king's initiative prompted princes, the nobility and the upper classes to follow suit, resulting in the spacious area today called the district of Dusit. Within this area, on Rajdamnoen Nok Avenue, are the offices of the **Tourism Authority of Thailand (TAT)**, where the friendly staff may be consulted on anything pertaining to travel in Thailand. They have numerous brochures free of charge, slides of various sites around the kingdom, which may be purchased for 10 baht a slide, and schedules of trains and buses. They can also make reservations for facilities operated by TAT, like the Bangphra Golf Course and Khao Yai Motor Lodge.

About two kilometers past the TAT offices down Rajdamnoen Nok is the imposing domed **National Assembly** build-

Above: This is where Jim Thompson, the Thai silk king once dwelled.

ing, earlier mentioned as the Throne Hall commissioned by King Chulalongkorn. Faced in marble imported from Italy, this impressive building is today used for ceremonial state functions. The parliament is now housed in a modern, more functional, but less elegant building not far away.

Immediately behind the National Assembly building is **Vimanmek Palace**, built by King Chulalongkorn as an escape from the then crowded and antiquated Grand Palace compound. This breathtaking mansion, reputedly the largest golden teak building in the world, gives visitors an intimate glimpse of the lives of the former king and his queen and consorts at the turn of the century. The king lived here for several years before moving to the newly – built Dusit Palace nearby.

Her Majesty Queen Sirikit found this imposing building in a sad state of abandonment and began the job of restoration, opening the magnificent edifice to the public in late 1985. Please note that admission is included in the ticket price paid to tour the Grand Palace. Tours are conducted in English, Japanese, Chinese and French. For details see Guidepost.

Across the street is **Dusit Zoo**, a shady retreat from the sun and street noise. The collection of animals is rather meagre, but the park affords the tourist an interesting glimpse of Thai couples and families at leisure.

Not far from the zoo is **Wat Benchamabopit**, the **Marble Temple**. This jewel-like structure occupies one corner of the grounds of **Chitralada Palace**, the home of the King and Queen of Thailand.

In one corner of the intersection of Rama V and Rajwithi Roads are the grounds and colorful buildings of **Vajiravudh College**, built as a prep school by King Vajiravudh (Rama VI), the eldest son of King Chulalongkorn. Across from the College, in Rama V Road, is the **Royal Handicrafts Center**, where an enormous selection of arts and crafts products from each corner of the kingdom is offered for sale.

The entire area with its spacious attractions – Vimanmek, the zoo, the Marble Temple and the Handicrafts Center – offer the visitor a pleasant district of tree-shaded streets, huge old mansions with walled gardens and green *klongs*. It is definitely a more serene corner of the metropolis, but distances make walking unfeasible.

Old Teak Houses

Looking out across Bangkok's skyline, it is difficult to imagine the days when canals (*klongs*) were the favored transport route and life was a leisurely affair, spent sipping cool drinks on open teak verandas. But there are still a few old houses, which have been preserved, with their stilts, leaning walls and airy interiors. A visit to any one of them gives the visitor a taste of what gracious living was like in the days before the building boom

started in Thailand in the late 1950s.

Wang Suan Pakkard: This beautiful palace compound is located on Sri Ayutthaya Road, just down from the Victory Monument, east of Phya Thai Avenue. Wang Suan Pakkard, meaning Lettuce Farm Palace, is a collection of five old teak houses, which were dismantled at their original locations and reassembled at the current site. The home of Princess Chumbkot until her death in 1988, the palace was set up to house and display the extensive art collection that she and her husband assembled over the years. There are special exhibits of Ban Chiang ware, unearthed at a prehistoric site in the northeast of Thailand, and an extensive collection of seashells. Set in the midst of the late princess's favorite flowers and shrubs, this oasis of serenity is the picturesque home to ducks, swans and a picturesque pelican or two.

Jim Thompson's House: Just off Rama I Road, on Soi Kasem San 2 and within easy walking distance of Mahboonkrong Shopping Center, this house, like Suan Pakkard, has been created from several old teak houses, dismantled in Ayutthaya and re-erected in the gardens on Klong San Saep in the heart of Bangkok.

But these old buildings, besides housing artifacts and offering another glimpse of life during days gone by, have an air of mystery. They retain an added mystique, being the former home of the "Thai Silk King" Jim Thompson, who, one morning in 1967, went out for a walk in the Cameron Highlands in Malaysia, and was never seen or heard of again. The book, *The Legendary American – The Remarkable Career & Strange Disappearance of Jim Thompson*, by William Warren, gives a well-documented account of Jim Thompson's life, up to the point of his disappearance. It describes how he built up his silk business, introduced Thai silk to New York and assembled his art collection and houses. All

proceeds go to the Bangkok School for the Blind.

Kamthieng House (Siam Society): The Kamthieng House is a typical northern Thai dwelling and displays a small collection of northern crafts and tools from the old days. The Siam Society, which publishes the *Journal of the Siam Society,* has long been dedicated to preserving aspects of traditional Thai culture. The other attraction in the grounds, for those seriously interested in Thai history and culture, is the reference library operated by the Society.

Walking Tours

Walking is not a popular form of activity in Bangkok. The weather is usually too hot, sidewalks are crowded and crossing a street is positively lethal. It should be stressed that crossing big busy streets

Above: A Thai girl with an offering. Right: Business as usual in Chinatown.

should be done with extreme caution and, if possible, always via a pedestrian bridge. But if a view of life free of cars and street noise is what you are looking for, there are places where people are carrying on much as they have for centuries.

The first is a warren of old streets, crumbling Chinese temples and Thai *wats* (*wat* is the name for a Buddhist temple in Thailand), just next to the glitter of River City and the Royal Orchid Sheraton Hotel on the Chao Phraya River. The walker must be willing to dive into the lanes with eyes and ears wide open, using trial and error to wend his way through. But the effort will give a taste of the old **Chinatown**, which is fast disappearing. Visitors should keep their camera ready for shots of urchins splashing in the river, monks sitting on a temple wall or Muslims outside their mosque, killing time watching passersby.

Lumpini Park, opposite the Dusit Thani Hotel, is another great place for walkers, especially in the mornings. In this cool shady park, the stroller will encounter hundreds of joggers, Chinese of all ages doing their daily *tai-chi* exercises and entire classes of women doing aerobic exercises in unison.

If the sight of all this exertion has stimulated the walker's hunger, **Soi Sarasin**, the street running along the park's north side, has dozens of vendors selling a vast selection of local dishes. Two of the vendors appear early every morning, offering what the more elderly Chinese seem to crave most after a rigorous workout – snake gall. There, writhing safely in wire cages, are such toothsome specimens as pythons, cobras and the extremely venomous banded kraits. These serpents, once chosen by a customer, are gutted and the gall and glands drained into a glass of whisky, which is gulped down. This elixir, believed to have rejuvenating powers, is a popular aphrodisiac for old men bent on an evening's frolic.

The third area conducive to walking is the collection of streets and lanes (*sois*) running around **Wat Saket** or the **Golden Mount**, for many decades, and until the building boom started, the highest point in the city. First scale the stairs to the top of the Golden Mount for a view of the city's rooftops, especially interesting at dawn or sunset. Then plunge into the streets with their many shops around Wat Rachanada on Mahachai Road. There are numerous little stores selling rattan ware and intricate wooden decorative pieces. A walk down Bamrung Muang Road brings one past the **Giant Swing**, a reminder of the ceremonies of earlier times, when young men risked life and limb swinging at dizzying heights. This area is rich in temples and just past the corner of Ti Thong Road, is the Kanit House Restaurant, which serves excellent pizzas, French cuisine, desserts and coffees.

The map which will serve the explorer best in Thailand is the Nelles Map "Thailand 1:1.5 Million". It includes a close-up map of downtown Bangkok, as well as a list of hotels and some important touristic information.

While the old houses of Bangkok and some of the walks around old neighborhoods give a glimpse of life of yesteryear, there is no better way to experience today's bustle of the common folk than to visit one of Bangkok's many markets.

The largest of them all is the **Weekend Market** at **Chatuchak Park** in the north of Bangkok. Formerly held at Sanam Luang, this weekend market was moved to its present location in 1982. This vast shopping area is open only on Saturdays and Sundays from 8:00 in the morning till sunset. Crowded and hot, the weekend market has something for everybody and tourists can expect to find any kind of souvenir, antique or handicraft. Clothing stalls are numerous, selling anything from traditional Thai items to factory rejects and second-hand shirts, imported from abroad in bulk, and reconditioned. Food stalls offer a prodigious array of dishes. Much of the area is given to plant, animal, bird and live fish vendors. In

Kampaeng Phet Road, across from the Weekend Market, is **Atok Market** which runs the length of the street and specializes in potted plants, gardening supplies and giant ceramic and terracotta pots. Unlike the Weekend Market, it is open throughout the week and has some good open air eating places.

The **Flower Market**, locally called *Talaat Tehweht*, runs along the mouth of Klong Krung Kasem canal. This permanent plant and flower market is open throughout the week from dawn to dusk. The stalls display an amazing variety of orchids and flowering shrubs.

Pratunam Market extends around the Petchburi-Rajdamri-Rajparop Roads crossing where, throughout the whole area, usually in small second and third floor rooms, hundreds of sewing machines whirr until late at night. They churn out millions of shirts every year, which are then sold right there by hundreds of busy street vendors.

Sampeng Lane or Soi Wanit 1 is a narrow alleyway crowded with sellers and shoppers, running from Pahurat, where Bangkok's Indian community gathers, right through Chinatown. Once again, for a detailed guide to this thriving lane, Nancy Chandler's colorful map is a must. Close to the beginning of the lane are some of the city's best Indian restaurants and sweet shops.

Klong Toey market, close to Bangkok's riverside port, is a hive of commerce with many imported items for sale. Located just off Rama IV Road, this market also offers the largest selection of fresh produce at the best prices in the city. A stroll will be rewarding.

The more upmarket shopping districts in Bangkok are in two different areas, one along Sukhumvit Road and the other in Silom Road. Airconditioned buses or taxis are the best mode of transportation to skip along these lengthy thoroughfares, which have some excellent luxury outlets, boutiques, department stores,

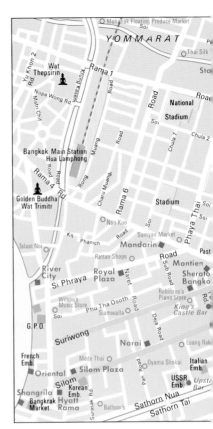

shopping malls and speciality shops. Finally, shoppers can find a vast array of shops in an area known as **Siam Square**, right in the heart of Bangkok on Rama I Road. Across from the chic Siam Center, bordering on the huge Mahboongkrong Shopping Center and opposite the Siam Intercontinental Hotel, Siam Square has many fast food outlets, clothing and shoe shops, book and computer stores, movie theaters and rows of stalls selling leather goods, audio tapes, clothing and fashion jewelry.

Museums

Bangkok, although not particularly known for its art galleries and museums,

BANGKOK
ENTERTAINMENT AND SHOPPING

0   1 km

does have several which present different facets of Thailand's fascinating history and culture during its development into a modern nation.

The most important is the **National Museum**, already mentioned in the section on Sanam Luang and the Grand Palace. Recently expanded, the museum is rated as one of the best of its kind in Southeast Asia. Housed in a series of buildings which were formerly the palace of the second king, usually a brother of the reigning king, the museum has guided tours in all major languages. For the details consult the information section of the museum's guidebook.

The displays are arranged according to the various historical periods of Thai art.

Buddhist sculpture makes up most of its collection, but its exhibits also contribute greatly to the understanding of Thai habits, tradition and lifestyle. Artifacts from royalty are displayed along with the most humble utensils of upcountry rural life. Prospective purchasers of Thai art or antiques would do well to familiarize themselves with the styles explained at the museum, before you are venturing into the marketplace.

Siriraj, Thailand's first modern hospital, opened in 1888 by King Rama V, is still one of the largest in the country, and contains ten museums, including its best known, the **Museum of Forensic Medicine**. Here, rather frightening examples of misdeeds are shown, including the pre-

served body of a Chinese mass murderer, executed about forty years ago. The museum is near Bangkok Noi station.

A new addition to Bangkok's museum scene is the **Imaging Technology Museum**, located near the main gate of Chulalongkorn University on Phya Thai Road. It was constructed in close cooperation with large multinational photo supply and camera companies from Japan and the US. Intended as a working museum, and providing a home for the Department of Photographic Science at the university, the museum has an extensive display of old cameras, some having belonged to the kings of Thailand. The photo displays have examples dating back to the last century and separate sections show the very latest photographic technology, set up by major companies. A must for photo buffs.

Above: Rikshaw driver waiting for customers in front of the cinema. Right: An orchestra plays on original instruments during the cultural show in the Rose Garden.

Also near the main gate of Chulalongkorn University on Phya Thai, is the **Natural History Museum**, a little-known gem, housed in an old building of the Faculty of Science. It is open only on request and has impressive collections of fossils, butterflies and stuffed birds and mammals. For information in English, on either of the above two museums, call the university's Office of International Affairs, Tel:215-0870/3, ext. 3331.

The **Thai Imagery Museum** in Thonburi is somewhat like a wax museum, but the figures are sculpted in fiberglass and are amazingly life-like. The kings of Thailand are a central display.

Bangkok, with its many markets, interesting old neighborhoods, temples and waterways, is sadly lacking in public parks and gardens, although the Thais are great lovers of flowers and plants. Thailand is after all one of the world's largest exporters of orchids and has developed several species unique to the kingdom. Visitors interested in plants native to Thailand and exhibits from abroad will

find no better place than the new Rama IX Park on the outskirts of Bangkok.

TAT will give directions to this huge area in the northeastern suburbs of the city. The **Rama IX Park** or **Suan Raw Kao** is the newest park in Bangkok and was completed in honor of the king's sixtieth birthday in 1987. It has been landscaped to display the many Thai plants to their best advantage and includes everything, from trees and shrubs to orchids.

In one pavilion are only shade-loving plants such as ferns and bromeliads. In a geodesic dome, donated by the US government and many American companies, a cacti collection has been planted, with specimens flown in from the Arizona and New Mexico deserts. Behind the upswept central pavilion of the park, which houses a collection of mementoes and photographs commemorating the life and hobbies of His Majesty the King, is a large artificial lake, in which aquatic plants native to Thailand have been planted. Chinese and Japanese gardens were donated by the governments in Beijing and Tokyo. The park is open everyday but is crowded on weekends, although it is too vast for this to matter.

Another garden, west of Bangkok, is the famous **Rose Garden**. Depending on traffic conditions, it is about an hour's drive (about 30 km) away. Known as **Suan Sam Phran**, this garden is really an assortment of attractions, the large landscaped flower beds being merely one of them. There is a modern hotel, a golf course, convention center and several Thai-style bungalows. Other recreational facilities include a swimming pool, bowling alley and river sports on the Tachin River. Thai cultural shows are presented as well. Located on Route 4, it is easy to reach by car, or by bus from the Thonburi southern bus terminal.

Already mentioned in the section on old Thai houses, the **Suan Pakkard Palace** also has a rich botanical collection. Its gardens were designed by Princess Chumbhot of Nagara Svarg, who, in addition to being one of Thailand's leading art collectors, was also an

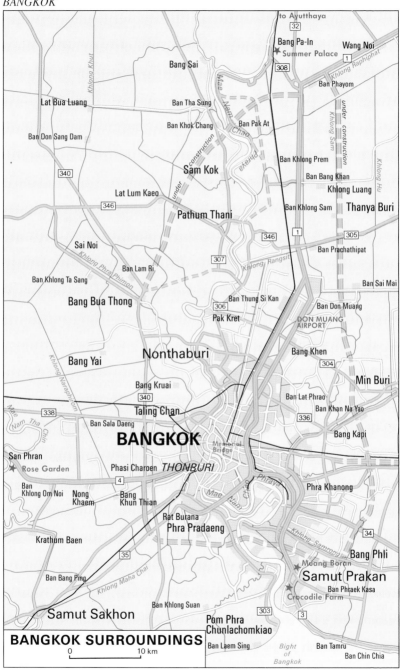

BANGKOK SURROUNDINGS

0   10 km

avid gardener. Many of the rarer trees and plants are labeled.

On the Thonburi side of the river, especially along the numerous canals, are acres of orchid gardens, where plants and cut flowers are cultivated for both the local markets and export. Thailand has over a thousand varieties of native orchid in its jungles, and experts are constantly trying to create new hybrids. The gardens along *klongs* are best visited by boat. Water tours can easily be arranged.

This leads to the next form of sightseeing, which Bangkok shares with cities like Amsterdam and Venice. Bangkok was, and to some extent still is, a city of waterways. Many of its canals (locally called *klongs*) are still in use, especially on the Thonburi side, and all are connected with the Menam Chao Phraya, the River of Kings.

A good and cheap way to get a feel for riverine Bangkok is by the **Chao Phraya Express Boats** or *Ruea Duan*. These boats run up and down the river at regular intervals (usually every 15 minutes), and offer an inexpensive way to see life on the main river of the country. Most visitors pick up the Chao Phraya Express at piers at the Oriental Hotel, the Royal Orchid Sheraton Hotel, or the stops nearest the Grand Palace. The boats start running at dawn and stop at sunset. Fares start at 5 baht and increase according to the length of the journey.

Ferries crossing the Chao Phraya, the *ruea kham fak*, operate at many of the same stops. They are used mostly by locals, but they can provide tourists with a glimpse of certain parts of Thonburi. For example, one interesting walk is through the old Portuguese section of Bangkok, around the Church of Santa Cruz on the Thonburi side. Merely by boarding a boat at Tha Saphan Phut and crossing the river, visitors will soon find that they have stepped into a quiet oasis, which seems far from the city. Long-tailed **taxi boats** or *ruea hang yao* can be seen roaring up and down the river, sending up a rooster's tail of spray. Some of these boats have regular schedules with fares starting at 3 baht.

Klong tours are becoming a standard feature for visitors to Bangkok. At **boat landings** like the Oriental Pier, Tha Maharaj or Tha Pra Chand near the palace, boat operators wait to transport tourists up the *klongs* in Thonburi. Such tours can be short trips, or can go as far as the Crocodile Farm in Samut Prakarn, the Floating Market, the Ancient City, to orchid gardens or fruit plantations.

Bargaining for fares is the rule with a minimum for one hour around 250 baht. Since one boat can accommodate at least ten persons comfortably, a group trip can be a real bargain. Refreshments can be purchased along the way from canalside shops. It is best to start out early, around 7:00. Many hotels can arrange such boat hire for guests.

River trips are an enjoyable way to tour Siam's ancient capital of **Ayutthaya** and the summer palace at **Bang Pa-in** (see p. 89). Several services have sprung up, but the pioneer of these luxury trips, the Oriental Hotel, operates two boats, leaving early in the morning. A buffet lunch is served on board. On reaching Ayutthaya, the boat, meets a tour bus, which transports passengers to the main points of interest, before returning to Bangkok in the late afternoon. It is recommended to go by bus in the morning, when it is still cool enough to tour Ayutthaya, and then return by air-conditioned boat, cruising back to Bangkok in the afternoon, having lunch and sipping drinks on deck as the river flows by.

At one time a large part of Thailand was covered by jungle and was home to an enormous variety of wildlife. Alas, the forest cover of the kingdom has been depleted, which had a disastrous effect on its wildlife. In 1988 for instance, because of excessive logging in the hills above Surat Thani in the south, floods destroyed

Serum containing antibodies to the venom is then taken from the horses and purified, before being distributed around Thailand and abroad as an antidotes for snakebite.

A notable animal attraction in Samut Prakarn, about 33 km from Bangkok on the Sukhumvit highway going southeast, is the **Crocodile Farm**, rated as the largest in the world. Started by a man who used to hunt crocodiles in the wild, it has been emulated by other countries to keep their crocodile populations from becoming extinct.

Today it is extremely rare to see any of the four species native to Thailand in their wild state. One of the farm's specimens is rated as the largest crocodile in the world by the *Guinness Book of Records*. The farm puts on regular performances throughout the day, featuring wrestling between man and crocodile plus other animal acts.

A sideline of the farm, raising crocodiles for their skins, has been boosted by the addition of a snake farm, to raise snakes for their skins. The main feeding of the crocs takes place late in the afternoon. Buses for Samut Prakarn leave Ekamai bus station on Sukhumvit Road at the end of Soi 61.

One other attraction in Samut Prakarn, which can be combined with a trip to the Crocodile Farm, is the **Ancient City** or *muang boran*. A favorite stop on the itinerary of Bangkok tour companies, this vast outdoor museum offers miniature versions of the major architectural attractions of Thailand, covering 80 hectares with beautifully crafted replicas.

The Ancient City idea was the brainchild of the owner of the largest Mercedes Benz dealership in Thailand. The company's offices are near the Democracy Monument on Ratchadamnoen Avenue. Public buses are the same as those going to the Crocodile Farm, or the company can arrange personal transportation.

villages and killed many people. This disaster provoked the government to declare a ban on logging operations, and suddenly ecology has become a major issue. Nevertheless, zoos and animal farms give the visitor an opportunity to see many species of tropical fauna, which in some cases are being kept from extinction by being re-introduced into the wilderness.

One of the oldest **snake farms** in the world is operating in the very heart of Bangkok and actively encourages visitors to come and see its show. Situated at the Pasteur Institute on Rama IV Road at the corner of Henri Dunant Road, the Institute raises venomous snakes to extract their venom. Snakes such as the banded krait, Siamese cobra, king cobra, pit and Malayan vipers are milked and fed every day at 11:00. The venom is collected and injected in small amounts into horses.

Above: Milking a cobra for its poison at the Pasteur Institute. Right: The Wat Arun, Temple of Dawn, at the Mae Nam Chao Phraya.

GLITTERING TEMPLES EVERYWHERE

The intricate, ornate Siamese architecture, that makes Thai temples so distinctly different, is almost exclusively reserved for Buddhist religious structures, particularly temples sponsored by royalty. The willingness to carry the extra expense and longer time involved in the construction of a temple, as compared to an ordinary building, is in part due to the Thais' belief in the power of merit-making and the deep-rooted tradition based on the fact that temples, in days gone by, were a community's most important building, not only as a religious center, but also as the heart of community activities and education.

Most of the more famous *wats* seen around Bangkok were built or renovated in the early Rattanakosin period, particularly during the reign of the first three Chakri monarchs, who were determined to restore a sense of continuity, and uphold the glory that was Ayutthaya.

Under subsequent reigns, royally sponsored construction projects focused more on modern institutions, such as schools, hospitals and government buildings.

The following selection of *wats* (temples) offers a good example of classical Siamese art and architecture:

1. **Wat Phra Kaew** (The Temple of the Emerald Buddha). Upholding Ayutthaya's tradition of having a temple within the grand palace compound, King Rama I built Wat Phra Kaew in the 1780s. The *ubosot* (sanctuary) houses the Emerald Buddha, the most revered image in the kingdom. This 75-cm tall statue is not, as is commonly supposed, one huge emerald, but is carved from some kind of, as yet undetermined, green stone. Three times a year, at the change of seasons, the

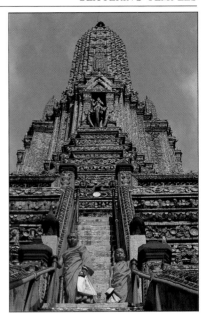

Left:The gigantic Reclining Buddha at Wat Po. Right: The Prang of the Wat Arun is covered with Chinese porcelain.

image is dressed in a ceremony performed only by the King.

In this, the kingdom's most famous temple, the buildings are adorned with glass mosaic and gilt, displaying typical Rattanakosin designs. The mural paintings in the cloisters show episodes from the *Ramakien*. Six pairs of 6-m tall *yaks* (mythical giants) stand guard at the entrances to the inner court, each having his individual marks and attributes. In the compound is also a replica of Angkor Wat. Detailed guidebooks are readily available. Proper dress is essential.

2. **Wat Po** (*Wat Phra Chetupon*). Bangkok's oldest and Thailand's largest temple, Wat Po, then called Wat Potaram, was built during the Ayutthaya period. King Rama III made it the center of medicine, traditional massage, literature and astrology, thus establishing the kingdom's first open university. Located next to, and on the south of, the Grand Palace, Wat Po has a gigantic reclining Buddha image, measuring 46 m in lenght and 15 m in height. The soles of the statue's feet

are beautifully decorated in mother-of-pearl. In the compound is also a school teaching traditional Thai massage, where the tired tourist can have his waning energy restored.

3. **Wat Suthat**. This temple was started by King Rama I and completed by Rama III. Originally conceived to match Wat Panan Cherng, a former temple in the heart of Ayutthaya, Rama II has been responsible for its present layout. It has some impressive mural paintings of legendary creatures, which were recently restored with aid from the German government. The *ubosot*, surrounded by 28 Chinese pagodas, representing 28 aspects of the Buddha, is considered the largest and longest in Thailand.

In front of Wat Suthat, in Bamrungmuang Road, stands "**Sao Ching Cha**", the **Giant Swing**. Made of huge teak logs, it was formerly used once a year in

Above: Wat Saket capping the Golden Mount. Right: A monk kneels at the feet of the statue of Buddha in the Wat Indraviharn.

a Brahmanical ceremony, where young men, swinging to a height of over 20 m, tried to snatch a bag of money. The practice was stopped in the 1930s.

4. **Wat Arun** (Temple of the Dawn). Wat Arun is associated with the reign of King Rama II, because of his extensive involvement in its restoration. Dating back to the Ayutthaya period, the temple, then called Wat Chaeng, was right next to King Taksin's palace before he moved his residence to Bangkok. The 86-meter-high *prang* (*chedi* or pagoda), one of Bangkok's symbols is a beautiful sight in the glow of sunset, if seen from the Bangkok side of the Chao Phraya River.

5. **Wat Ratchabopit**. This richly ornate temple was built in 1869, its interior being a blend of Versaille and Thai styles. The main chapel's door and window panels feature unusual mother-of-pearl inlays. Of special interest is the royal cemetery in the grounds, with its Khmer, Thai and Gothic structures. Wat Ratchabopit is close to the Ministry of Industry on Ratchabopit Road.

6. **Wat Benchamabopit** (The Marble Temple). Already an ancient seat of religion when Rama II had it renovated, this temple was completely rebuilt at the turn of the century. In 1899, when two old temples were torn down to make way for an expansion of Dusit Palace, King Chulalongkorn (Rama V) ordered an all out restoration of Wat Benchamabopit as an act of atonement. Prince Narit, the king's half-brother, was charged with the creation of a perfect Thai-style temple and succeeded to everyone's delight.

The graceful, modern-looking *ubosot* was built in white Carrara marble from Italy. It houses a replica of *Phra Buddha Shinnarat*, in the base of which are the ashes of King Rama V. Unconventional are the stained glass windows and the large collection of Buddha statues representing, in either original or replica, all periods and styles from all parts of Thailand.

The temple is the premier meeting place for visiting foreign Buddhist monks of different sects and has been a center for religious discussion, sometimes of a controversial nature. The Marble Temple is on Si Ayutthaya Road near Chitralada Palace.

7. **Wat Traimit** (The Temple of the Golden Buddha). Situated near Hualumphong Railway Station, Wat Traimit was just an ordinary old temple until an accident opened a crack in the stucco covering of a Buddha statue, revealing solid gold inside. The 3-m high statue, weighing 5 1/2 tonnes, had been considered rather unsightly, and had been offered to and turned down by many other temples before Wat Traimit finally agreed to house it. This is not the first incident of its kind and it is thought that the plaster was applied to this valuable 13th century Sukhothai style image to hide it from the looting Burmese.

8. **Wat Bovornnivet.** Wat Bavornnivet was established in 1832 to house the *Phra Buddha Shinnasi* statue from Pitsanuloke. It is the seat of the Mahamakut Rachawittayalai, a Buddhist university set up by King Rama IV as the first of

two seats of higher religious learning in Thailand. Located in the Banglampoo area, a strong Chinese influence is evident, as seen by the Chinese style gateways with *siaw gung* or Chinese entrance guardians painted on the door panels. The *ubosot* features frescoes by one of the finest *Rattanakosin* mural painters, *Krua-in-kong*, who was the first artist to apply Western techniques to classical Thai paintings.

9. **Wat Mahathat**. Previously called *Wat Salak*, this temple houses the Mahachulalongkorn Rachawittayalai, the second Buddhist university in Thailand. The temple dates back to the Ayutthaya period, but has underwent considerable restoration work in 1844, during the reign of King Rama III. Wat Mahathat was the place where major revisions in the Buddhist scriptures were carried out during the reign of King Rama I. It was also a cre-

Above: The massive gold Buddha in the Wat Traimit. Right: A classical dancer at the Erawan shrine.

matorium for royalty. For those interested in meditation, a visit to Section V in the compound may be interesting, as it is the headquarters of the Burmese version of Vipassana Buddhist meditation in Thailand. It is also one of the very few religious institutions in the country where instruction in English is readily available. Visitors will also find a thriving open air market in the temple grounds, offering herbs, medicinal drinks, precious stones, antiques, amulets and plants.

The temple is on Na Phrathat Road between the Fine Arts Department and Thammasat University. The grounds are excellent for spending a relaxing afternoon and entry is free.

10. **Loha Prasart** (The Metal Palace). The first metal palace, a two-storey building with a golden roof, was built in India as a retreat for the Buddha and his followers during the Buddhist Lent. The second was a nine-floor structure, also with a golden roof, erected in Sri Lanka 382 years after the death of the Buddha. And Loha Prasart, in the compound of Wat Ratchanaddaram, is the third and only surviving metal palace. It was built in 1846 to commemorate a princess, niece of King Rama III and the first consort of King Rama IV.

The three-storey, brick and limestone building in the style of the earlier metal palaces, with 37 spires, is now easily visible again, since the old Chalerm Thai movie theater, which had blocked the historical building from view for decades, was demolished in 1989. Curious visitors may also want to see the amulet market in the inner temple compound, where all kinds of Buddha images, religious objects and talismans are sold.

This rather sparse glimpse of Bangkok's temple scene may whet your appetite to venture out on your own, but if you prefer the convenience of air-conditioned transport and guided tours, there is no end to the variety of temple tours available. For details ask at TAT.

EXOTIC NIGHTLIFE

Bangkok has the reputation for having the most exotic and varied nightlife in the region, most of which can be enjoyed at very reasonable prices. Although entertainment after dark takes many forms, hostess bars of one sort or another have, for the last two decades, dominated the scene.

There are literally thousands of restaurants, clubs and massage parlors throughout the city. These are backed up by three major Muay Thai boxing rings, illegal casinos, cinemas, theater performances and even a symphony orchestra. There is something to appeal to everyone, but despite the variety, if one objective was to describe Bangkok's nightlife, it would have to be "physical".

We will not describe the endless string of lobby bars, discos and restaurants, that belong to hotels, because these are basically the same all over the world. They are characterized by the hotel chain operating them, rather than the country in which they are located.

But outside Bangkok's big hotels, things start to become interesting. Specifically, the night scene caters mostly for the unattached of both sexes. It is very easy to find someone who appears to want to talk and get to know you better. There is never any reason for being lonely. Conversations can be held sipping vintage French champagne underneath a crystal chandelier in an exclusive membership club, or over a beer in a sparsely decorated noodle shop, where the only item identifying the place as a night spot is a battered Vietnam-war-era jukebox. The intrepid tourist will soon discover that the similarities between these two extremes are more numerous than the differences.

Left: Sanam Luang and the Grand Palace by night. Right: Patpong makes no attempt to hide what is available.

The Thais are a naturally sociable people who do a lot of entertaining. The idea of having fun, or *sanuk*, as it is called, is ingrained in the local culture. What the Thai really likes doing best is having a party with friends, and this is the basic underlying reason why night life in the City of Angels has become legendary the world over.

But how are you, the tourist, going to experience what is on offer in the short period of your stay? The safest bet is to adhere to established entertainment centers, unless someone you know and trust is taking you to a specific destination somewhere else. Most forms of Bangkok nightlife are to be found in Patpong Road and the alleys leading off it, between the two major shopping areas of Silom and Suriwongse Roads.

Although it would be unfair and inaccurate to suggest that all that is on offer at Patpong after dark is fast-food, booze and easy sex (cheap by Western standards at that), Patpong makes no attempt to hide what is available – despite the fact that

83

prostitution is illegal. Attempting to understand how the after-dark section of Thailand's mega-million-dollar tourism industry operates, is confusing at best. Don't even try.

Seasoned veterans suggest you should see things as they appear, and avoid value judgements. If you find something overly bizarre or even distasteful, simply accept it and reserve your criticism for later.

Realize that you won't be able to change things as they are. You could never play an influential role. Whatever the appearance, Thailand's nightlife is exclusively operated by the Thais themselves, something which many a would-be Western publican has learnt to his great disadvantage.

Although the sexual side of Thailand's tourism industry is just part of the overall picture, it is what tends to interest many male visitors the most. Immigration

statistics reveal that nearly a third of all tourist arrivals in Thailand are unattached males: from which information you can draw your own conclusions.

Generally speaking, night life centers around go-go bars, cocktail lounges, discos and late night cafes, some with live music and vocalists. In recent years, a few other varieties of entertainment, such as discos masquerading as restaurants to circumvent licensing laws, have sprung up, but these are just refinements on proven formulae.

The most recent development is the yuppy bars and "pubs", many with live music, frequented by young middle class Thais. These tend to spring up in clusters, the best known being **Silom Plaza**, a five-minute walk from Patpong. A number of rather pleasant, yet usually crowded, bars and clubs offering food and music, can be found on Soi Lang Suan and Sarasin Road, along the north side of Lumpini Park.

But the focal point of night life in the City of Angels is unquestionably **Pat-**

Above: Day after day they are waiting for customers. Right: Dinner at the Shangrila.

pong Road, a 200-meter long strip with its side lanes teeming with about 250 establishments. Most of these are go-go bars, where scantily clad girls gyrate their bodies to the beat of the latest rock music, while trying to catch the eye of the more a fluent looking patrons.

Up until the end of the Vietnam War, into the mid 1970s, Patpong retained some sense of amateurism, but now things are strictly professional. The girls working here are increasingly likely to have been born in the capital and have an education approaching high school level. With few exceptions, they are trying to make as much money as they can, and in the shortest time possible.

If you have any dealings with Patpong's bar girls, this is something to bear in mind. Like ladies of the night the world over, they realize that sentimentality doesn't pay the bill, and if given the opportunity, they will take you for every penny you have. It is easy to take a girl out of a bar, but infinitely more difficult to get the bar (mentality) out of the girl.

However, this has not always been the case. Twenty years or so ago, the several thousand girls working in Patpong were mostly poor farmers' daughters with only a primary education, if any at all. They had migrated to the city in search of a better life and on arrival discovered that their only saleable assets, besides their native charm, were their alluring looks and bodies.

Patpong has also seasonable variations, with cheaper prices and a more relaxed atmosphere from April to September. Conversely, business becomes most frenetic over the end-of-the-year festive season, when the girls work particularly hard to earn enough to tide them over during the lean months.

If you want to know what Patpong was like a decade or so ago, spend an evening in **Soi Cowboy**, a somewhat smaller collection of bars with a couple of restaurants on a lane connecting Sois 21 and 23 off Sukhumvit Road. Most of the girls here live in dormitories above the bars in which they work. Soi Cowboy is less glamourous than Patpong, but it is also less hectic and, in general, cheaper. Married couples are welcome and the girls will happily come and talk to you without insisting that you buy them drinks.

A word on drinks seems warranted at this point. With the exception of hotels, up-market cocktail lounges and membership clubs (where you don't actually have to be a member in order to get in), the prices of drinks in Bangkok are very reasonable.

Expect to pay between 40 to 60 baht for locally brewed beer or spirits and a little less for a soft drink. The price of drinks bought for girls (or boys) working in a bar is slightly different, because they earn a comission on every glass. Don't be surprised if your and her glass of gin and tonic have a different price tag.

The sheer number of go-go bars has led to fierce competition and thus the need to offer different attractions. The more adventurous visitors might consider visiting a "live-show" bar, where all sorts of amazing things go on. These bars tend to be upstairs to give the performers a few vital seconds to cover themselves, should the police raid the premises.

There was a time when live shows meant striptease, with some innovative performers using the aid of cigarettes, pingpong balls, blow pipes, eggs and lit candles to enhance their shows. All that has changed though, as rival establishments constantly dream up a succession of new acts, some involving two or more performers, in the hope of attracting more customers.

Gay clubs are found everywhere in Bangkok with a fair concentration in a short *soi* two lanes north of Patpong, often called *Patpong III*. Some of them offer sophisticated entertainment and have no objection to straight customers.

For up-to-date information on the night scene in general, consult the weekly *Trink Page* in the Saturday issues of the *Bangkok Post* .

BANGKOK
Accommodation

LUXURY: **Airport Hotel**, 333 Chert Wudthakas Rd, Don Muang, Tel:566-1020; **Ambassador** 171 Sukhumvit, Tel:251-0404; **Asia**, 296 Phyathai Rd, Tel:215-0808; **Central Plaza**, 1695 Phaholyothin Rd, Tel:541-1234; **Dusit Thani** 946 Rama IV Rd, Tel:236-0450; **Hilton International Bangkok**, 2 Wireless Rd, Tel:253-0123; **Imperial**, Wireless Rd, Tel:254-0111; **Indra Regent**, Rajaprarob Rd, Tel:252- 0111; **Landmark**, 138 Sukhumvit, Tel:254-0404; **Le Meridien President**, 135/26 Gaysorn, Tel:253-0444; **Mandarin**, 662 Rama IV Rd, Tel:234-1390; **Menam**, 2074 New Road, Tel:289-1148; **Montien**, 54 Surawongse Rd, Tel:233-7060; **Oriental**, 48 Oriental Ave, Tel:236- 0400; **Rama Gardens**, 9/9 Vibhavadi Rangsit Rd, Tel:579-5400; **Regent of Bangkok**, 155 Rajadamri Rd, Tel:251-6127; **Royal Orchid Sheraton**, 2 Captain Bush Lane, Siphya Rd, Tel:234-5599; **Royal River**, 670-805 Charansanitwong Rd, Tel:433-0300; **Shangri-La**, 89 Soi Wat Suan Plu, New Road, Tel:236-7777; **Siam Inter-Continental**, Rama I Rd, Tel:253-0355; **Tawana Ramada**, 80 Surawongse Rd, Tel:233-5160.

MODERATE: **Bangkok Center**, 328 Rama IV Rd, Tel:235-1780; **Bangkok Palace**, 1091/336 New Petchburi Rd, Tel:253-0510; **First Hotel**, 2 Petchburi Rd, Tel:252-5010; **Florida**, 43 Phyathai Square, Tel:245- 3221; **Impala**, 9 Sukhumvit Soi 24, Tel:259-0053; **Manhattan**, Sukhumvit Soi 15, Tel:252-7141; **Manohra**, 412 Surawongse Rd, Tel:234-5070; **Narai**, 222 Silom Rd, Tel:233-3350; **Plaza**, 178 Surawongse Rd, Tel:235-1760; **Silom Plaza**, 320 Silom Rd, Tel:236- 8441; **Windsor**, 8-10 Sukhumvit 20, Tel:258-0160.

BUDGET: **Collins House - YMCA**, 27 South Sathorn Rd, Tel:287- 1900; **YWCA**, 13 South Sathorn Rd, Tel:286-5764; **Century**, 9 Rajaprarob Rd, Tel:245-3271; **Grace**, 12 Nana North, Soi 3, Sukhumvit, Tel:253-0651; **Liberty**, 215 Pradipat Rd, Tel:271-0880; **Malaysia**, 54 Soi Ngamduplee, Rama IV Rd, Tel:286-3582; **Nana**, 4 Nana Tai, Sukhumvit, Tel:252-0121; **Royal**, 2 Rajdmanern Ave, Tel:222-9111.

Hospitals
Bangkok Adventist, 430 Phitsanulok, Tel:281-1422; **Bangkok Christian**, 124 Silom Rd, Tel:233-6981; **Bangkok Nursing Home**, 9 Convent Road, Tel:233-2610; **Samitivet Hospital**, 133, Soi 49 Sukhumvit, Tel:392-0010; **St.Louis Hospital**, 215 South Sathorn Rd, Tel:211-2769.

Museums / Art Galleries

National Museum, Sanam Luang, Tel:224-1333, open daily, except Mondays and Fridays, from 9:00 - 16:00; **National Arts Gallery**, Chao Fa Road, Tel:281-2224, open daily, except Mondays and Fridays, from 9:00-16:00; **National Theatre**, next to the National Museum, Tel:224-1342; **Thai Imagery Museum**, 43/2 Mu 1, Pinklao, Nakhon Chaisri Rd, Thonburi, Tel:211-6261. **Vimanmek palace**, open daily 9:00-16:00. **Wang Suan Pakkard**, open daily exept Sundays 9:00-16:00. **Jim Thompson House**, open Monday-Friday, 9:00-16:00. **Kamthieng House** (Siam Society) 131 Soi Asoke (Sukhumvit 21), open Tuesdays and Saturdays, 9:00-12:00, 13:00-17:00. **Museum of Forensic Medicine**, open Monday-Friday, 9:00-16:00.

Other Places of Interest

Snake Farm, open daily 8:30-16:00.
Crocodile Farm, open daily 8:00-18:00.
Ancient City, for transporte phone 222-8143, 221-4495.

Bookstores and Libraries

Asia Books, 221 Sukhumvit; branches at Peninsula Plaza, Rajdamri Rd, and Landmark Hotel, 138 Sukhumvit; **DK Books**, Siam Square, Mahboongkrong Center, Alliance Francaise, Patpong/Suriwong corner; **Booksellers**, Patpong 1; **AUA Library**, 179 Rajdamri Rd, Tel: 252-7067; **British Council**, 428 Siam Square, Soi 2, Tel:252- 6136; **Neilson Hayes Library**, 195 Surawong, Tel:233-1731; **National Library**, Samsen Rd, 281-3614. In addition, all branches of **Central Department Store** have an extensive book section.

Post / Telegraph / Telephones

Central Post Office, Charoen Krung (New Road) open 8.00 to 20.00, Sat.& Sun. 8.00 - 13.00 (also telegraph and long distance phone service). For long distance calls within Thailand, use blue phones in booths and dial area code before number. International calls easiest through hotels or at Central Post Office. Most hotels have postal services and stamps for sale. The Indra-Regent Hotel at Pratunam has a small post office in the basement.

Access and Transport

At **Bangkok International Airport**, 24 kms from the city center, airport limousines are available as soon as one exits customs. An information desk will give details. Regular air-conditioned buses (Route 4, 13, 29) are the cheapest way of getting into the city, but have no provision to take on a lot of luggage. Taxi fares from the International Airport are usually 250 baht and up, whereas right next door, at the domestic terminal, fares are somewhat cheaper. Visitors are cautioned to take only authorized taxis as unmarked pirate cabs are not too reliable and may even be dangerous.

Taxis in Bangkok may appear rather neglected, but are usually reliable. They do not use meters and bargaining is the only way to agree on fares. Tourists can expect to pay more than the going rate, and it is wise to obtain current fares from your hotel information desk or the Tourism Office. Whenever possible, have the hotel reception write the destination in Thai. For an easy return, carry your hotel's card with its location written in Thai.

Samlors or motor-tricycles (also known as tuk-tuks) are a common sight in Bangkok, but are not recommended for the weak of heart, nor those worried about their hair style. These agile little vehicles do give a thrill to the adventurous though. Fares are proportionately cheaper than taxis and they are best for short rides or in narrow lanes. Samlors are less than ideal in heavy rain and during rush hours, when pollution is heaviest and traffic slow.

Buses will get you anywhere in Bangkok and are the most economical way of getting around. The route network is extensive and many buses run throughout the night. There are three fare classes in use. The blue and cream non-air-conditioned and the somewhat smaller, green-colored buses cost a flat 2 baht for any distance, the red and cream normal buses are 3 baht and the big blue air-con buses cost between 5 and 15 baht, according to the distance traveled. Most visitors prefer the air-con buses, but you must tell the conductress your destination for the fare to be computed. Several maps showing current bus routes are readily available.

For points along the river or on canals, the easiest way of travel is by boat. A recently published book, *Bangkok Waterways* by William Warren, will not only give details of the different boats and fares, but has many interesting tips on where to go and what to see.

Tourist Information

For tourism-related information of any kind contact the **Tourism Authority of Thailand (TAT)** Head Office, Ratchadamnoen Nok Avenue, Bangkok 10100, THAILAND. Tel:282-1143/7, FAX: (662) 280-1744, or the TAT counter at Bangkok International Airport, Tel:523-8972/3. When in trouble while in Bangkok, contact the **Tourist Police** at Tel:281-5051 or 282-8129.

RICE BOWL OF A NATION

THE CENTRAL PLAINS

THE CENTRAL PLAINS

Draw a circle on a map of Thailand with Bangkok as the center and the radius going south as far as Hua Hin or Prachuab Khirikan, or to Nakhon Sawan in the north. Within that circle is an area of vital importance to the nation, as it is not only the rice bowl of the kingdom, but also that part of the country with the greatest economic growth potential. At the same time there are some wonderful historic and natural sites of interest, many of which may be visited on day trips out of Bangkok.

Scattered across this area of river-fed paddies are thousands of small hamlets, which, in spite of their proximity to Bangkok, still regulate their lives according to the cyclical seasons of rice planting and harvesting. This region – unlike the poorer parts of the north, and even more so the northeast – has been blessed by fertile soils and an abundant water supply from the Chao Phraya River and its tributaries. Hence there exists a solid commitment to the land, without too much interest in anything new. Natural resources have been abundant here for centuries, so why bother with imported ideas.

Left: Rice paddies as far as the eyes reach.

Because the frequent flooding of the Chao Phraya River made these plains so fertile, major Thai civilizations have flourished here, with many of their ruins still visible today. If day trips from Bangkok are not appropriate, many of the following towns and historic sites may serve as stop-overs on trips further away.

Bang Pa-in

Journeying north from Bangkok by rail, bus, car or boat, three historic sites – Bang Pa-in, Ayutthaya and Lopburi – are among the most popular and interesting of Thailand's attractions. The first to be reached is **Bang Pa-in**, only some 60 km from Bangkok. The main attraction here is the royal palace enclosure, one of the most photographed sights in Thailand.

Bang Pa-in dates all the way back to the Ayutthaya period. The original palace was founded by King Prasat Thong, who was born in the area. It became a summer residence for the Ayutthaya kings, because it was in easy reach by river. After the destruction of Ayutthaya, Bang Pa-in was abandoned until King Mongkut (Rama IV) found its salubrious situation inviting. He began its restoration in the mid-nineteenth century, a process continued by his son, King Chulalongkorn. Both are responsible for most of the

89

Ye
Three Pagodas Pass 1980
Sankhla Buri
Sadaik Taung 1283
Khao Laem Res.
Natkyizin
Chai Nat
1210
Ban Rai
Han Kha
Sing Buri
Khok Samrong
Lop Buri

HEINZE BOK ISLANDS
Heinze Channel
Khao Daen 1249
Thong Pha Phum
Krasieo Res.
Srinagarind Res.
Dan Chang
Pang Hok Khon
Don Chedi
Sawaengha
Ang Thong

MAUNGMAGAN ISLANDS
River Kwai Village Hotel
Myitta
1257
Si Sawat
621
Suphan Buri
Pa Mok
PHRA NAKHON SI AYUTTHAYA

LAUNGLON BOK ISLAND
Launglon
Khao Ro Rae 1125
Sai Yok Waterfall
Sathani Nam Tok
Nong Khao Ngai
Phanom Thuan
U Thong
Song Phi Nong
Bang Pa-in
Prac

TAVOY
1558
Sai Yok
Kanchanaburi
River Kwai Bridge
Nong Khao
BANGKOK (KRUNG THEP)
Pathum Thani
Thanya Buri
Nonthaburi

MYANMAR (BURMA)
Myinmoletkat Taung 2072
Ban Pong
Photharam
NAKHON PATHOM
Bang Yai
Taling Chan
Min Buri
Chachoeng

Tavoy Pt.
Palauk
RATCHABURI
Bang Phae
Damnoen Saduak
Krathum Baen
34
Samut Prakan

MALI ISLAND (TAVOY I.)
1050
Pak Tho
SAMUT SAKHON
Samut Songkhram

TANINTHARI (TENASSERIM)
KABOSA I.
Investigator Passage
KADAN ISLAND
Kyaukpya
Palaw
Khao Yoi
944
Phet Buri Res.
PHETCHABURI (Phet Buri)
Hat Chao Samran
KO SI CHANG
Bight of
Siracha
Bang Lamung

THAMIHLA I.
TENASSERIM I.
MAINGYI I.
Pawut
Kaeng Krachan Dam
Cha-am
Bangkok (Ao Krung Thep)
Pattaya
3

THAYAWTHADANGY I. (ELPHINSTONE I.)
Kyataw
KALA
Mergui
GRANTS I.
Auckland Bay
Hua Hin
Pran Buri Res.
KO KHRAM YAI
KO SAMAESAN

BAILEY I.
MERGUI
SAGANTHIT I. (SELLORE I.)
PARKER I.
SABI I.
Taninthari (Tenasserim)
Khao Yai 1204
Ban Nong Sano
THAILAND

KUNTHI I. (HAYES I.)
BENTINCK I. (PYINZABU I.)
KANMAW I. (KETTHAYIN I.)
Manoron
Theinkun
Three Hundred Peaks N.P.
696
Kui Buri

GREAT WESTERN TORRES IS.
LETSOK-AW
PAWE-GYI
Lenya
876
Thap Sakae
Prachuap Khiri Khan
Ban Huai Yang

BUSHBY I.
SIR J. MALCOLM I.
OWEN I.
Bokpyin
Bang Saphan
4
116

ARCHIPELAGO
KAU-YE
LANBI KYUN I. (SULLIVAN I.)
SIR ROBERT CAMPBELL I.
Karaturi
582
GULF

CLARA I.
WA-ALE I.
Tha Sae
Pathiu

PILA I.
BUDA I.
Khao Nam Noi 755
Chumphon
GULF O

LORD LOUGHBOROUGH I.
Investigator Channel
Kra Buri
Ao Sawi
Sawi
KO TAO
Chong Tao

ZADETKALE I. (ST. LUKE'S I.)
Maliwun
610
La-un
Ulu
Lang Suan
KO PHANGAN

ZADETKYI I. (ST. MATTHEW'S I.)
ISTHMUS OF KRA
Ranong
Phato
Chong Phangan
KO SAMUI

THAN I.
KO CHANG
553
Kapoe
635
KO PHALUAI

BRUER I.
KO PHAYAM
Chong Samui

CHRISTIE I.
KO PHALUAI
Ao Ban Don

Surat Thani
Kanchanadit
Khanom
•1028

CENTRAL THAILAND

0   100 km

buildings seen in the compound today. On a lake in the middle of what was once an island, the palace has five buildings, with the oft-photographed lake pavilion in the center of the lake. This typical Thai-style building, called **Aisawan Thi Phaya**, contains a bronze statue of King Chulalongkorn.

Ayutthaya

Most visitors include Bang Pa-in in a day trip to **Ayutthaya**, which lies only a few kilometers further north by road or river. When Bangkok was truly a "Village of the Wild Plums", Ayutthaya was the royal capital of the kingdom of Siam, and a stupendous sight it must have been. European visitors who recorded their observations at the time, compared it favorably with Venice because of its elaborate system of canals and the luxurious houses and palaces lining them. As the capital of a rich agricultural kingdom, Ayutthaya had grown to a size greater than Paris or London by the time it received its first European visitors around the fifteenth century.

Situated at the juncture of three rivers, its site had been chosen in 1350 because it was easy to defend. A canal was cut between two of the rivers, thus forming an island. In the four centuries after its founding, the relatively stable prosperity of the land contributed to the accumulation of great wealth. Each successive king added his own temple or palace. And throughout the city more canals were dug to connect each district and neighborhood. By the time Europeans were sailing up the Chao Phraya to pay homage to the kings of Siam, Ayutthaya had reached a level of opulence which not only astounded foreign visitors, but excited the envy of neighbors as well.

In 1767, the Burmese laid siege to Ayutthaya, keeping the city sealed for months and starving the population into submission. Once they breached its

defenses, they went on a spree of destruction and left little of the city intact. Palaces, temples, priceless pieces of art, libraries with ancient scrolls and historical records were ransacked and put to the torch. The destruction was so complete that the newly emerging Chakri dynasty, after having re-established control over Siam, decided on a new capital further south, considered less exposed to possible future invaders.

Located 85 km north of Bangkok on the Chao Phraya, Ayutthaya sits astride all major routes going north. It can be reached in slightly more than an hour and a half from Bangkok by either road or rail. It is one of the favorite points of interest for Bangkok tour operators, and is the destination of several luxury river cruise services.

Buses for Ayutthaya leave the Northern Bus Station at Morchit every ten

Above: Chedis in Ayutthaya. Right: Buddhist monks in Ayutthaya.

minutes. Trains to Ayutthaya can be boarded at Hualampong or Samsen stations. Schedules are available at the information counters at either station. Generally, trains leave every half hour, from early morning till night, with the journey taking only an hour and fifteen minutes.

Boats for Ayutthaya can be found at the Tha Thien pier, but up-river trips can take a long time. Many travelers prefer to go by bus or train and then return in a leisurely three hours by boat during the heat of the afternoon. Departure times and fares can be obtained at the boat landing in Ayutthaya near the Chandra Kasem Palace. At the same landing, boats can be hired for a circular tour of the river/canal island.

The temples visible on a river tour are **Wat Phanam Choeng**, **Wat Phuttaisawan**, **Wat Kasatrathira** and **Wat Chai Wattanaram**. Detailed information is available at Chandra Kasem Palace, in the museum, or from TAT in Bangkok.

One of the most visited sites is **Wat**

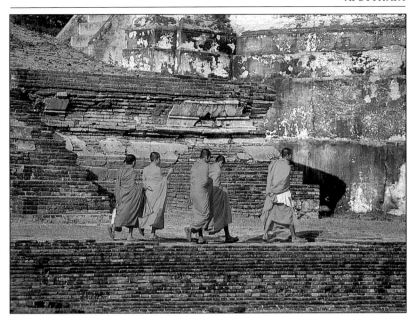

Raj Burana in the heart of the island. It was built in 1424 by King Boromraja II, the seventh of the Ayutthaya kings. Two of its *chedis* (pagodas) house the ashes of his two sons, killed in battle. During restoration in 1958, many jewelled ornaments and gold artifacts were unearthed, which are now displayed in the National Museum in Bangkok.

Wat Mahathat, across the road from Wat Raj Burana, has confused historians as to its origin, but is generally considered the work of King Boromraja I, around 1374. Excavations of its foundations also produced many Buddha images and gold objects, now housed in the National Museum.

Wat Phra Sri Sanphet was the most important temple within the palace compound, with a similar function to that of the Emerald Buddha Temple in Bangkok today. Inside the temple, King Ramathibodi commissioned the construction of a 16-m standing Buddha in 1500. It was cast in bronze and covered with beaten gold, weighing an estimated 170 kilogrammes. He called the image Phra Sri Sanphet. When the Burmese invaded, they set the bronze image on fire to melt the gold and destroyed the temple.

Wat Yai Chai Mongkol, **Phra Mongkol Bopitr**, one of the largest bronze statues in Thailand, and **Khun Phaen's House**, a Thai-style dwelling built in conformity with a house described in a popular work Thai literature, are further attractions in central Ayutthaya.

There are many other temples and ruins scattered throughout the island. Across the river are numerous other sites in varying states of decay. Specialized guidebooks can lead the visitor to these, as well as to the sites where Ayutthaya's foreign communities – the Portuguese, the French and Japanese – were resident.

In addition to its temples, Ayutthaya has two museums worth visiting, especially before beginning a sight-seeing tour.

Chandra Kasem Palace is located in the northeast corner of the town, near the river and not far from the U-Thong Hotel.

The palace is a museum unto itself and was built by the seventeenth of the Ayutthayan monarchs for his son, who became King Naruesan. The complex was destroyed by the Burmese and went unrepaired until King Mongkut commissioned its partial reconstruction for his own residence.

The **Chao Sam Phraya National Museum** is on Rojana Road opposite the City Hall. It has a collection of bronze, stone and terracotta statues, which are well described in a pamphlet written for the Fine Arts Department by Prince Subhadradis Diskul.

Lopburi

15 kilometers north of Ayutthaya, and about 155 from Bangkok, is **Lopburi**, where neolithic and Bronze Age artifacts have been unearthed. From the 6th to the 11th century – the Davarati Period – Lop-

Above: Temple dancers in the Monkey Temple of Lopburi.

buri was an important town, and during the 11th and 12th centuries, when much of central Thailand was part of the Khmer Empire centered in Angkor, Lopburi was a regional capital. Once Siam became Thai, with its capital in Ayutthaya, Lopburi evolved as the kingdom's second important city.

Lopburi's most illustrious period was during the reign of King Narai, between 1657-88. Called Louwo at the time, the city was graphically described by the many European missions which came to establish links with Siam. The Chevalier de Chaumont, emissary from Louis XIV, gave a letter from his king to King Narai. At the same time King Narai appointed as his Chief Minister a Greek, Constantine Phaulkon (Chao Phraya Vichayen) who was later executed in a coup d'etat.

The ruined walls, gates, temples and palaces testify to the size of the former capital. One of the best known sights is **Prang Sam Yod**, meaning Temple of the Three Spires. It was constructed as a Hindu shrine and later used by Buddhists.

Wat Prasri Ratana Mahathat has in its compound a laterite Khmer-style *prang* and numerous *chedis* from King Narai's time. His palace, called **Narai Radja Niwes**, is behind Wat Prasri Ratana Mahathat. It took 12 years to build (1665-1677) and is located in the center of town, between Ratchadamnoen and Pratoo Chai roads. The entire compound is a national museum. TAT has a brochure on Lopburi, giving details of each pavilion.

Lopburi can be reached from Bangkok by following the instructions for Ayuthaya. Air-conditioned buses leave from the Northern Bus Station every 20 minutes from 05:00 to 20:30.

A Trip to Nakhon Nayok

Northeast of Bangkok and about 140 km from the capital, is the province of **Nakhon Nayok**, which offers scenic attractions often overlooked by non-Thais, but not by resort developers. Several picturesque temples, some waterfalls and a beautiful park and botanical collection make this a pleasant destination. For those driving, Highway 305 provides the most scenic route to the town of Nakhon Nayok. From here, Route 33, which runs to Aranyaprathet on the Cambodian border, leads to the waterfalls and the **Wang Takrai Park**. From the mainroad turnoff, which is clearly marked, it is another 20 kms to the **Salika Falls**, at their most spectacular near the end of the rainy season in October or November.

Wang Takrai Park, along the same road that leads to the waterfalls, is rated as one of the finest in Thailand. It was established in 1955 by Prince Chumbkot of Nagara Svarga, who died in 1959. He and his wife also established **Suan Pakkard Palace**, mentioned in the Bangkok section. After his death, his wife, Princess Chumpot, opened the park to the public in memory of her husband. Over the years she planted here a large variety of plants and trees she had brought back from her travels abroad. For 2 km the park runs along the banks of a stream, an ideal walk in a valley surrounded by hills. Bungalows can be rented in the park and there is a restaurant and picnic tables.

Five km past **Wang Takrai Park** is **Nang Rong Waterfall**, coming down from the mountains in a long stream. Steps lead to a good viewpoint, where the entire falls can be seen.

Kanchanaburi and the River Kwai

Just after Nakhon Pathom, about 60 km from Bangkok, both highway and the railway split, with the main route going south to Malaysia and Singapore, and the other branching off to the west towards **Kanchanaburi** and the Burmese border.

Today, Kanchanaburi, the largest town in western Thailand and site of the famous **Bridge over the River Kwai**, bustles with a constant stream of the curious. They come from all over the world to pay homage to those who labored and died. For those interested, there are many books describing the inhumane ordeal the prisoners endured while building the 415 km of railway, which ran along the valley of the River Kwai from Thailand into Burma, during the Second World War.

Because of the fame generated by Pierre Boulle's book and the movie, *Bridge over the River Kwai*, Kanchanaburi has become one of Thailand's premier attractions. But in spite of its notorious place in war annals, it is the sleepy, yet prosperous, center of a rich agricultural and mining area, that stretches all the way to Burma.

Recently, a proposal to rebuild the old railway to Burma sparked a controversy especially since the company making the proposal was Japanese. At present, visitors can go by rail only halfway up the valley, as the stretch of the line from the village of Nam Tok to Burma was torn up

several years ago. Visitors get a thrilling ride up the valley, over creaking trestles built in niches carved out of the rock by prisoners of war, only to stop in the middle of nowhere. Now the government has proposed rebuilding the line, to follow the original route up the valley of the Kwai, all the way to Three Pagodas Pass and the Burmese frontier.

Although it is feasible to see the sights on a one-day trip, Kanchanaburi really requires two or three days to do it justice. Located 120 km northwest of Bangkok at the junction of the Rivers Kwae Yai and Kwae Noi, the town dates back to 1833. It is the Kwae Yai River which is spanned by the infamous bridge on the outskirts of town.

Kanchanaburi can be reached from Bangkok in about two hours by car or bus, but the train ride is still the recommended way to go, at least one way.

Above: The famous bridge over the River Kwai near Kanchanaburi. Right: Floating market at Domnoen Saduak.

Trains leave from Hualampong or Thonburi and air-conditioned buses from the bus station on Nakhon Chaisri Road in Thonburi.

Information on both services may be obtained at TAT offices. Numerous tour operators offer package tours to Kanchanaburi at reasonable prices, and for those with little time to spare, these might be the better alternative.

On arrival in Kanchanaburi, the first stop should be at the **TAT** office on the main road, opposite the Allied War Cemetery. Detailed brochures give information on the main sights in town and up the valley. Rented bicycles or motorcycles are available for those who wish to tour at their own pace. A number of ferries cross the river for a recommended visit to the **Temple of the Limestone Cave**. The **Chongkai Allied War Cemetery**, where 1,740 Allied prisoners are buried, is close by. They are part of the 16,000 who died during the construction of the railway. Of those, 7,000 are buried in and around the area in cemeteries which are maintained by an international committee.

A reminder of the war is the **JEATH** (Japanese, English, American, Thai, Holland) **War Museum**, in the grounds of a riverside temple compound. The photos and paintings depicting the life in the prison camps are displayed in a replica of a typical prisoners' hut. Don't forget to scan the visitors' book for its entries of international anti-war cliches: "Forgive, but don't forget"; "They tortured – but we bombed".

As for the bridge itself, the original was bombed by the US air force on February 13, 1945. Today's replacement is the setting for the always popular light and sound shows, staged after dark during the River Kwai Bridge Week in late November or early December. The show reenacts war scenes, with the train crossing, bomb attacks and all.

After exploring the town, a trip north is recommended. Highway 323 runs northwest and closely parallels the path of the Kwae Noi River. This route leads to the Burmese border, only a short distance from **Three Pagodas Pass**, where the railway crossed into Burma. To reach the actual pass requires an arduous off-road trek. Ask at the TAT office for details regarding the situation around the border, which is often in control of Burmese insurgent groups.

Closer to town, is the **Muang Sing Historical Park**, about an hour's drive from Kanchanaburi. The park contains some newly renovated thirteenth century Khmer ruins and other archaeological sites, some prehistoric. Further north on the same route is the **Sai Yok Waterfall**, which can also be reached by boat. During, and immediately after, the rainy season, these falls are at their most spectacular. Close by the falls are the newly-discovered **Wang Badarn Caves** with some impressive stalactites. The entrance to the caves is small, but inside the underground chambers are vast. The dis-

coverers of the caves, Lam Yurit and his son, are in permanent residence and ready to guide visitors and provide lighting. There are seven chambers in all.

Up the valley is the **River Kwai Village Hotel** where travelers, going by train to Nam Tok, which is also the end of the line, can arrange to be picked up by minibus. The hotel is built on the bank overlooking the river, with air-conditioned rooms built around a swimming pool. To add to the sense of jungle isolation, monkeys, owls and parrots squawk at passersby from perches in the gardens. Jungle treks and visits to Karen and Mon tribal villages or the nearby caves are offered by the hotel.

Damnoen Saduak Floating Market

Damnoen Saduak, 110 km south of Bangkok in the Province of Ratchaburi, is a town with a genuine floating market, where vendors in hundreds of little boats peddle their wares. They sell fruit, vegetables, kitchen utensils, household

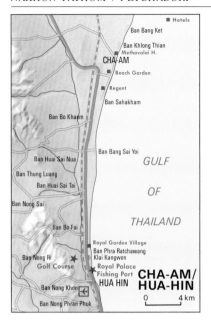

Nakhon Pathom

Lying less than 60 km west of Bangkok, **Nakhon Pathom** is regarded as the oldest of Thailand's existing cities, dating back to at least 150 BC. It is also said to be the place where Buddhism was first established. Nakhon Pathom was used as the model for Phnom Penh, Cambodia, in the movie *The Killing Fields*. On approaching the city, the first thing one notes is the towering **Phra Pathom Chedi**, said to be the highest pagoda in the world. It rises to a height of 127 m and is covered with thousands of golden-colored glazed tiles, brought here all the way from China.

Several other temples are in the vicinity of the giant *chedi* and are open to visitors. In November each year, a fascinating temple fair is held, the carnival attracting many thousands of visitors from all over the country.

Regular buses leave the Southern Bus Terminal every ten minutes, while air-conditioned buses leave every half hour between 07:00 in the morning and 22:30 at night. Trains can be boarded at Hualampong station or at Bangkok Noi on the Thonburi side. For further details contact the local TAT.

goods and what is best described as the local version of fast food.

It takes about two hours to get there from Bangkok, buses leaving from the Southern Bus Terminal on Nakhon Chaisri Road in Thonburi every 20 minutes. The best time to visit the market is between 08:00 and 10:00 in the morning. When arriving at Damnoen Saduak bus station, disembark and follow the walkway along the canal on the right hand side. Taxi boats may also be hired to take you to the market. The trip to Damnoen Saduak can be combined with a visit to Nakhon Pathom or the Rose Garden not far away, which is described in detail in the section on Bangkok. For convenience, all of these excursions can be arranged through a tour operator at any leading hotel.

Petchaburi

On the main coastal highway going south, and 130 km from Bangkok, is the town of **Petchaburi**, easily reached by road or rail. The most prominent attraction of the town, and one easily visible from the highway, is the newly restored royal palace on a hill, overlooking the town and coast. Called **Khao Wang**, it was built by King Mongkut (King Rama IV) in the nineteenth century. The various buildings are joined by walkways and the beautifully landscaped grounds have been planted with the king's favorite trees and flowering shrubs. From the astronomical observatory at the summit, visi-

Right: Hauling a boat across the sand on a beach near Hua Hin.

tors can enjoy a panoramic view of the coast of the Gulf of Siam.

South of Petchaburi town and formed by the **Kaeng Kracham Dam**, is a large reservoir where visitors can hire boats for fishing or visit a Karen tribal village across the lake. To get to Kaeng Kracham, drive south on the Petchkasem Highway for about 50 km and make a right turn at the easily seen sign post. Bungalows are available for rent at the site, making this a pleasant destination for family outings.

Cha-am Beach

Forty km south of Petchaburi is **Cha-am**, one of the older, yet still expanding, beach resorts on the western coast of the Gulf of Siam. It has a 3-km-long, sandy, casuarina-tree-lined beach with a rather unremarkable collection of bungalow complexes, beachfront hotels, motels, restaurants and food stalls. But with the rise in tourism, some first class hotels, with their own private beaches, have also sprung up. Some of them, like the luxurious Regent Cha-am, offer every connience imaginable. The soon-to-open Dusit Cha-am even features a polo club.

Hua Hin

Cha-am's next door neighbor, 200 kms from Bangkok by road, is **Hua Hin**, the first and oldest of Thailand's beach resorts. It was established in the 1920s and quickly became the favorite summer playground for the wealthy. A royal palace was constructed on the beachfront and an excellent 18-hole golf course drew the Bangkok élite, many of whom built their own bungalows along the beach. The State Railways of Thailand built an enormous beach hotel with long open balconies.

Hua Hin had become the "in" place. The annals relate that in 1932, when a group of young military officers declared an end to the absolute monarchy, King Prajadihok (Rama VII) was informed of his changed status while playing golf in

Hua Hin. Apparently His Majesty went on to finish his game.

For some time Hua Hin was eclipsed by the rapid development of resorts on the eastern side of the gulf. In the late sixties and throughout the seventies, new places southeast of Bangkok, like Bang Saen and Pattaya, gained favor with young Bangkokians, because they were easier to reach by road. But during the past few years, change has come to Hua Hin as well, and its beach front is alive with several new hotels.

Even the staid old Railway Hotel has gone through a remarkable facelift. Only a few years ago it was used as a set in the movie *The Killing Fields* when it served as *Hotel Le Phnom* in Phnom Penh, capital of Cambodia.

Shortly afterwards, it was leased from the State Railways by a group of Bangkok businessmen, who, together with a well-known French hotel chain, transformed it into a spectacular resort, adding a new wing, while staying more or less faithful to the original colonial-style architecture.

Bordering on the south of Hua Hin lies the province of **Prachuab Kirikhan**, traditionally thought of as the gateway to the south. Here Thailand reaches its narrowest point. Standing on the beach in Prachuab looking inland, one can see the mountains only a few kilometers away, marking the Burmese border.

Pranburi Beach

Between Hua Hin and the provincial capital Prachuab Kirikhan, is **Pranburi**, the center of a number of luxury coastal resorts and site of the Three Hundred Peaks **National Park** (*Khao Sam Roi Yot*). This park is definitely worth a visit, but access is not easy, unless one has one's own transport. Motorcycles may be rented in Hua Hin for the day and it is quite feasible to visit this park by motorbike.

There are some fascinating caves and a long beach. The main cave is close to the beach and clearly marked. It is reached after a steep climb, where, at the top, children are usually waiting with kerosene lamps to light the way inside the cave's enormous chamber, with its truly remarkable stalactites and stalagmites. After the climb, the beach may look like a good place for a refreshing dip, but the sand is muddy and swimmers tend to sink up to their knees wading to where the water is deep enough for a swim.

Prachuab Kirikhan

Prachuab Kirikhan is surrounded by hills and plantations and looks like most Thai provincial towns, with all its nondescript shops, banks and administration buildings. It sits on a bay with a long, curving beach, with a bluff at each end, sheltering it from the gales off the gulf.

A long fishing pier is constantly busy with boats unloading their catches, and in the evening the town market is filled with fishermen and village folk, eating barbecued seafood and getting drunk on local whisky.

A road runs along the bay, and if one has transportation, a number of small fishing villages along the coast make for an interesting visit.

Not far from the pier is a hill with a small, well-maintained temple at its summit. From here one has a sweeping view of the town and the bay, and can, on clear days, even look into Burma. Along the beach are several bungalow complexes and seafood restaurants, which attract families with cars, who come from Bangkok for the weekend.

The attraction here is a rural life style not at all touched by tourism. Although easily accessible by train and road, whether from Bangkok and Hua Hin or the south, local transportation is scarce and a definite problem. Nonetheless, Prachuab is well worth a visit.

AYUTTHAYA
Accommodation

BUDGET: **U-Thong Hotel**, 86 U-Thong, Tel:215- 136; **U-Thong Inn**, 210 Mu 5, Rotchana Rd, Tel: 242618; **Wiang Fa**, 1/8 Rotchana, Tel:241-353.

KANCHANABURI
Accommodation

BUDGET: **Kasem Island Resort**, 27 Chaichumphon Rd, Tel:511-603; **Rama River Kwai**, 284/3 Saeng Chuto Rd, Tel:511-269; **River Kwai Village**, (Bangkok reserv – 1054/4 New Petchburi Rd, Tel:251-7828; **Chiangcome Erawan Hotel**, Kwai Yai River, just before Erawan Falls; **River Kwai Family Camp**, Tel:512-733.
BUDGET: **Prasopsuk Bungalow**, 277 Saeng Chuto, Tel:511-411; **P.Si Rungruang**, 218/14 Saeng Chuto, Tel:511-655.

Tourist Information

TAT Office, Saeng Chuto Rd, Tel:511-200 – ask about accommodation up the valleys, raft trips and motorcycle rentals.

Restaurants

Esan, (serves Northeastern food) Saeng Chuto Rd; **Sabay-chit**, next to River Kwai Hotel on Saeng Chuto Rd, (menu in English);
Raft restaurants along the river front serve good freshwater fish dishes.

LOPBURI
Accommodation

Asia, 1/7-8 Surasak, Tel:411-892; **Holiday Hotel**, 3 Soi Suriyothai 2, Narai Maharat Rd, Tel:411-343; **Thai Pe**, 24.6-7 Surasongkhram Rd, Tel:411-524.

NAKHON PATHOM
Accommodation

Rose Garden, 21 Mu 2, Phetkasem Rd, Tel:321-684; **Nakhon Inn**, 55 Rajwithi, Tel:251-152; **Whale**, Tel:251-020.

CHA-AM
Accommodation

LUXURY: **The Regent Cha-Am**, Cha-Am Beach, Tel:471-480; **Cha-Am Garden**, 256 Ruamchit Rd, Tel:471-046; **Cha-am Methavalai**, Ruamchit, Tel:(Bkk) 280-2581.
MODERATE: **White Hotel**, 263/32 Ruamchit, Tel:471-118; **Cha-am Cabana**, 186 Hat Khlong-Thian, Tel:471-614; **Happy Home**, 241/34 Ruamchit Rd, Tel:471-393; **Cha-am Villa**, 241/1 Ruamchit Rd, Tel:471-241.
BUDGET: **Rung Aran Bungalows**, 263/26 Ruamchit, Tel:471-226.

HUA HIN
Accommodation

LUXURY: **Royal Garden Village**, 43/1 Phetkasem Beach Rd, Tel:512- 412; **Royal Garden Resort**, 107/1 Phetkasem Road, Tel:511-881; **Sofitel Central**, 1 Damnoen Kasem Road, Tel:511-012.
MODERATE: **Golf Inn**, 29 Damnoen Kasem, Tel:512-473, **Sailom Hotel**, 29 Phetkasem, Tel:511-890.
BUDGET: Many guest houses are to be founded along Narretdumri Road near the beach.

Restaurants, Bars, Discos

Besides sophisticated dining at any of the top hotels, there are some cheap Western restaurants – like the Head Rock Cafe – on Narretdumri Road. Seafood restaurants are found along Damnoen Kasem Road, at the usually very crowded Night Market on Dechanit Road, and best of all near the main fishing pier, Tha Thiap Reua Pramong at the end of Chosin Road.
Here the reputation of the basic, but very comfortable seafood resaurants is such, that Bangkok gourmets do not hesitate to drive the over 200 kilometers for an exceptional meal. The freshly caught and well-prepared shrimp, crab and lobsters, as well as the friendly service, usually merit a 10 to 15 per cent gratuity.
For night owls there is live jazz at the Sofitel and a very popular disco at the Royal Garden Resort. Many small bistros and open air bars, in a lane near the Sofitel entrance, serve a lively clientele till the early hours of the morning.

Post / Telegraph / Telephone

Hua Hin Post Office, Damnoen Kasem Rd, Domestic trunk calls at blue phone box across the street from the Post Office.

Tourist Information

There is a local government Tourist Office next to the Police Station on Damnoen Kasem Rd.

PRANBURI
Accommodation

Club Aldiana Siam, 9 Parknampran Beach, Tel:621-701. Aldiana is the German answer to the very successful French-managed Club Med resorts. First class accommodation, excellent food and various entertainment facilities.

PRACHUAB KIRIKHAN
Accommodation

Casa Sally, Hat Wa-Ko (12 kms from town), Tel:601-296; **Suk San**, 131 Su-Suk Rd, Tel:611-145; **Tesaban Bungalow**, Su-Suk Rd, Tel:611-150; **Provincial Govt. Bungalows**, Su-Suk Rd, Tel:601-014.

THE PLEASURE COAST OF THE GULF

PATTAYA
EASTERN GULF
KOH SAMET

PATTAYA

Pattaya is not a place for the meek and mild. It offers something for everyone, and at the same time it seems to encourage strong opinions. Like Waikiki, Australia's Gold Coast, the Costa Del Sol, or the French Riviera, Pattaya is rapidly becoming something more than a beach resort. It is becoming an extraordinary experience.

Only 140 km southeast of Bangkok (a two-hour bus ride), Pattaya's proximity to the capital has made it one of Asia's premier glitz resorts. Those seeking tranquil moments strolling on miles of unsullied beach, had better forget Pattaya, at least during the hours when the Pattaya crowd is usually awake. Granted, in the wee hours of the morning, when dawn is tinting the horizon, or late at night under the moon, the beaches of Pattaya are practically empty. But by midday, when hangovers have been tranquilized by a late breakfast, the beaches are packed, and calm and tranquility will not be too evident.

Thus Pattaya is a honky tonk beach town, it is the R&R venue for the US

Left: A quiet sunrise on Pattaya beach, some hours before the tourists flock.

Seventh Fleet, it is home to thousands of entertainers, hosts and hostesses. It is also an upmarket condominium site, mecca for the down and out, boomtown of Southeast Asia. It does have fine beaches, palm trees, sun and sea breezes. It also has hotels of every category, the finest cuisine next to hot dog stands, bars with juke boxes adjoining cocktail lounges with piano players. Depending on your mood and inclination, there is a certain magic about the place. But do not go to Pattaya and hope to write a thesis on Third World development. It is Fun City and brooks no opposition.

While Pattaya itself is a swinging resort, catering to every fancy, it is also within easy reach of a number of attractions in the surrounding areas. Tour companies are numerous, and car and motorcycle rental shops abound. Thus many tourists use the resort as the center for excursions, either on their own or in tour groups.

Beaches Everywhere

Pattaya Beach, running from North to South Pattaya, is 4 km long with a beach road paralleling its sands, usually filled with cruising minibuses (*songthaews*) looking for passengers. The North Pattaya end is the more upmarket part with

103

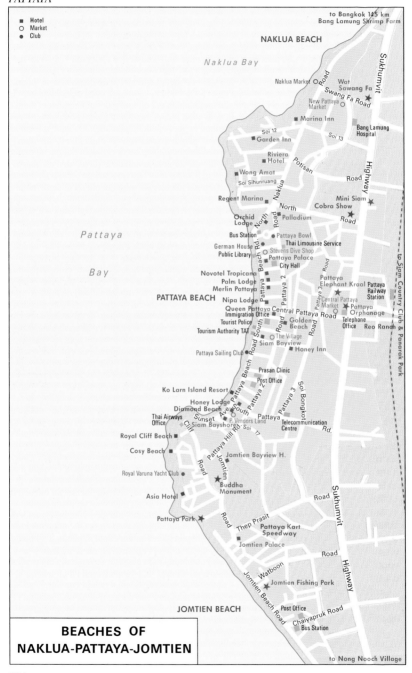

- ■ Hotel
- ○ Market
- ● Club

NAKLUA BEACH

Naklua Bay

to Bangkok 145 km
Bang Lamung Shrimp Farm

Naklua Market
Wat Sawang Fa
Swang Fa Road
New Pattaya Market
Marina Inn
Bang Lamung Hospital
Soi 12
Garden Inn
Soi 13
Riviera Hotel
Wong Amat
Soi Sihunruang
Potisan
Regent Marina
Mini Siam
Cobra Show
Naklua North Road
North Road
Orchid Lodge
Palladium
Bus Station
Pattaya Bowl
German House
Thai Limousine Service
Public Library
Stevens Dive Shop
Pattaya Palace
City Hall
Novotel Tropicana
Palm Lodge
Merlin Pattaya
Pattaya Elephant Kraal
Pattaya Railway Station
PATTAYA BEACH
Nipa Lodge
Central Pattaya
Central Pattaya Market
Pattaya Orphanage
Queen Pattaya
Immigration Office
Golden Beach
Telephone Office
Reo Ranch
Tourist Police
Tourism Authority TAT
The Village
Siam Bayview
Honey Inn
Pattaya Sailing Club
Prasan Clinic
Post Office
Ko Larn Island Resort
Honey Lodge
Diamond Beach
Sunset
Pattaya
Thai Airways Office
P. Vendors Land
Telecommunication Centre
Siam Bayshore
Soi 17
Royal Cliff Beach
Cliff
Cosy Beach
Pattaya Hill Road
Royal Varuna Yacht Club
Jomtien Bayview H.
Jomtien
Buddha Monument
Asia Hotel
Pattaya Park
Thep Prasit
Pattaya Kart Speedway
Jomtien Palace
Watboon
Jomtien Fishing Park
Jomtien Beach Road
Sukhumvit Highway
JOMTIEN BEACH
Post Office
Chaiyapruk Road
Bus Station

Pattaya Bay

Pattaya 2 Road
Central Pattaya Road
Pattaya Beach Road South
Pattaya 2 Road South
Pattaya 3 Road
Soi Bongkot
Sukhumvit Highway

to Siam Country Club & Panarak Park

to Nong Nooch Village

BEACHES OF
NAKLUA-PATTAYA-JOMTIEN

its swankier hotels, better and more expensive restaurants, and patches of sand that are just a little less crowded.

South Pattaya is a totally different kettle of fish. Tina Turner music accompanies the beckoning calls of thousands of bar hostesses, intent on plying the passerby with happy-hour drinks. Happy-hour is not a South Pattaya institution. It is just that here it never seems to end.

Jomtien Beach, about 4 km from town, is further south along the coast, and the site of frantic condominium development. It seems that new projects are announced every day. The beach is 6 km long, and is served by a constant flow of *songthaews*. Windsurfing, water scootering and parasailing are a few of the more active water sports to be found here.

Koh Larn, the island clearly visible from Jomtien Beach, is 45 minutes away by speed boat. It is the largest in the group of nearby islands and the water sports of Jomtien are supplemented here with snorkeling and scuba diving, or viewing the coral reefs from glass-bottomed boats. On the island's main beaches, a lot of seafood restaurants provide fresh fare straight from the briny and some bungalows are available if a longer stay is desired.

About 3 km from central Pattaya, at km 143 on Sukhumvit Highway, is **Mini-Siam**, featuring exhibits similar to those at the Ancient City in Bangkok – downscaled replicas of the most famous cultural and historic sites in Thailand. Also on Sukhumvit Highway, just behind the Pattaya Orphanage, is the interesting **Pattaya Elephant Kraal** with demonstrations of elephants being trained and at work. The kraal is open daily from 10:00 to 14:30.

On the road to the Siam Country Club golf course is the **Pattaya Elephant Village** with shows similar to, but somewhat

Above: Anything goes on the beach of Pattaya, even parasailing.

more elaborate than, those at the kraal. On the same road is also **Panarak Park**, a tropical garden with a well-stocked fish pond, from which visitors are encouraged to catch their supper. A fee is charged for the use of the fishing equipment. A restaurant, bungalows, a putting green, jogging and cycling paths and boating are available to visitors.

The **Jomtien Fishing Park** also offers fresh water fishing and is open from 8:00 to 24:00. It has an excellent restaurant, where you can have your catch prepared to perfection.

Pattaya Park is a water-centered amusement park, an entertainment paradise for the entire family. It has colorful water slides, whirlpools and large wading pools for youngsters. Restaurants and fast food stalls keep visitors fed. The park has game rooms and lockers. Conveniently, it is right on the beach, so you can also have a dip in the ocean.

Some 12 km from Pattaya town is **Wat Yansangwararam**, a unique example of modern Thai temple architecture. The

wat, under the patronage of His Majesty the King, offers Buddhist meditation courses, especially recommended for those needing a rest from the rigors of Pattaya nightlife. The *wat* is open for visitors daily from 6:00 to 18:00.

Nong Nooch Village, about 20 km from Pattaya, is a vast garden estate of some 240 hectares. This idyllic resort has an orchid nursery, cactus garden, and beautifully landscaped park, styled in different designs. An arts and crafts center demonstrates Thailand's many handicrafts and in a large auditorium, cultural performances, folk and classical Thai dances and martial arts shows are presented. There is also an elephant show. Show time is daily at 10:00 and 14:30. Tickets and transportation may be booked at the Nong Nooch Village Pattaya Office, opposite the Nipa Lodge Hotel, Tel:422-958.

Above: The tropical wilderness struggles with modern tourism. Right: Condominiums have mushroomed at Jomtien beach.

Sporting Life

While Pattaya's reputation centers mainly on its nightlife, many visitors, after a few hectic rounds of bars and snacks, are reminded of their expanding waistline. Here the numerous and varied sporting facilities come in handy. The following is a list of various activities available here.

Jogging: At the foot of Pattaya Hill is the Pattaya Fitness Park. In addition to its green and landscaped gardens, the park offers a hilly jogging track shaded by large trees. In late afternoon, when a nice breeze lowers the temperature, you can jog down the sidewalks of Beach Road, or along the 6 kms of Jomthien Beach. Recommended around sunset or early morning.

Car and Motorcycle Racing: At km 14 on Route 36, on the way to Rayong, is the **Bira International Circuit**, named after Prince Bira, one of Thailand's best known motor racing enthusiasts. The 2.4 km circuit, ideal for Formula 3 races,

stages several international events a year. The circuit is open to those who like to race their own machines. Fees range from 500 baht for two hours to 1,000 baht for four hours. Bike riders may use the track from 8:00 to 12:00 for from 300 to 500 baht.

Golf: Bangphra International Golf Club, often said to be Thailand's most beautiful, has a challenging 18 holes, 6,000 m, par 72. Open from 6:00 to 18:00. Facilities include a 60-room hotel, swimming pool, restaurant, pro-shop etc. Tel:321-332; Siam Country Club course, rated locally as a very tough course, is 5,900 m long with par 72. A 30-room hotel, driving range, restaurant and pro-shop are available. Tel:428-002; Phlu Ta Luang (Royal Thai Navy Golf Club) at 6220 m, par 72, is the kingdom's largest. Dense vegetation covering its hills makes lost balls a common problem. Facilities include driving range, restaurant and pro-shop. Tel:601-185; the Asia Hotel right in Pattaya has a 9-hole course, 970 m, par 27. Tel:428-602.

Tennis: If tennis is your game, make your booking at any of the 14 hotels in Pattaya which have courts, primarily reserved for hotel guests. Several also have tennis coaches and instructors.

Go-kart Racing: Go-karts can be rented and run on the 400 m track of the Pattaya Kart Speedway at 212 Mu 9, Pattaya 2 Road, Tel:423-062.

Squash: At present, only the courts of the Cherry Tree, on Siam Country Club Road, offer squash facilities.

Snooker: Snooker can be played at Pattaya Bowl on Pattaya 2 Road, Tel:429-466; the Palladium, Tel:424-955; Palace Bowl, Tel: 428-487; Jomtien Bayview Hotel, Tel:425-889; and at A.R. Snooker, Tel:422-373.

Badminton: The Pattaya Badminton Court on Soi 17 is open 24 hours a day.

Bowling: There are three bowling alleys in Pattaya: Pattaya Bowl, Tel:429-466; Palace Bowl, Tel:428-487; OD Bowl, Tel:423-612.

Archery: There is an outdoor archery range at Nong Nooch Village.

Shooting: Tiffany's on Pattaya 2 Road has an air-conditioned shooting range with 19 fully-equipped galleries. Handguns and field rifles can be rented. Tel:429-642.

Windsurfing: Windsurf schools and suppliers are scattered all along the 6 kilometers of Jomtien Beach. The Pattaya Windsurf Club stages frequent competitions, some of them international events.

Sailing: Contact either the Royal Varuna Yacht Club, Tel:428- 959, or Sundowner Sailing Services, at km 157 on Sukhumvit Highway,

Parasailing: Many hotels offer parasailing facilities. In addition, private operators offer their services all along Pattaya Beach, at Jomtien and on Koh Larn island.

Waterskiing: Along all beaches, speedboat operators and boards can be hired.

Above: Fun, games and competition – a windsurfer's regatta. Right: Transvestite show in Pattaya.

Scuba Diving: Four outlets in Pattaya offer equipment, supplies and instruction: Dave's Den, Tel:423-486; International Divers' Center, Tel:423-325; Seafari Dive Shop, Tel:428-126; Steven's Dive Shop, Tel:428-392. The most popular locales for dives are the islands of the Koh Larn archipelago, but the uncontrolled traffic of motor boats, waterskiers and scooters make the area increasingly dangerous. Some divers complain about debris littering the coral. The above listed dive shops can give information on the better and less frequented islands, many of which are administered by the Royal Thai Navy and lie south of Pattaya off Sattahip. There are also several wrecks in the area for underwater exploration.

Game Fishing: Several operators organize deep-sea expeditions. Ask at Deutches Haus on Beach Road, Tel:423-486; Jenny Bar, Tel:429-645; and Shamrock Bar, Tel:425-417 for details. Trips are made to the islands of Maniwichai, Rin, and Khram. Although the Gulf of Thailand is suffering increasingly from

overfishing, enthusiasts can still count on a rich catch of Maylin king mackerel, shark and barracuda, all of which can be expected to put up a great fight.

Fresh Water Fishing: The Jomtien Fishing Park on Jomtien Beach Road, Panarak Park and the Bang Lamung Shrimp Farm offer visitors fishing in their well-stocked ponds.

Horseback Riding: Located on Sukhumvit Highway, is the Reo Ranch, which is stocked with horses from Australia. Riding trails meander through the countryside with some running down to the beach.

The rates for the above-mentioned facilities vary according to the season and some can be subject to negotiation. The Tourism Authority (TAT) office in Pattaya , 382/1 Chaihat Road, South Pattaya, Tel:428-750, can usually supply rates and other up-to-date information. Current activities and prices can be obtained from the weekly tourist publications *Pattaya This Week* and *Explore Pattaya*, available free at most hotels and restaurants.

Events and Festivals

Like the rest of the country, Pattaya celebrates national festivals like *songkran*, the old Siamese New Year, with gusto. For a few days in the middle of April, when the weather is hottest, water is thrown at all and sundry, but not before various acts of religious merit making and honoring the elders have been performed.

On full moon during late October or early November, *loy krathong*, the Festival of Light, is held, when everyone floats a little raft with a candle, some jossticks and perhaps a small coin, where ever there is some water.

Pattaya also celebrates its own week-long **Pattaya Festival** in early April. Mile-long parades, numerous beauty contests for men and women, concerts and fireworks displays, tests of skill and various games, international kite flying competitions and Formula Two motor races draw visitors from all over the kingdom and many parts of the world.

PATTAYA
Accommodation

LUXURY: **Royal Cliff Beach Resort**, Tel:421-421; **Asia Pacific**, Tel:428-602; Dusit Resort, Tel:428-541; **Merlin Pattaya**, Tel:428-755; Montien Pattaya, Tel:233-7060 (BKK); **New Siam Pattaya**, Tel:428-580; **Nipa Lodge**, Tel:428-195; Ocean View, Tel:428-084; **Orchid Lodge**, Tel:428-161; **Pattaya Lodge**, Tel:421-988; **Regent Marina**, Tel:428-015; **Siam Bayshore**, Tel:428-677; **Siam Bay View**, Tel:428-728; **Novotel Tropicana**, Tel:428-645; **Wong Amat**, Tel:426999.

MODERATE: **Beach View**, Tel:422-660; **Cosy Beach**, 280 Cliff Rd, Tel:429-334; **Diamond Beach**, 373/8 S.**Pattaya**, Tel:428-071; **Golden Beach**, 519/27 Pattaya 2nd St, Tel:428-891; **Honey Inn**, 528/8 Pattaya 2nd St; Tel:429-133; **Koh Larn Island**, Booking Office 183/82 Soi Praisani, Tel:428-422.

BUDGET: **Honey Lodge**, 598/8 Pattaya 2nd St, Tel:429-133; **Palm Lodge**, North Pattaya Beach Rd, Tel:428-779; **Pattaya View Inn**, 183/57 Moo 10, Soi Chaiyasit, Tel:429-380; **Queen Pattaya**, Pattaya 2nd St, Tel:428-234; **Travel Lodge**, 583 Pattaya Beach Rd, Soi 13, Tel:428-040.

Clinics
Pattaya Nua Clinic, 129/1 Pattaya Klang Rd, Tel:428-876; **Rama Polyclinic**, 205/8 Pattaya 2 Rd, Tel:429-662; **Prasarn Clinic**, Pattaya Soi 13, Beach Rd, Tel:429-123; **Praxis Pattaya**, 1/20 Pattaya Center, opposite Nipa Lodge Hotel, Tel:429-357.

Hospitals
Banglamung Hospital, Talad Mai, Sawangfah Rd, Tel:428-325; **Cholburi Hospital**, Sukhumvit Rd, Cholburi, Tel:282-008; **Pattaya International Clinic,** Pattaya Soi 4, Beach Rd, Tel:428-374; Pattaya Memorial, Pattaya Klang Rd, Tel:429-422; **Somdej Memorial Hospital**, Jermjompol Rd, Sri Racha, Tel:311-009.

Post / Telegraph / Telephones
The Pattaya Post Office and International Telephone, Telegraph and Telex Office is at Soi Chaiyasit, Beach Rd, Tel:429-341. To contact the Pattaya Telephone Exchange, phone 428-111.

Radio
Pattaya Radio Station (FM 107.75) - Tel:429-281.

Newspapers
The Bangkok Post, 186/26 Soi Post Office, Tel:429-904.

Access to and Transport in Pattaya

Air-conditioned and regular buses leave the **Eastern Bus Terminal** at Ekamai (Soi 63, Sukhumvit) in Bangkok regularly throughout the day, taking somewhat over two hours to reach Pattaya. For information on departure times and fares phone 392-2391 for air-conditioned and 391-2504 for regular buses. Travel agents in Bangkok and Pattaya will gladly arrange for a tour bus to pick you up at your hotel for the trip to or from Pattaya. In Bangkok this service involves a bus going around the city to pick up passengers at the various hotels which can be very time consuming because of heavy traffic jams.

Travel in Pattaya

Mini-buses *(songthaews)* make getting around in Pattaya very easy, although this form of transport may be the most comfortable. Fares are supposed to be 5 baht per person per ride, but if you go beyond the Beach Road limits, prices have to be negotiated, a complicated procedure if you are new or unfamiliar with the surroundings. Not being able to communicate in the local language will complicate matters further. Consult the local tourism brochures or TAT office for the rental of motorcycles or jeeps. Prices vary widely. Also beware of shady deals when a faulty vehicle is offered which is bound to break down. You may be made responsible for any repairs, although the fault is not yours.

Boat trips to Koh Larn can be arranged through travel shops. Tickets are 250 baht per person for a round trip, which includes lunch. Boats leave at 9:30 and 11:30 and take 45 minutes. Without lunch the trip costs 100 baht. Boats and junks can be chartered, but prices depend on season and the type of boat you prefer. Junks travel to Koh Larn as well, leaving at 9:30 to view the coral reefs and return at 16:30. The trip costs 250 baht including lunch.

Bor Kor Sor air conditioned buses out of Pattaya depart every 30 minutes from the new bus station at the North Pattaya Road Terminal between 6:00 and 21:00. The fare to Bangkok is 50 baht. There is also a service running straight from Pattaya to Bangkok International Airport from 7:00 to 19:00 for a cost of 100 baht.

Diamond Coach buses leave from the Nipa Lodge Hotel at 8:30, 12:30, 17:00, dropping passengers off at major hotels in Bangkok. The fare is 110 one way, 220 baht return. The Erawan Coach Co. offers daily services from the Siam Bayview Hotel at 9:00, 13:00, and 17:00 to its Gaysorn Road terminal in Bangkok with drop offs at major hotels.

Trips to the island of Koh Samet (refer to special section on that island) can be arranged through Cleo International, Malibu Travel Service or Fly Bangkok bus service. Buses usually depart Pattaya daily at 8:30 and 13:30 and return at 10:30 and 18:30. One way fare is 120 baht.

Tourist Information

Tourism Authority of Thailand (TAT), Pattaya Office, 382/1 Beach Road, Tel: 428-750 or 429-113. (open seven days a week including holidays).

Police / Government Offices

Tourist Police (bi-lingual assistance for visitors), Office attached to TAT office, Tel:429-371.
Immigration Office, Soi 8, Beach Road, Tel:429-409. Pattaya Police Station, Beach Road, Tel:428-223.

Restaurants

Pattaya has a vast range of eateries, ranging from one end of the spectrum to the other. Even the strangest and most outlandish of dishes are to be found in restaurants so varied and numerous, that it is impossible to list them all.

The acknowledged leaders in their particular cuisine are as follows:

THAI: **Nang Nual Seafood**, Pattaya 2 Rd, Tel:428-478; **Nang Nual Jomtien Beach**, Tel:231-548; **Krua Suthep**, Pattaya 2 Rd, Tel:418- 137; **Kruatalay**, 345 Jomtien Beach, Tel:423-000; **PIC Kitchen**, Soi 5, Beach Rd, Tel:428-374.

CHINESE: **Narissa**, Siam Bayview Hotel, Tel:428-728; **Tam Nak Nam Floating Restaurant**, Pattaya Central Rd, Tel:429-059; **Villa Seafood Restaurant**, Soi 7, Pattaya Beach Rd, Tel:422-523.

JAPANESE: **Akamon**, 468/19 Pattaya 2 Rd, Tel: 429-598; **Yamato**, Soi Yamato, South Pattaya, Tel: 429-685.

KOREAN: **Koreana**, 436/6 N.Pattaya, Soi 1, Tel:429-635.

GERMAN: **Alt Heidelberg**, 273 Beach Rd; **Drei Jahreszeiten**, Beach Rd; **Hafen Stueble**, Beach Road.

FRENCH: **Orient Express** (in two railway cars), Beach Rd. between Montien and Nipa Lodge Hotels, Tel:428-195.

INTERNATIONAL: **O'Hara's**, 463/8 Srinakhon Shopping Center, Tel:422-264. **Dolf Riks**, Srinakhon Shopping Center, Tel:428-586; **El Toro Steakhouse**, 215/31-32 Pattaya 2 Rd, Tel:426-238; **Green Bottle**, Pattaya 2 Rd.

Shopping

South Pattaya has numerous shopping centers, department stores and boutiques, but visitors should be cautioned that prices here are by no means the fairest in the kingdom.

Nevertheless, for those anxious to purchase gems, beachwear, handicraft items, leather goods and footwear, and who don't have the time or opportunity to shop elsewhere, South Pattaya has a wide range of products to offer.

Bargaining is still the best way to obtain a realistic price, except in department stores, where prices should be fixed. Westerners, unfamiliar with the practice of bargaining, would be wise to visit several shops and compare prices, before making a purchase

The huge multi-million-baht - as yet not completed - shopping complex on North Pattaya Road is patterned after the Night Bazaar in Chiang Mai and has a handicraft center, bazaar and shopping arcade with small bars, nightclubs and outdoor seafood restaurants.

The best guide for shoppers is the bi-monthly, pocket-sized "Shopping Guide" put out by the TAT. Free to visitors, it contains useful information on shopping, major shopping centers, and a list of TAT-approved retail outlets and sightseeing destinations.

Excursions

From Pattaya, many one, two or more day trips by road, rail or water are possible to a number of other resorts, islands and parks. The following destinations are treated in more detail in the section on the Southeast Coast

Bangsaen Beach, Nong Mon Market, 42 km from Pattaya, is a huge seafood market. Vendors also sell handicrafts of bamboo, rattan and ceramics.

The **Khao Khiao Open Zoo**, on the road to Bangphra Golf Course is 18 km from Bangphra which itself is 35 km from Pattaya. The open zoo has over 50 animal species roaming in large enclosures.

Chan Ta Thian Waterfall, a few km from the Open Zoo is an open park and wildlife preserve. Koh Samet and Ban Phe, Sri Racha, Koh Sichang, Chantaburi and Trat all make interesting outings from Pattaya.

Entertainment

Pattaya This Week and *Explore Pattaya*, two regular publications, available free at hotels, restaurants and tour agents, give details of shows, buffet specials, theater, sporting events and other happenings.

EASTERN GULF

Following the shoreline curving from the mouth of the Chao Phraya all the way south to the Cambodian border, one sees a string of provinces with a fascinating and varied array of sights and experiences. From the glitter and noise of Pattaya, to the deserted islands of Trat, this stretch presents maritime Thailand in all its diversity. Running through this region, Sukhumvit Highway starts in Bangkok and goes all the way to Cambodia. Once the road leaves Bangkok's suburbs, especially the vast industrial estates in Bangna, the countryside changes and rice paddies, salt pans, and shrimp farms become frequent sights.

Chonburi

Closest to Bangkok is the province of **Chonburi** with its rapid development as the location of the vast Eastern Seaboard Project, one of Thailand's most ambitious industrialization schemes. The town of Chonburi itself is an unspectacular provincial capital, much like many others around the kingdom. It is 85 km from Bangkok and the first major town reached by bus on trips further south. Visitors may well remember Chonburi as nothing more than the place where traffic suddenly drew to a crawl, midway on the trip south, because the town presents a time-wasting bottleneck.

Beginning with Bangsaen Beach, the coast from here on is a long string of pleasant bays, islets, beaches and resorts, the most precious gem on the necklace being Pattaya (some nasty tongues suggest that it's just an artificial stone). This line of resorts stops at Sattahip, where the coastline makes a wide sweep, with less intensive development continuing after Rayong.

Left: He is fishing the hard way. Right: Fishing the easier way, with boats.

Bangsaen Beach

Bangsaen, once the premier beach resort for Bangkokians, has seen better days, before new roads, luxury buses and fast cars shifted the focus to Pattaya. Seven km out of Chonburi, or 3 km off Sukhumvit Highway from the Nong Mon market, it can be reached from the Chonburi bus terminal by hailing a minibus or *tuk-tuk*. From Bangkok, buses leave for the resort regularly throughout the day.

Popular now with many Thai families, mainly on long weekends, foreigners would find the resort a disappointment. The beach itself can be very crowded, but swimming is unpleasant because of excessive mud close to shore. Nevertheless, Baengsaen is worth a visit, if only for a few hours and as an escape from the pollution of Bangkok.

The beach is lined with coconut palms and casuarina trees and beach chairs and umbrellas may be hired. The nearby **Ocean World** is one of those water amusement parks much appreciated by

113

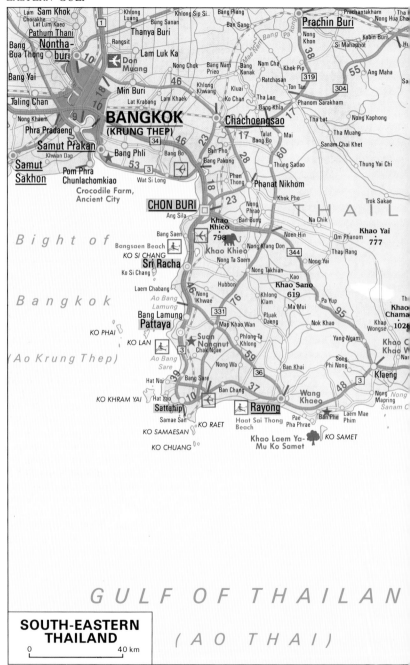

SOUTH-EASTERN THAILAND

0   40 km

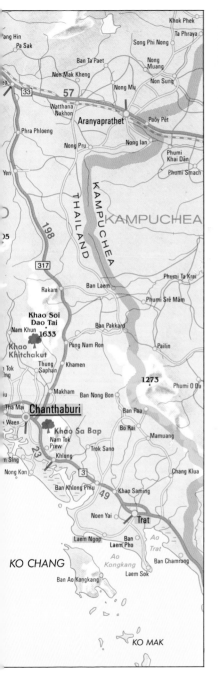

parents and their children. There is a roller coaster and enormous water slides. Restaurants, snack bars and a poolside bar are open dawn to dusk.

The **Marine Science Museum** is Bangsaen's other attraction. Located at Srinakarinwirot University, just before Ocean World on the road to the beach, the institute encourages tourists to visit. Its aquarium provides an educational side-trip from the rigors of a visit to Ocean World. For details phone Tel:377-671.

Sri Racha and Koh Sichang

Following the Sukhumvit Highway south, the next place of interest is **Sri Racha**. This busy seaport and trading post has won awards as the cleanest town in the kingdom. It also has a unique fleet of vehicles serving as taxis – huge rumbling and noisy tricycles, built from Harley-Davidson bikes. Lining its main street are numerous seafood restaurants, whose reputation draws people all the way from Bangkok, just for a meal. Few have menus with prices on, so hungry visitors should mark each dish and ask the price before ordering. That way there will be no confusion when the bill is presented to you.

The harbor is, unfortunately, a collecting point for debris, but just out of town there is a pleasant walk towards the causeway leading to **Koh Kaeo Pi Sodarn**, a small island with an interesting temple. Sri Racha is also the departure point for **Koh Sichang**, visible offshore. This long, narrow island has a unique history and a climate best described as arid, with prickly pear cactus and other desert plants in abundance. The pink sandstone, limestone cliffs and dry terrain are all unlike any other island in the gulf. On the boat trip over, passengers will see many ships anchored offshore, offloading cargo too heavy to be shipped up the shallow river to Bangkok. Many of the vessels will take on tapioca for the return trip.

Halfway down Koh Sichang, a picturesque village is strung around the harbor. On a hill above the town is a Chinese temple, famous among Bangkok Chinese as a point of pilgrimage. On special holidays, like Chinese New Year, the ferry boats are packed to the rim. Several narrow concrete roads run the length of, and criss-cross, the island and motor trishaws take you anywhere for 10 baht. About midway on the over 10 km long central road is **Tewpai Lodge** with bungalows, a restaurant and a rather noisy location. On one wall is a relief map of the island, giving an idea of its layout.

At the south end of the road are the grounds of **Chulalongkorn University's Marine Science Institute**. Nearby, several acres of the grounds are scattered with the ruins of gardens, terraces, aqueducts and several buildings, all part of a Summer Palace, originally built late last

Above: A small gas station, gasoline only gallon-wise. Right: Sundown is the best time for fishing.

century by King Chulalongkorn (Rama V). Across the site, a path meanders up to a small *wat*, where the king used to meditate. Concrete steps are all over the place, some leading to small caves, others going down to a bay with a rocky beach. Bathers should beware of spiny sea urchins. For a glimpse of the royal lifestyle at the time, refer to the Vimanmek Palace mentioned in the Bangkok section, which was reconstructed from the teak timbers of the palace on Koh Sichang.

The French occupied the island after a disagreement with the Thais in 1893 and did not leave until 1907. This convinced the king that the island was too vulnerable and therefore he never visited Koh Sichang again.

There is little accommodation available on Koh Sichang and only a handful of modest Thai-style restaurants cater to the hungry. Some hotels, basic in nature, can be found close to the harbor and a few bungalow complexes are at different locations on the island. Reservations, in Thai only, are made by telephone, of

which there are only two for the whole island.

Boats to Koh Sichang leave Sri Racha
every two hours, with the last boat back
leaving at 16:30. Buses from Bangkok go
directly to Sri Racha, leaving the Eastern
Bus Terminal near Soi Ekamai every 25
minutes. Air-conditioned buses going
back to Bangkok leave the Sri Racha terminal every hour, but on weekends, visitors should book a few hours ahead of the
intended departure time.

Rayong

The next province going south is **Rayong**. With its sea cliffs, rubber plantations, long sandy beaches and inland
parks, this province has much to offer.
Many large resorts are springing up along
the coast and the TAT office in Bangkok
can provide the latest information. The
town of Rayong is, like Chonburi, a
rather nondescript provincial capital, 220
km on the old Highway (Route 3) or 185
km on the newer Route 36, from Bang-

kok. Rayong Province is, like its eastern
neighbor Chantaburi, a fruit-growing
center, famous for durian and pineapple.
One will on occasion encounter the
heady odor of a fish sauce factory, since
this mandatory ingredient of Thai cuisine
is a major product of the province.

Rayong town has only few temples
which are worth visiting. The **King Taksin Shrine** at Wat Lum Mahachai Chumphon commemorates the early Siamese
king who rallied Thai fighters and freed
the country from Burmese occupation
after the fall of Ayutthaya. Many Chinese
come to worship here during Chinese
New Year.

At **Wat Pa Pradu**, located near the
town center is a large reclining Buddha
11.95 meters long. About 2 km from the
town center, at the end of Taksin Maharaj
Road is Pra **Chedi Klang Nam**, a small,
very old pagoda, built on an islet in the
Rayong River. Behind the city hall is **Pra
Buddha Angkirot**, the principal Buddhist image of the town, enshrined in a
traditional Thai pavilion.

117

Along the Rayong coast are numerous beaches and islands and even some luxury resorts. **Haat Sai Thong**, the "Golden Sand Beach", has some bungalows and is very quiet and very clean. Turn right at km 208 to get to this idyllic stretch of golden sand which is definitely off the beaten track.

Koh Saket is a small island immediately offshore and a 20 minute boat ride from Haat Sai Thong. There are some bungalows, but it is advised to book at least a week ahead. There is a small restaurant but fresh water must be transported from the mainland. Ferries to the island start operating from 9:00 and the last return trip is at 17:00.

The **Sobha Botanical Garden** has a well-laid-out display of indigenous and transplanted species. It is only 70 km from Pattaya and not far from the ferry

Above: Family outing in a tuk-tuk. Right: A pint-size hawker offering snacks on the beach.

landing for Koh Samet. In the grounds are also some 100 year old Thai houses, furnished with traditional utensils.

Right around the corner from the gardens is the luxurious **Rayong Resort** with first class accommodation, sophisticated dining and a host of leisure time facilities, including a disco. There is a very long fishing pier going straight out into the sea and boats may be hired to hop over to Koh Samet.

Only a few km further on and 15 km from Rayong, is the small town of **Ban Phe**, the jumping off point for Koh Samet. If the wind is right, you will smell Ban Phe before you actually set eyes on it. This hamlet is a busy fishing port. It has a large market, where its many sea-based products, such as fish sauce, dried cuttlefish, dried shrimp and shrimp paste are sold. Beyond Ban Phe are long stretches of sand. Strung along the highway, numerous bungalow complexes sit beneath casuarina trees. They are busy with weekenders from Bangkok who usually drive their own cars.

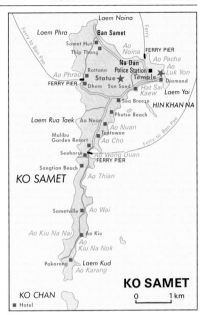

KO SAMET

KO CHAN
■ Hotel

0   1 km

KO SAMET

KOH SAMET

This beautiful nature park, about 6.5 km offshore from Ban Phe, is a magnet for Bangkok's young, especially on long weekends, when students, mainly in groups, invade the island. Seven km long and shaped like a narrow triangle, it can be clearly seen from the pier, where boats leave at regular intervals for the half hour trip. Discovered by budget travelers a few years ago, it has just about replaced Koh Samui on the other side of the gulf as the haven for nature lovers.

Koh Samet figures in Thai literature as Koh Kaeo Phitsdan in the story of Pra Apaimanee, written by Sunthon Phu, Thailand's great nineteenth-century poet. The island has been administered by the Forestry Department since October 1981, and is the most popular part of a National Park that also includes the nearby islands of Kudi, Kham and Plai Tin. Being strictly regulated, it has, so far, escaped the clutches of real estate tycoons and has practically no infrastructure.

While recent reports suggest that Koh Samet's coral reefs are suffering from overfishing and pollution, skin divers still find the reefs filled with schools of colorful fish. Information on walks, beaches, bungalows and local folklore can be gleaned from an interesting small booklet, *Samet,* by Alan Alan, available in many Bangkok bookstores or on the island itself.

Chantaburi

Leaving Rayong, Highway Route 3 runs to **Chantaburi**, the next province along the east coast. About 320 km from Bangkok, Chantaburi, because of its proximity to Cambodia, has figured frequently in Thai history. It was the site of repeated cross-border skirmishes between the Thais and French.

Rich in natural resources, Chantaburi is off the tourist track, yet offers two prime attractions. First, it is one of the leading fruit-growing areas of Thailand and holds a very popular annual Fruit

119

Festival, usually in April. Durian, custard apple and pineapple are the main crops. In addition, the town is the center of a leading gem mining area, famed particularly for its star sapphires.

In **Chantaburi town**, the main market is where to buy the province's many fruits and fruit products, as well as locally made handicrafts and fresh seafood, caught along the coast.

Along a street called Sichan, known locally as "Gem Street", is an area, right in the heart of Chantaburi, where gem stones are traded. On most days between 9:00 and 12:00, but especially on Fridays and Saturdays, large crowds of gem buyers, from Bangkok and abroad, inspect and purchase locallymined sapphires and rubies from the pits across the border in Cambodia.

Only recognized buyers are trusted and will be allowed into the shops to inspect the stones for sale in bulk. Tourists interested in purchasing the odd stone may do so in a few retail outlets.

Outside the town, several gem mines may be visited, but inquiries should be made at the hotel. A national park, several waterfalls and the Laem Singh cape, 30 km from town, are further points of interest. At **Laem Singh** are the remains of two forts, dating to the Rama III era. On the road leading to the fishing pier is a rectangular building of red brick (Kook Khee Gai or the Chicken Droppings Jail), used by the French to imprison captured Thai soldiers when the area was occupied at the end of the last century. The jail's ceiling consisted of slats serving as a chicken roost, and the droppings were meant as additional punishment for the prisoners below.

Trat

Because of its remoteness, Thailand's southeastern most province has yet to get onto a tourist itinerary. But this moun-

Above: Entertainment for the whole family, a folk theater performance.

tainous province might offer just what is needed after the attractions of Bangkok and Pattaya have paled. From Bangkok's Ekamai station, air-conditioned buses cover the 400 kms in a little over six hours, the trip taking the better part of a day.

The main purpose for going to Trat is to visit some of the islands and it is recommended to ask, first thing on arrival, which boat goes where, leaving when and from where.

Enquiries may be made at the hotel or at Laem Ngob, the boat pier, where boats leave for some of the islands, including Koh Chang, Koh Koot, Koh Kradat and Koh Rad. The latter two islands are about two hours from Laem Ngob jetty and are untouched, with beautiful beaches and coral reefs. Tel:331-921 for further information.

Koh Koot is 45 minutes by boat from Laem Ngob and is well known for the Than Sanuk waterfall.

Koh Chang, the largest of the islands off the Trat coast, is Thailand's second largest island (after Phuket) and some 30 km in length and 8 km broad at its widest point. Dense vegetation covers the mountainous interior, with some of the hills reaching a height of 800 m. Some spectacular waterfalls and a number of totally secluded beautiful beaches are worth a visit.

There is usually only one boat per day going to Koh Chang and there is no accommodation available except some bungalows at the Forestry Department, usually reserved for its own staff. Call the Forestry Department in Bangkok at Tel: 579-0529 for information. It is wise for anyone intending to visit Koh Chang to carry his own camping equipment.

Trat Municipality operates a tour to the island and this can be contacted at Tel:511-282. It is essential to make arrangements through a Thai friend or a local agent, as the operator does not speak English.

Accomodation at:
CHONBURI PROVINCE
CHONBURI TOWN: **Buraphaphon**, 844/100 Sukhumvit, Tel:282-664; **Chonburi**, 728/22 Sukhumvit, Tel:282-488; **Chonburi Diamond Palace**, 123 Moo 1, Soi Supphamit, Tel:272-037; **Eastern**, 888 Sukhumvit, Tel:283-713.
BANG SAEN: **Bang Saen Beach Resort**, 55-150 Bangsaen Beach Rd, Tel ;376-675; **Villa**, 190 Mu 13, Bangsaen Beach Rd, Tel:377-088.
SRI RACHA: **Grand Bungalow**, 9 Choemchomphon Rd, Tel:312-537; **Si Racha Lodge**, 4 Choemchomphon Rd, Tel:311-647; **Si Wichai**, Choemchomphon Rd, Tel: 311-212.
KOH SICHANG: **Champ Bungalows**, House 74/1 Koh Sichang, Cholburi, Tel:272-987; **Bungalow Sripitsanu**, 30 Moo 3 Koh Sichang, Tel: 272-987.

RAYONG PROVINCE
RAYONG TOWN: **Asia**, Sukhumvit, Tel: 611-022; **Rayong Otani**, Sukhumvit, Tel: 611-112; **Tawan-Ok**, 52/3 Sukhumvit, Tel:611-167.
BAN PHE: **Rayong Resort** *(luxury)*, Laem Tarn, Ban Phe, Tel:211-0855; **Chao Le Cottages** *(moderate)*, Tel:437-2974; **Rungnapha Resort**, Tel: 671-729; **Coral Reef Resort**, Tel: 511-4010.
SAMET ISLAND:*MODERATE:* **Vongdeuan Resort**, Tel:250-0424; **Malibu Garden**, Vongduan Beach, Tel:321-0346; **Ao Phrao Bungalows**, Paradise Beach, Tel:613-540. **Samet Villa**, Sea Breeze Beach, Ao Phai. *BUDGET:* **Naga Bungalows**, communal showers; **Tub Tims Bungalows**, Ao Tub Tim.

CHANTABURI PROVINCE
CHANTABURI TOWN: **Chantaburi Hilton**, 41/210 Raksak-Chamun Rd, Tel:311-064; **Chantaburi Hotel**, 42/6 Tha-Chalab Rd, Tel: 311-300; **Chanta Nimit**, 116-118 Rimnam Rd, Tel:312-388; **Eastern**, 899 Tha-Chalab Rd, Tel:312-218; **Kasem San 2**, 23 Sri Rongmuang Rd, Tel:311-173; **Travel Lodge**, 14 Raksak-Chamun Rd, Tel:311-531.

TRAT PROVINCE
TRAT TOWN: **Muang Trat**, 4 Sukhumvit, Tel:511-091; **Thai Rungrot**, 296 Sukhumvit, Tel:511-141; **Tung Nguan Seng**, 66-77 Sukhumvit, Tel:511-384.
ISLANDS
Koh Kradat: Tel:311-3668; **Koh Chang**, National Parks Division of Forestry Dept, Tel:579-0529; Bangbao Beach Resort, Tel:511-597; **Koh Pui,** Chan Prapha Tours, Tel:252-5629.

A JOURNEY INTO HISTORY

PHITSANULOK
SUKHOTHAI
TAK

Approaching the north from Bangkok, the traveler will pass through a region with many sites of historical significance, worth visiting. Geographically, this part of Thailand, which includes the provinces of Phichit, Khampaengphet, Phitsanulok, Tak, Sukhothai and Uttaradit, is often considered part of the north, but is historically not a part of Lannathai (the country's eight northernmost provinces), whose people speak their own, distinctly different dialect.

PHITSANULOK

This provincial capital is of little interest to the tourist, but the town does have a TAT office with information on the rich historic sites in the adjoining provinces. Located 390 km north of Bangkok, it is an important commercial center, as well as a transit and transportation hub for the region. The train stops here, but does not stop in Sukhothai. Two flights a day connect Pitsanulok with Bangkok.

Running through town is the Nan River, on the banks of which is the town's main shrine, **Wat Phra Sri Ratana Mahathat**, with a large bronze Buddha statue, cast in the Sukhothai style. The

Left: One of the highly venerated statues of Buddha in Phitsanulok.

image is famous and much revered throughout Thailand. Two km out of town are the ruins of **Wat Chulamani**. This temple dates back to the Sukhothai period, but has some structures built in the earlier Khmer style.

Opposite the Buranathai Buddha Image Foundry on Wisutkasat Road is the **Dr. Tawi-Pim Buranaket Folklore Museum**, well known for its extensive collection of local folk arts and crafts items such as basketry, ceramics and ancient kitchen utensils. Visitors interested in purchasing local handicraft products would do well to visit the museum, to study the genuine articles, before buying fakes in the markets along the river.

SUKHOTHAI

Meaning "The Dawn of Happiness", **Sukhothai**, 425 km north of Bangkok, was the capital of the first truly Thai kingdom. Founded around 1240, the Sukhothai kingdom lasted for 120 years, before becoming a vassal of Ayutthaya. King Ramkamhaeng, the third of the eight Sukhothai monarchs, ascended the throne in 1278 and reigned for 40 years. A skilled warrior, he was also a patron of the arts. He transformed the young kingdom into a powerful state and greatly extended its boundaries.

123

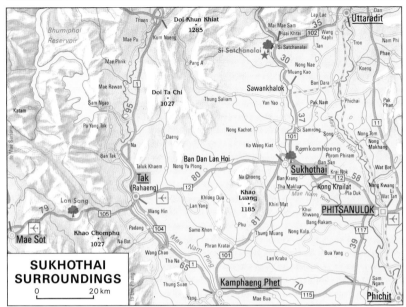

On his first trip to China in 1282, he visited the all-powerful Kublai Khan, and in 1300, returning from a second visit, he brought back Chinese craftsmen to teach the Thais the art of carving stone and making earthenware. "Sankhalok Pottery", as this form of celadon ware is known, is prized highly by collectors. The king is also credited with having invented the Thai alphabet.

Sukhothai, like Ayutthaya, is a city of **ruins**, most of which are located in the **Sukhothai Historical Park**. From the scale of the monuments and ruins, one can easily imagine the glory Sukhothai attained in its brief history. Within the area of restoration are the remains of palaces, temples, city gates, moats, dams, irrigation ditches, ponds and canals. The dykes, which formed part of the water control system, have been restored by the Fine Arts Department with the cooperation of UNESCO.

Right: The famous Wat Mahathat in Sukhothai.

Much of the outer wall of the old city still stands. The four gates are largely intact, and within the walls are 35 monuments. The **Ramkamhaeng National Museum**, built in 1960, displays Sukhothai art and pottery. It also has a well-made miniature model of the Sukhothai site, giving a good idea of relative distances between the monuments. A detailed guide book is on sale in the museum or at the entrance to Wat Mahathat.

The **ruins of the royal palace** and **Wat Mahathat** are in the center of town with the palace grounds covering some 160,000 square meter While searching through the ruins of one of the buildings in the nineteenth century, King Mongkut (Rama IV) found a stone tablet bearing ancient Thai script. He also unearthed part of the stone used as King Ramkhamhaeng's throne, from which, according to legend, he conducted the affairs of state under the trees.

The most photographed ruin in Sukhothai is probably that of **Wat Sri Chum** with its 11 m tall seated Buddha. Located

to the west of the town, there are old inscriptions in the ceiling of an interior passageway, which are only visible with a torch. **Wat Saphan Hin** crowns a 200-meter- high hill 2 km to the west of Sukhothai. This hill presents an excellent overall view of the ruins of Sukhothai. There is also a 12-meter tall standing Buddha surrounded by laterite columns.

About 20 km south of Sukhothai is the 340 square kilometer **Ramkamhaeng National Park**. It lies at 1,200 meters above sea level, with waterfalls and a wide variety of flora and fauna. The park is on Highway Route 1 coming from Bangkok. Bungalows and tents are available through the National Park Section of the Forestry Department in Bangkok. Tel:579-0529.

Si Satchanalai

Having once been the most northern outpost of the Sukhothai kingdom, the ruins in **Si Satchanalai** are more neglected than those in the former capital,

but they are still worth a visit. Si Satchanalai is to the north of Sukhothai and, once in town, signs indicate where to find the ruins across the Yom River.

Wat Chang Lom is a monastery in Si Satchanalai town, its main attraction being the great pagoda in Sri Lankan style with 39 stucco elephants around its base. **Wat Khao Phanom Phloeng** sits above Wat Chang Lom with its large seated Buddha on a hill overlooking the town. From this vantage point, the layout of the old city can be visualized.

Si Satchanalai was originally called Sawankhalok, as it was here that the Chinese potters first produced the Sankhalok celadon. An excursion to Si Satchanalai requires a visit to **Wat Prasi Ratana Mahathat** at Chaliang, about 2 km from the ferry going to the main ruins. A pleasant walk brings you to the point where a ferry boat is usually waiting to take visitors to the *wat* on the other side. Situated on a promontory at a bend in the Yom River, the thickness of the walls suggests that the original structure

Pra Keo, almost next door, is the main temple within the walls. It is rich in Buddha statues in various stages of decay. Outside the walls are **Wat Chang Rob** and Wat Phra Si Iriyabot. The former is surrounded by elephants and has a large *chedi*, which is artistically remarkable in itself. The pattern of decoration, stucco elephants, bo trees and demons, so characteristically Sukhothai, is nowhere as well preserved as in Wat Chang Rob.

Wat Phra Sri Iriyabot is dedicated to the four attitudes of the Lord Buddha. In this *wat* a standing Buddha has been left without restoration and is an excellent example of the original style of Sukhothai sculpture. The small **museum** opened by the Fine Arts Department is a must for a first-time visitor who wishes to understand the ruins. It also has some excellent examples from all periods of Thai art.

must have been a fortress. In the courtyard are two sanctuaries, a *chedi* and a large *prang*. Architecturally, the monuments are of the Ayutthaya period, but with a strong Khmer influence.

Kamphaeng Phet

Because this town was, along with Sukhothai and Si Satchanalai, one of the three main centers of the Sukhothai kingdom, it is worth including in an itinerary involving Sukhothai. Sitting on the left bank of the Ping River close to the highway to Chiang Mai, it may well be the first stop on a tour of the region.

The **ruins** are strewn about a site surrounded by remarkably well-preserved walls of laterite and sandstone. After walking past the provincial hall, the first ruin you come to is **Wat Prathat**. Its round *chedi* is surrounded by columns and flanked by two smaller *chedis*. **Wat**

Above: Another Buddha reclining, here in Kamphaeng Phet.

Along the Burmese Border

This region consists of a number of districts which still have the feeling of the wild, untamed frontier. There are still periodic skirmishes on the border, mainly because the Burmese government is trying to suppress ethnic minorities such as the Karens, who continue to resist absorption. Sometimes this fighting spills over into Thailand.

Since Thailand has become one of the most fashionable destinations, its better known sights are often overrun by tourists, and have, for many travelers, lost their original charm. Looking for new destinations, many off-the-beaten-track sights have been re-discovered and made accessible by good roads, comfortable buses and new regional airports. Like other parts of rural Thailand, the mountainous areas along the Burmese border are within a few hours of Bangkok or Chiang Mai, and more visitors are discovering the untouched beauty of these little known places.

TAK

This province, 425 km north of Bangkok, is the gateway to that part of the border region known for its night time smuggling of Burmese teak into Thailand. It also sits astride the Pan-Asia Highway, which runs across the border and was planned as the main link between the countries of the region. The **Bhumibol Dam** (Yanhee Dam), with a length of 200 km, Thailand's largest water reservoir, has excellent fishing and boating facilities and a good hotel. The dam site is some 50 km beyond the town, which is relatively dull.

Mae Sot, 85 km from Tak and 500 km from Bangkok, is a district town with a considerable cross-border trade. The nearby Moey River, forming the border between Thailand and Burma, is dry for part of the year, and traders from either side simply walk through the river bed to peddle their wares. A busy **market** along the banks offers Burmese rubies and other gems, handicrafts and cloth from across the border. Prospective gembuyers should beware of fakes.

In town, the large market behind the Siam Hotel is the place to go for Burmese clothing and some good Indian and Burmese food. Treks to hill tribe villages are being organized from Mae Sot, offering a glimpse of tribal life as yet completely unspoilt by tourism. These trips also offer some spectacular views of ever changing mountainscapes.

A highway, running along the border, passes through Mae Sot, going north towards **Mae Sariang**, but at present public transport is only available as far as **Tha Song Yang**, some 180 km or a little more than half the distance.

Going south, the road runs for 150 km, ending at **Um Phang**. A branch road goes to the town of **Waley** on the Burmese border, a well-used, but even more remote smuggling center. It can be reached by *tuk tuk* out of Mae Sot.

SUKHOTHAI & SI SATCHANALAI
Accommodation
Chinnawat, 1-3 Nikon Kase, Tel:611-385; **Kitimongkol**, 39 Singhawat, Tel: 611-193; **Sawat Phong**, 56/2-5 Singhawat, Tel:611-567; **Sukhothai**, 15/5 Singhawat, Tel:611-133; **River View,** 92/1 Nikon Kasem, Tel:611-656.
Museums
Ramkhamhaeng National Museum. Open daily except Mon, Tue from 9:00-12:00, 13:00-16:00.
Local Festivals
Loy Kratong (mid-November) is celebrated by setting small rafts of flowers and candles adrift on the ponds of Sukhothai. An annual event, it attracts thousands to Sukhothai so reservations are a must. *Songkran* (12th April) is the former Thai New Year and is still celebrated vigorously by people throwing water at each other.

PHITSANULOK
Accommodation
LUXURY: **Thep Nakhon**, 43/1 Srithammatraipidok, Tel:258-507; **Amarin Nakhon**, 3/1 Chao Phraya Phitsanulok, Tel:258- 588; **Ratchaphruk**, 99/9 Phra-Ong Dum, Tel:258-788. *MODERATE:* **Pailin**, 38 Baromtrai Lokkanat, Tel:252-411. *BUDGET:* **Indhra**, 103/8 Srithammatraipidok, Tel:259-188.
Tourist Information
TAT Office, 209/7-8 Surasai Trade Center, Boromtrailokanat, Tel:252-742.
Local Events / Festivals
During the first weekend of October, boats from all over Thailand come here to race. Races take place in front of Wat Yai.

TAK
Accommodation
MODERATE: **Wiang Tak**, 25/3 Mahadthai Bamrung, Tel:511-950. *BUDGET:* **Mae Ping**, 231/1 Mahadthai Bamrung , Tel: 511-807; **Tak**, 18/11 Mahadthai Bamrung, Tel: 511-234.

MAE SOT
Accommodation
MODERATE: **Mae Sot Hills**, Tel: 532-600. *BUDGET:* **Siam**, 185 Prasat Withi, Tel: 531-376; **First**, 444 Inthakhiri, Tel:531-233.
Excursions
Cruising on Mae Ping Lake behind Bhumipol Dam: Boats and raft cruises travel the upstream part of the lake from the Dam to the Doi Tao Self Help Settlement in Chiang Mai Province, a distance of 140 km. For hiring boats or rafts contact the Education Tour Center, Tel:221-5183; or Far East Queen Co, Tel:511-1872.

LANNATHAI,
A NORTHERN LAND,
A DIFFERENT
PEOPLE

CHIANG MAI
THE NORTH

CHIANG MAI

As Thailand's second largest city and – some say unfortunately – the fastest growing commercial center in the north, **Chiang Mai** has become a leading attraction for tourists, local and foreign. It lies on the banks of the Ping River, in a flat, rice-growing valley at a height of about 300 m above sea level. The surrounding mountain ranges are only a short distance away, with the 1,675 m high, lushly forrested Doi Pui to the west, dominating the town.

Historically, Chiang Mai has not been in the mainstream of Thai events. Because of the mountainous terrain it remained isolated from the rest of the country, but developed independently, somewhat influenced by Burma, as the center of a northern kingdom. It was only with the advent of roads and the construction of the railway to the north, that Chiang Mai became incorporated into a larger and more unified Siam.

Before the northern rail line pushed into the Ping Valley in the 1920s, journeying to Chiang Mai was a major expedition over poorly marked trails and across rivers without bridges. In the

Left: The golden Chedi on the Doi Suthep near Chiang Mai.

1940s, Germaine Krull, then manageress of the Oriental Hotel in Bangkok, took many days to drive north. She often found the road impassable, with bandits and tigers being additional obstacles. In the early 1950s, it took Harold Young, the creator and owner of the first Chiang Mai Zoo, three days to drive a Landrover from Bangkok to Chiang Mai – and the tigers were still a pest.

The travelers who did brave the wilds and got to Chiang Mai, found an idyllic town, nestling in a fertile valley. Hence its reputation as the Rose of the North – a city of ancient temples, inhabited by a relaxed people, innocent and unspoilt by the outside world, and with customs and crafts refined over a millenium.

Today, tourist literature still attempts to preserve the myth and to some extent it really is applicable. Chiang Mai still seduces visitors with its mountains, temple bells and relative tranquility. But the city is growing rapidly. While the temples are still there and Doi Suthep does rise into the cool mists overhead, the modern city has spilled far beyond its ancient walls, and a walk through the Night Market with its blaring music and touts illustrates how far Chiang Mai has moved beyond its isolated past.

The city's physical layout is no longer dominated by the remnants of days gone

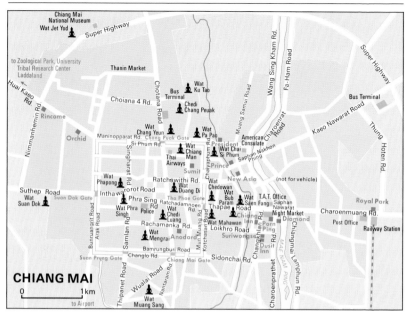

by. Once a walled city about a kilometer off the west bank of the Ping River, its ancient walls, which had been breached several times during its 700-year-old history, are broken and crumbling. The moat, still relatively intact, has been re-lined in recent years, and the five main city gates have been restored. In the area between the eastern wall and the Ping River, the modern town of Chiang Mai has developed, especially along Ta Pae Road. The railway station, together with the main post office and the bus terminal, is on the east side of the river, which is now spanned by four bridges.

The early history of Chiang Mai and northern Thailand is not too clear and only an outline may be given here. When the Mongols started to conquer China in the early thirteenth century, Kublai Khan, on his move to the south, demanded the allegiance of all chieftains who had formerly been vassals of China. One of

these chieftains was Prince Mengrai, who, himself of mixed blood – Thai and Lawa – had unified several small tribes and began pushing south from his base near Chiang Saen on the Mekong River. In 1262 he founded Chiangrai, making it his first capital. In 1292 he finally succeeded, after many attempts, in defeating the old Mon kingdom of Haripunchai (Lamphun), and decided that his by now extensive kingdom, Lannathai (meaning "a million rice fields"), deserved a new capital.

With the assistance of two allies, King Ramkamhaeng of Sukhothai and King Ngam Muang of Payao, King Mengrai laid out his new capital. By the time of his death in 1317, Chiang Mai was firmly in place as the capital of the region comprising most of the territory north of Sukhothai.

In the south, the kingdom of Ayutthaya had been established, and by the four-teenth century was putting pressure on the southern flanks of the region control-led by Sukhothai. The Lannathai armies

Right: Two young monks in their digs.

130

went to the aid of their southern allies several times, but eventually Sukhothai fell to Ayutthaya in 1378. For the next two centuries the rival kingdoms in the north and south fought many battles with neither gaining the upper hand. In the meantime, Burma had consolidated its power and by 1556 overwhelmed and absorbed Lannathai. For the next two centuries, Chiang Mai was ruled by a succession of Burmese overlords, although during this period it fell once for a brief time to Ayutthaya.

With their foothold in the north, the Burmese began to eye the wealth of Ayutthaya, and in 1767 they overran and sacked the city. But the Thais, under their new leader, Taksin, re-grouped and by 1775 had pushed the Burmese back and retaken not only Ayutthaya, but also Chiang Mai. At this point Chiang Mai became, like Ayutthaya before it, an abandoned capital, a dead city. The repeated wars had broken the city's spirit and the remaining inhabitants abandoned their homes and moved south to Lampang.

Chiang Mai lay dormant for 20 years before the first of its old inhabitants started to move back. Slowly it regained its former status as the capital of the north. Under powerful overlords, who owed allegiance to Bangkok, Chiang Mai remained the northern outpost of the new Siam for over a century. It was only with the advent of modern transportation that this quasi-independent city was brought within easier reach of Bangkok and thus truly incorporated into the kingdom.

Even today, along the borders with Burma and in the more isolated valleys, life and custom hearken back to those times, not so long ago, when Chiang Mai was the only center of civilization in a vast mountainous no-man's land.

Chiang Mai's attractions are amazingly varied, with something for every taste. The **TAT Office** is the first destination visitors should go to before starting to explore the sights. Located at 135 Praisanee Road, on the corner of Ta Pae Road near Nawarat Bridge, the office can assist in planning an itinerary based on interests

and time available. They will also caution visitors on possible hazards in the hills and may recommend reliable trekking companies and current prices.

Chiang Mai is first of all a city of temples. There are 36 *wats* within the old city walls, and another 85 in town, with many more in the surrounding country-side. **Wat Phra Singh**, on the corner of Singharat and Rajdamnoen Roads, is one of the two most important temples in Chiang Mai. Built in 1345 during the reign of King Pha Yu, the seventh of the Mengrai dynasty, it is the most illustrious of the city's religious buildings. Its elaborate woodcarvings and stucco figures were restored in 1927. Behind a large circular *chedi* is a small chapel housing the image gave the *wat* its name. The image of the Phra Buddha Sihing was supposedly made in Ceylon and transported to Siam

during the Sukhothai period. The original head was stolen in 1922, and replaced with a replica. On the walls of the chapel housing it are vibrant frescoes dating from the sixteenth Century.

Wat Chedi Luang on Phra Pokklao Road has a large number of resident monks and is, together with Wat Phra Singh, the most highly revered temple in Chiang Mai. Near the entrance is a *viharn* with a deep porch and two *nagas* on either side of the steps leading to the shrine. Behind the *viharn* is the impressive *chedi*, originally built in 1411. It reached a height of over 85 m before it was partially destroyed by an earthquake in 1545. It now reaches a height of 60 m.

Wat Chiang Man has the distinction of being the oldest temple in Chiang Mai, and was built by King Mengrai in 1297. The king is said to have resided in the temple during the construction of the city. Located on Rajaphakinar Road, the *wat* has a stone slab, which is said to mark the spot where King Mengrai died. This stone is covered with old Thai characters,

Above: An inspired art student in Chiang Mai. Right: The weary glory of the Wat Suan Dok.

which until now have never been correctly deciphered.

Wat Cha Si Phum is on the northeastern corner of the old moat near the President Hotel on Wichayanon Road. Its attractions are a well-preserved *chedi*, a wooden library and a *viharn* or main hall with some outstanding woodcarvings.

Wat Pa Pao is noteworthy for its Burmese-Shan style architecture. Surrounded by a low wall, its gates are elaborately decorated and in the paved courtyard are several *chedis* arranged around a central pavilion. **Wat Chieng Yuen** is not far from Wat Pa Pao on the same road. It has a large brick *chedi* decorated with stucco and broken porcelain. At the entrance is an octagonal Chinese pavilion decorated with peacocks and leaves.

The temples on Ta Pae Road, Chiang Mai's main business street, may be visited while on a shopping spree. **Wat Saen Fang** is built in Burmese style and is reached down a quiet lane which opens into the *wat's* serene courtyard. Opposite is **Wat Bupparam** with an elaborately decorated main hall. **Wat Mahawan**, only a few meters further up the road, has a large Burmese-style *chedi* and intricate woodcarvings, while **Wat Chedovan**, almost opposite and down a short alley, has three Burmese-style *chedis*.

Outside the town there are four temples of interest. **Wat Suan Dok**, about one kilometer west of the Suan Dok Gate on Suthep Road, has spacious grounds and a tranquil atmosphere. It has a Chiangsaen-style Buddha dating from 1504. **Wat Umong** (the Underground Temple) is situated 1.2 km beyond the turnoff for Wat Suan Dork. This *wat* sits in a quiet grove, many trees bearing little labels with words of wisdom in Thai, Chinese and English. Although this *wat* has suffered from the centuries, it has a basement crypt hollowed out of the flat rock sitting behind a ruined *chedi*, where monks used to meditate.

Wat Chet Yot can be reached by going up Huey Kaew Road and then turning right at the Rincome Hotel. Just off the

Superhighway to Bangkok and near the National Museum, this *wat* was built in the fifteenth century and is somewhat similar in design to the Mahabodhi Temple at Bodh Gaya in India. Built in 1455, it has seven spires. Beautiful decorations adorn the sides of the *chedi*. The temple was the site of the eighth Buddhist Council held in 1477 which revised the teaching of the Enlightened One. The grounds are quiet and relaxing.

Wat Koo Tao, the last on the list, can be easily reached from Wat Chet Yot turning off the Superhighway on Chotana Road and going towards the Provincial Stadium. It has a unique *chedi* built in 1613 to contain the ashes of a Burmese ruler. It is in the form of five globes of diminishing size, each containing a niche with a Buddha statue.

Above: Thai woman diligently working at her weaving loom. Right: Parasol-making in the village of Bo Sang.

Within and around the city are several other attractions worthy of a visit. The small and well-maintained **Chiang Mai National Museum** has a good collection of Buddha images and a large display of ceramics and northern household and work utensils. Open from 9:00 to 12:00 and 13:00 to 16:00, Wednesdays to Sundays. Admission is free on weekdays.

The **Chiang Mai Zoological Park** has been designated for expansion, although it is already the largest city zoo in Thailand. It has a wide variety of animals which can be viewed from paths running through its rather hilly site. Nearby is **Huey Kaeo Arboretum** featuring shady walks through a botanical garden.

For those planning on trekking to hill tribe villages, the Chiang Mai University **Tribal Research Center** is a must. It has a small museum, which displays tribal crafts products and artifacts, giving a good introduction to the various hilltribes. **Laddaland** is a fun park about 2 km outside the city. To get there, go up Huey Kaew Road and turn right at the ir-

rigation canal. Like similar parks elsewhere in Thailand, it has landscaped gardens, Thai cultural performances, shops, restaurants, a children's playground and some typical northern Thai houses. Good for family outings.

Around Chiang Mai, visitors have within a short distance a choice of destinations. Most travelers consider **Doi Suthep** a must. The hilltop lies 16 km north of the city and can be reached by minibus from the White Elephant Gate, Pratoo Chang Pueak. The cost is 30 baht going up and 20 baht coming down. Ask at the TAT office for details.

At the top is **Wat Phra That**, a temple established in 1383 by King Ku Na. A *naga*-guarded staircase of some 300 steps leads up to the *wat*, from where, on clear days, the entire Chiang Mai valley can be seen. Visitors can easily check visibility by looking at the *wat* from the town below. If it can be seen clearly, visibility will probably still be good on arrival at the top. Also on Doi Suthep is the **royal palace** still used by the Royal Family

every winter. It lies a further 5 km up the mountain road beyond the *wat*. Its gardens are open on weekends and holidays except when members of the Royal Family are in residence. The rose gardens are at their best in January.

A Hmong village on Doi Pui, locally referred to as Meo City because of its modern ways, is on a dirt road which splits off just before the palace. The descending road is rough and only passable by minibus or jeep, and only during the dry season.

The village, although peopled by authentic Hmongs, demonstrates what can happen when the hilltribes' daily lives become routine fixtures for the benefit of tourists. Being the tribal village nearest to Chiang Mai, it is the most visited. Sites are labeled "Typical Village Hut #1", "Typical Village Meeting Hall #2", or of course "Typical Opium Field". Nevertheless, a walk into the farther reaches, beyond the souvenir hawkers, can provide a glimpse of traditional dress and ways of life.

135

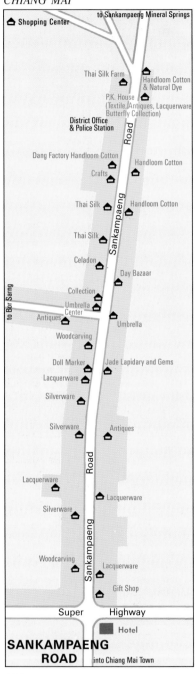

On the western routes out of the city, Routes 108 and 1009, there are attractions ranging from the Cultural Center on Wua Lai Road next to the Chiang Mai Gate, to *wats*, craft shops and factories.

Also to the west is **Doi Intanont National Park** and numerous turnoffs to waterfalls. On the Chiang Mai-Hang Dong Road are earthenware and lacquerware shops, selling products made at the small factories in the area.

Further on, about 58 km from town, is **Wat Phrathat Si Chom Thong**, built in 1451, and housing a Buddhist relic. In the area of the Doi Inthanont National Park are the **Mae Klang** and **Vachiratarn Water Falls**. The park itself covers over 1,000 square kilometers and offers truly spectacular scenery.

North of Chiang Mai, on Routes 107 and 1096, the **Thai Celadon Factory** sells some of its products straight from the kiln. Lying about 6 km from town on the Chiang Mai-Fang road, it is closed on Sundays. Nearby are several **orchid farms** which display a huge variety of wild and hybrid orchids, with flowers and plants for sale.

East of town on Route 1026, many villagers specialize in crafts like ceramics, weaving and umbrella-making. One center is **San Kampaeng**, 13 km from town, famous for its hand-woven cotton and silk. Lining both sides of the road on the way are numerous handicraft factories and stores which encourage visitors to browse and watch the craftsmen at work. A further 23 km from San Kampaeng village are the **San Kampaeng Hot Springs**, where one can soak out the aches of a long day of sightseeing. A spa, Roong Aroon Hot Springs, has been established not far from the springs, where hot mineral water is supplied straight to the rooms for the comfort of guests.

Right: Hilltribe hut with thatched roof in the northern mountains.

The Hilltribes

Whether travelers venture down the Kok River from Tha Thon near the Burmese border to Chiangrai, or merely go for a stroll through Chiang Mai's Night Market, the presence of members of the various tribal minorites will become quickly apparent.

On treks through the jungle hills, visitors will come through their villages and may stop for a rest or even the night. In town, they are easily spotted in their colorful tribal costumes, purchasing supplies in the market or selling their distinctive silver jewelry or tribal craft products in the streets and night bazaars.

For a quick introduction to the hill people, there is no better place to start than the **Tribal Research Center** at Chiang Mai University, which has done extensive research and displays maps and literature on the tribes of northern Thailand.

Historically, the tribes are linked to migratory movements from Tibet, Laos, China and Burma during the last two centuries, not ignoring the fact that some tribes have been in the region much longer. Some of the tribal people are technically stateless, and, being mostly seminomadic with their own language, culture and religion, they are in some ways comparable to the North American Indians, or, perhaps even more so, the gypsies of Europe.

The Tribal Research Center estimates the tribal population to number over 450,000 people. The six major tribes, the *Akha* (called Igor by the Thais), *Lahu* (Musur), *Lisu* (Lisaw), *Hmong* (Meo), *Karen*, (Kalieng) and *Yao*, have a number of sub-groups, all with distinctly different costumes and customs. The Karen came originally from Burma and are still migrating into Thailand. They are divided into four sub-groups and generally live in valleys, where they are cultivating rice and vegetables.

On the mountain ridges of the north can be found the Akha or Igor, perhaps the least advanced or developed of the tribes. They are resistant to change and live mainly on rice, corn and opium cultivation. Originating in Tibet, they are scattered throughout the mountains of Laos, Thailand, Burma and south China and are considered poor even by tribal standards.

The Hmong or Meo are the most numerous of the northern tribes. They are also avid opium growers and can be found in Thailand, Laos and south China, the latter being their original home. Divided into several sub-groups, their different clans may be recognized by the dress of their women.

The Lahu, locally called Musur, are found mainly on high mountain ridges, living on corn, rice and opium. They, like the Karen, have four sub-groups.

Linguistically somewhat related to the Akha and Lisu, they originally came from Tibet and today live in the higher hill regions of Thailand and China. They are, like most of the tribes scattered throughout Thailand, animists, believing in spirits and ancestor worship.

Perhaps the most colorful of all the tribal groups in the northern mountains are the Lisu, whose womenfolk wear a large, intricate head-dress and elaborately decorated garments of a blue or greenish shade, with the men hardly less ornately clad, at least on festive occasions. Opium cultivation is still very much part of their life, although not to the same extent it was twenty or even ten years ago.

The Yao are by far the culturally most sophisticated of the tribes and originated in China. Their religion is a combination of old animistic rites, a diluted form of Taoism and ancestor worship. Although their spoken language is distinctly different from Chinese, they do use Chinese script, being the only hilltribe in Thailand with a written language.

Besides the mentioned tribes, there are a number of other, often unrelated groups, who, mainly because of their remoteness and small numbers, are hardly ever encountered.

CHIANG MAI
Accommodation

LUXURY: **Rincome,** 301 Huey Kaew Rd, Tel:221-044; **Chiang Inn**, 100 Changklang Rd, Tel:235-655; **Chiang Mai Orchid**, 100-102 Huay Kaew Rd, Tel:222-099; **Chiang Mai Plaza**, 92 Sridonchai Rd, Tel:252-050; **Dusit Inn**, 112 Changklang Rd, Tel:251-033; **Poy Luang**, 146 Super Highway, Tel:242-633.

MODERATE: **Chiang Come**, 7/35 Suthep Rd, Tel:211-020; **Chiang Mai Hills**, 18 Huey Kaew Rd, Tel:235-0240 (Bkk); **Northern Inn**, 234/18 Maneenopparat Rd, Changphuak Gate, Tel:210-002; **Prince**, 3 Taiwang Rd, Tel:236-744; Suriwongse, 110 Changklang Rd, Tel:251-051.

BUDGET: **YMCA**, 2/4 Mengrai-Rasni Rd, Tel:221-819; **Sri Ratchawong**, 103 Ratchawong Rd, Tel:235-864; **Muang Thong**, 5 Ratchamankha Rd, Tel:211-438; **New Chiang Mai**, 22 Chaiyaphum Rd, Tel:236-561; **Nakhon Ping**, 43 Taiwang Rd, Tel:236-024; **Anodard**, 5 Ratchamankha, Tel:211-057.

Tourist Information

Tourism Authority of Thailand (TAT), 135 Praisani Rd, Tel:235-334

Access and Local Transport

By Road: Two modern highways connect Chiang Mai with Bangkok, both just under 700 km long. Air-conditioned buses leave the Northern Bus Terminal in Bangkok 5 times daily between 9:10 and 21:30 and take about 8 hours. (Phone 279-4484/7 for details).

There are also several tour companies offering air-con non-stop service to Chiang Mai: Chiang Mai Golden Tour, Tel:247-1051; Ambassador Tour, Tel:252-0402; Indra Tour, Tel:251-6187; Thanchit Tour, Tel:279-6768 and Poy Luang Tour, Tel:252-0200.

For buses to nearby provinces: contact Chiang Mai Arcade Bus Station, on the Superhighway. Tel:241-449, 242-664.

By Rail: Depart Bangkok at 15:45 (Rapid Train) or 18:00 (Express Train); depart Chiang Mai, 15:20 (rapid), 16:50 (express).

For more information contact: Rail Travel, Tel:223-7010, 223-7020 in Bangkok, or Tel:242-094, 242-795 in Chiang Mai. For reservations, tickets in all classes may be purchased up to 30 days in advance at the Advance Booking Office in Hualampong Station, Bangkok, from 8:30 to 18:00 on weekdays and mornings only on weekends and holidays.

By Air: In Bangkok contact Thai Airways International, Larn Luang, Tel:280-0070, 280-0080 and in Chiang Mai, Tel:211-044/7. There is a minimum of 5 flights a day.

Local Festivals
Throughout the year, Chiang Mai celebrates many festivals, but three are of particular interest for visitors.

The "Flower Carnival" is held on the first Friday, Saturday and Sunday of February and celebrates the height of the blooming season with parades of beautifully designed floral floats, troupes of dancing girls and traditional musical bands.

Songkran, the Thai New Year, is celebrated everywhere in Thailand, but in Chiang Mai it is a particularly exuberant 7 day festival with everyone throwing water at everybody else.

Loy kratong is celebrated throughout Thailand on the full moon day of the twelfth lunar month, generally between end of October to mid-November. In Chiang Mai, not only individuals float their tiny rafts of flowers and candles, but a long line of giant floats is paraded through the city before arriving at the river, where all floats are judged before being let into the water.

Trekking Companies and Excursions
Youth's Tour, Chiang Mai Youth Hostel, Manee Nopparat Rd, Tel:221-800; **July Travel Tour**, Suriwongse Hotel, Tel:236-733; **Chiang Mai Nice Travel**, Je T'aime Guest House, Charoenrat Rd, Tel:234-912; **Summit Tour & Trekking**, Thai Charoen Hotel, Tapae Rd, Tel:233-351.

Tour Companies
World Travel Service, Rincome Hotel, Tel:221-044; **Thai International Tours**, Chiang Inn, Tel:235-655; **Chiang Mai Golden Tours**, Pornphing Hotel, Tel:235-099; **Tourismo-Thai**, Chiang Inn, Tel:235-655.

Museums / Cultural Centers
National Museum, on Superhighway near Wat Jet Yod. Open: Wednesdays to Sunday 9:00 to 12:00 and 13:00 to 16:00. Good collection of local bronzes and ceramics. **Tribal Research Center** at Chiang Mai University has small tribal museum. The **Old Chiang Mai Cultural Center** on Wualai Road presents tribal dances nightly.

Restaurants
NORTHERN THAI: **Aroon Rai**, Kojchasarn Rd; Thanam, (excellent, but no sign in English) between the Chiang Mai Hotel and Tha Pae Gate; Serimit, opposite Poy Luang Hotel on the road to San Kamphaeng, specializes in seafood; **Lung Thaworn**, Wiang Kaew Road near Wat Chiang

Man serves Thai and French food; **Galae**, Northern Agricultural Development Center, 65 Suthep Rd, good food in beautiful surroundings; For the best Khao Soi noodles, a northern speciality, go to a ramshackle shop in Soi Fin (OpiumLane) just past the mosque in Changklang Road, or try **Lam Duang**, in Charoen Rat Road on the other side of the river. **Khantoke dinners** (A khantoke is a low, round table, around which a group of people, sitting on the floor, share several dishes) are a northern institution and are best at the Old Chiang Mai Cultural Center, 185/3 Wualai Road. Unlike at some other restaurants, at Old Chiang Mai, particular attention is paid to authenticity, where dancers, musicians and instruments must be oritginal Lannathai. Nothing less will do. Phone 235-097 for reservations.

CHINESE: **Ruam-mit Phochana**, Sithiwong Rd; Canton Suki, Huey Kaew Rd; **Today Restaurant** (serves dim sum lunch only) Viang Ping Bazaar, Chang Klan Rd.

INDIAN: **Al-Shiraz**, 123 Chang Klang Rd (opposite Night Bazaar).

FRENCH: **Le Coq d'Or**, 18-20 Chaiyapoom Rd; Le Chalet, 71 Charoenprathet Rd.

GERMAN: **Haus München**, 115/3 Loi Kroa Road.

ENGLISH: **The Pub**, 88 Huai Kaeo Rd.

VEGETARIAN: **Mangsawirat**, Suthep Rd; **Ngam Nit**, Chang Moi Dat Mai; **Whole Earth**, 88 Sridonchai Rd.

Budget shops for cheap *WESTERN* meals: good for breakfasts is the **Thai German Dairy**, 33 Moon Muang Rd; Daret Restaurant, 59/63 Moon Muang Rd; **Galae Guesthouse**, 7 Charoenprathet Rd.

Shopping
The Night Bazaar on Changklang Road draws vendors from all over the city and the outlying regions. Excellent selection of northern handicrafts, hill tribes jewelry, blue farmers shirts, lacquerware etc. Bargaining a must.

Hospitals
McCormick Hospital, 135 Kaew Nawarat Rd. (English speaking staff), Tel:236-010, 236-107; **Suandok Hospital**, Suthep Rd, (Provincial Hospital and Center for Malaria Treatment).

Post / Telegraph / Telephone
General Post Office, Charoen Muang Rd. (near Railway Station) has full postal services and telegraph. Overseas telephone calls can be made from the telephone office on Praisanee Rd, weekdays during working hours. After hours and weekends phone from hotel.

THE NORTH

Lan-Na-Thai (A Million Rice Paddies), as the people of the north prefer to call their region, embraces eight provinces: Chiang Mai, Mae Hongson, Lamphun, Lampang, Phayao, Chiang Rai, Phrae and Nan.

The hilly, partly jungle-covered region covers an area of just under 90,000 square kilometers and borders on Burma in the west and north, and the Mekong River and Laos in the east. More and more of the never-ending flow of tourists visiting Chiang Mai, the region's principal economic and administrative center with its international airport, venture out to explore the provinces after having absorbed the sights in the city.

Provincial airports in Mae Hongson, Lampang and Chiang Rai, together with the constantly expanding network of modern roads, reaching into the remotest corners of the region, have opened up areas of interest and magnificent landscapes, formerly only accessible on foot. But the easy access has also resulted in ecology becoming an ever-growing concern, mainly because of uncontrolled deforestation in the hills.

The north's main attractions for the visitor are the many ancient ruins of cities and temples, and the colorful hill tribes, whose villages are found on the mountains of all the region's provinces. Their cultures are undergoing a gradual change in the face of tourism and Thai modernization, forcing tour operators to alter old itineraries and go further afield to find more authentic and traditional villages.

Parts of northern Thailand have long been used by the tribes for opium cultivation, especially the Golden Triangle, which is not a geographical entity, but a loosely defined area, where Burma, Thailand and Laos meet. But this aspect of the

Left: A longtail boat takes off at dusk over the River Kok.

region's (underground) economy is also changing. Under constant pressure from the authorities, the tribes are slowly switching from poppies to cash crop cultivation, selling their produce at the local markets or to middlemen for export.

The best time to visit the north is the cool season, November to February, when the days are clear and sunny, but cooled by breezes from the hills. The evenings may require a sweater and blankets will be needed when sleeping. The rainy season, from June to October, is also favored by many visitors, as the hills are lush with new growth and the rains are sporadic showers, often falling at night. During the hot season, from March through May, the temperature rises higher than in Bangkok, but the lower humidity makes the heat more bearable.

Although transportation in the region has improved enormously in recent years, many areas are still somewhat remote and tourism facilities away from the main towns can be very basic. At the same time, centers like Chiang Mai, Chiang Rai, Lampang, Lamphun and Mae Hong Son are firmly established on the tourist itinerary and definitely worth a visit.

Chiang Mai Province

Of the many established excursions out of Chiang Mai, Route 107, going all the way north to Fang and beyond, is probably the most widely traveled. Buses leave frequently from the White Elephant Gate for the 155 km trip to Fang, stopping at points along the highway, from where many interesting sidetrips can be made.

One of the most popular stops is at km 49, the turnoff to the **Chiang Dao Elephant Training Center** on the banks of the Ping River, where every morning a group of young pachyderms are put through their training routine. The Hilltribes Development and Welfare Center

A popular excursion for the energetic, seeking a taste of the wilderness, replete with mountains, caves, waterfalls and hilltribe villages, is a journey by boat down the Mae Kok River from Tha Thon to Chiang Rai.

Tha Thon is 24 km north of Fang on the banks of the Kok River. There is a landing stage, from which longtail boats leave daily for the trip down the River Kok to Chiang Rai. The trip takes four to five hours and fares are usually around 160 to 200 baht per person.

The best time to go is between October and January. Avoid the driest time of the year just before the rainy season, when the trip may well become an expedition over sand bars, with everyone having to bail out into the knee-deep river to dislodge the boat. Along the way, there are some interesting, but easily negotiated rapids and many hilltribe villages.

For more information on the numerous tours offered in Chiang Mai Province, ask TAT or enquire at your hotel's tour counter.

at km 61.5 is run by the Department of Public Welfare and provides the hilltribes with instruction on improving their lifestyles and the cultivation of cash crops, like coffee and flowers.

Near the district town of Chiang Dao, at km 72, is the 2,185 m high **Doi** (meaning mountain) **Chiang Dao**, with several tribal villages on its slopes. The nearby **Chiang Dao Cave** houses many Buddhist statues. For details, consult the TAT office in Chiang Mai.

Highway 107 becomes the main street of **Fang**, which, in spite of its 700 years of history, has little of interest. Just before entering the town, a turnoff to the left leads, after 8 km, to a horticultural station which supplies the tribes with coffee, apples and peach seedlings. A further 3 km takes you to **Baw Nam Rawn**, the well-known sulphur hot springs, set against a backdrop of forested hills.

Above: The famous statue of Buddha at Wat Hua Kuang.

Mae Hong Son

Mae Hong Son, the western most of the northern provinces, is rapidly developing with the advent of tourism, made possible via a new road and Thai Airways' 30 minute flight from Chiang Mai. About 275 km from Chiang Mai by car and 925 km from Bangkok, the provincial capital of the same name (in Thailand, all provinces are named after their provincial capitals, or perhaps the other way round), was until quite recently, a town in the misty mountains, famous for bandits and smugglers. Its isolation made it a posting for out-of-favor civil servants from Bangkok and political exiles. It was only in the late 1960s that an asphalt road was built from Chiang Mai, which at one point reaches the highest altitude of any major road in Thailand – 1,513 m – at Ban Ton Ngew. Several buses a day ne-

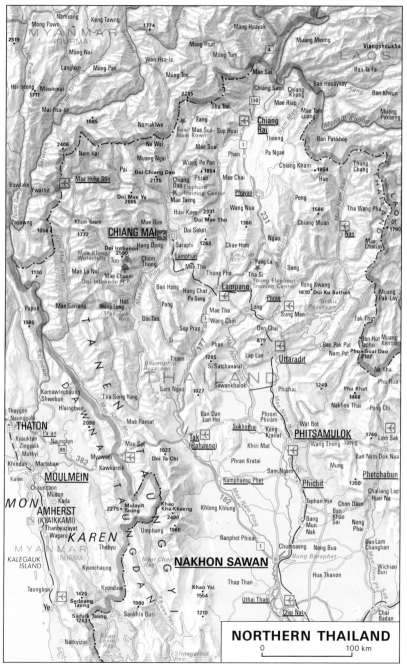

NORTHERN THAILAND

0   100 km

143

gotiate the winding route, which may take as long as ten hours from Chiang Mai to Mae Hong Son.

About 35 km from Chiang Mai, on Route 108 to Mae Hongson, Thailand's highest mountain, **Doi Inthanon** (2,576 m), can be clearly seen from the highway. The entrance to **Doi Inthanon National Park** and the **Mae Klang Waterfalls** is at km 57, marked in both Thai and English. The waterfall is 8 km from the highway, and the summit of the mountain another 40 km. Tolls are charged for vehicles going up the mountain. On the way, two other waterfalls, the lush vegetation, birds, wild flowers and a panoramic view provide ample reason to make the trip.

Highway 108 passes through Chom Thong and then Hot, a district town only worth mentioning as a rest stop or for a quick meal en route. Just outside of Hot is the turn off to **Doi Tao** and **Wang Lung**

Above: The Chedi on the Doi Kong Mu near Mae Hong Son.

(Route 1012). One km down this road another turn off (Route 1103) leads to Doi Tao, 33 km away. This village sits on the northern shore of the lake formed by the **Bumibhol Dam**, some 140 km to the south. Floating bungalows can be rented here, but reservations have to be made at least one week in advance. Ask the TAT office in Chiang Mai for details. The Chiang Mai Lake Tours Co. operates two large charter vessels for lake tours for 50 to 100 passengers. For information and bookings contact their office in Chiang Mai at 97-99 Charoenmuang Road.

Mae Sariang, the next town on Route 108, sits in a valley formed by the Yuam River, and was, until the opening of the highway in 1968, almost completely cut off from the rest of the country. It has one main hotel and a couple of Burmese temples of recent vintage. Mae Sariang is also close to the convergence of two rivers, the Moey and Salween on the Burmese border. Tours, including elephant rides, can be arranged, especially before the start of the rainy season, when

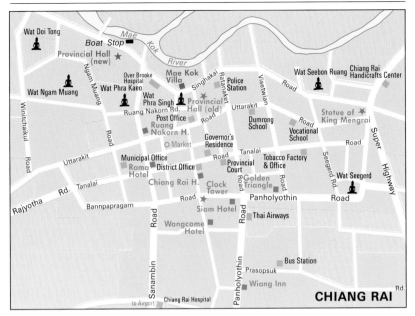

vast carpets of wildflowers cover the hills. TAT in Chiang Mai can give you up-to-date details.

Route 108, going almost due west from Chiang Mai to Mae Sarieng, now makes a sharp right turn, going straight north to **Mae Hongson**. Only slightly over a century old, this provincial seat administers a province whose population is only 2 per cent Thai, the remainder being Thai Yai or Shan and various hilltribes. The town was founded as a center for capturing and trading wild elephants. Today, Mae Hongson has become the new "Shangri-la" of Thailand, but the tranquil remoteness is slowly disappearing by courtesy of the many resort developers and an increasing number of tourists.

The busy morning market between 6:00 and 8:00 is ideal for observing the ethnic mix from the hills and surrounding villages. Hilltribe people in full regalia come down to sell and buy. Old women, chewing hand-rolled cheroots, encourage photographers to take their picture. On the outskirts of town is **Doi Kong Mu**, a 450-m high hill overlooking the valley. On the top are two *chedis* built last century. Local tour operators may be contacted for a number of trips through town and the surrounding area.

Chiang Rai and the Golden Triangle

One of the major draws in Thailand, the **Golden Triangle** is still a main conduit for opium and its by-products, with an estimated three-quarters of the world supply coming from the region. **Chiang Rai**, the destination of the River Kok trip from Tha Thon, is the closest tourism center to this area, and the most convenient jumping-off point for trips to the opium-growing hills.

From Chiang Mai, it is most easily reached via Route 1019 in three and a half hours by bus. Over the last two years, Chiang Rai has rapidly evolved as a resort town and hotel chains are building luxury hotels there. Frequent air connections with Chiang Mai and Bangkok

145

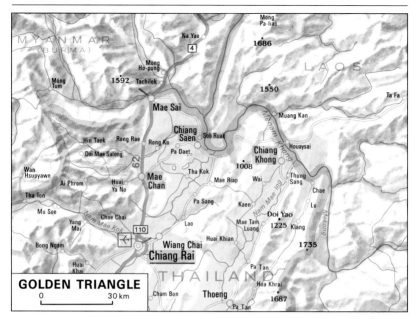

GOLDEN TRIANGLE
0   30 km

have made this possible. There are about five *wats* worth visiting in Chiang Rai, among them **Wat Phra Singh**,and **Wat Phra Kaeo**. **Wat Ngam Muang** and **Wat Doi Tong** are two temples positioned on hills with the latter commanding a fine view of the River Kok.

The real value of Chiang Rai is its location near the Golden Triangle region. In the town itself are a number of trekking outfits with offices in local guesthouses to which any of the major hotels will be able to direct tourists. To see the opium poppies in bloom or watch the harvest, you will have to time your visit for January-February.

Thailand's most northerly town is **Mae Sai**, at the very end of Paholyothin Road, which starts a thousand kilometers away, at the Victory Monument in Bangkok. On the same road, 28 km from Chiang Rai is **Mae Chan**, where the road forks; the left going to Mae Sai (32 km) on the Burmese

Right: The sun hanging like a balloon near Chiang Rai.

border and the right to Chiang Saen (31 km) on the Mekong River from where you can see Laos on the opposite bank.

Two km after Mae Chan on the Mae Sai route is the turnoff to the **Hilltribe Development and Welfare Center** 12 km down the road. This road also leads to Doi Mae Salong, passing Ban Pha Dua, a Yao village, and an Akha village called Ban Igor Sam Yaek, giving visitors a glimpse of hilltribe life.

Up the mountain past cultivated fields is **Mae Salong**, a Kuomintang Chinese settlement over 30 years old. The villagers are the remnants of Chiang Kai Check's 93rd Army, who fled here from Mao's forces. They support themselves by raising coffee and other mountain crops. The village has a Chinese-medium highschool and a movie theater, showing Chinese movies from Taiwan. On the mountain are several restaurants, some souvenir shops and even a small hotel.

Mae Sai is a typical border town and an ideal spot to observe a lively cross-border trade, with Burmese, Shans and Akha

tribesmen coming across the Nam Sai River to do their shopping in Thailand. Although Thais may wander freely over the bridge into Burma, foreigners are not allowed to do so. **Wat Phra That Doi Wao** is on a lane to the left of Phaholyothin Road and up a long flight of steps to the top of a hill, from where the town, the river and the Burmese village of Tachilek are clearly visible.

A good dirt road connects Mae Sai with Chiang Saen, but most visitors go back to the junction on the highway at Mae Chan and retrace their steps back up to **Chiang Saen**. This little town has a small, yet well-laid-out museum and an impressive collection of ruins on which restoration work is being done. The monuments have been tastefully incorporated into the townscape, which functions as an outpost on the Mekong, with Laos clearly visible on the other side of the river.

Entering Chiang Saen, one first sees the grass-covered ancient city gate. Beyond this, to the left, is a rough road lead-ing to **Wat Pa Sak**, Chiang Saen's oldest *chedi*, shaped in the form of a stepped pyramid with Buddhas in its niches. In the northwest corner of town, about 1 km from Wat Pa Sak, is **Wat Phra That Chom Kitti**. On top of a hill, which can be reached by a climb up 300 crumbling steps, this *wat* overlooks the town, the Mekong and its Laotian bank.

Going 11 km north on Route 1016, one arrives at **Sob Ruak**. From here one has a distant view of the Golden Triangle's supposed center, where the Ruak River flows into the Mekong, forming the point where the borders of Laos, Thailand and Burma meet.

Four km south of Chiang Saen, on Route 1129, is **Wat Phra That Pha Ngao**, where a fine Buddha image was discovered in 1976. The same route, paralleling the Mekong River for 50 km, reaches **Chiang Khong**, formerly a very busy trading center and crossing point for boats going to Huey Sai in Laos. From Chiang Khong, Route 1020 (107 km) goes back to Chiang Rai.

Leaving Chiang Rai on National Highway 1 going south, travelers will reach **Payao** after 95 km. Sitting on one side of a large shallow, fish-filled lake, 6 km long and 4 km wide, Payao is regarded as one of the oldest towns in Thailand. Artifacts unearthed here testify to a history going back to the Bronze Age. **Wat Si Khom Kham** has a 400-year-old Buddha with a remarkably serene face. The temple courtyard has some Buddha heads in sandstone.

A short 1 km away is the inviting lakeshore with a string of good restaurants where travelers can enjoy a tasty meal with the mountains beyond the lake as a backdrop. The local speciality here is roasted giant frogs fresh from the lake and as big and tender as young chicken. Would this be to your taste?

Further south on Highway 1 is the town of **Ngao**, 52 km from Payao. The route diverges here with the left fork becoming Route 103, leading to the provinces of Phrae and Nan.

If approaching from the south, coming up Highway 1 from either Bangkok or Chiang Mai, the traveler will come first to **Phrae**, a town of little interest besides filling your petrol tank and having a drink before continuing to Nan.

Nan

Nan is another remote but worthwhile destination in the north which is only just beginning to open up. Up to 1980, tourism was actively discouraged because of frequent insurgency activities in the hills. Today, the situation is no longer dangerous and Nan is attracting visitors, primarily because of its remoteness and untouched quality. Transportation from Chiang Mai is frequent with at least four regular buses per day, taking about seven hours to reach Nan from Bangkok.

The town was established during the Sukhothai period and lies 690 km north

Above: Bringing in the sheaves. Right: At the popular Nan boat races.

of the capital. Its attractions are the **Prathat Chae Haeng Pagoda** and the **Nan Provincial Boat Race**, an annual event in late October, which has gained increasing popularity. The boats are made from single tree trunks and are called war canoes. The races are the main event of the Nan Provincial Fair which attracts thousands of people annually.

One kilometer before Nan is **Wat Phaya Wat**. Behind a modern main hall is a *chedi* built in the form of a stepped pyramid. There are five tiers in all and along each level are Buddha statues in the niches (all of them somewhat reminiscent of the *chedi* in Chiang Saen).

Not far away from this temple, is **Wat Phrathat Khao Noi** with its distinctive pagoda sitting on top of Khao Noi Hill. It is 2 km west of the provincial administration building. From this point, 260 m above the town, one can gain an excellent perspective of the surrounding area.

To begin a tour of Nan and its sights, the **National Museum** is the best place to start. Located in a palace built for the local governor in 1903, the museum contains a famous black elephant tusk, regarded as the province's most valuable treasure.

Photos and texts in Thai and English describe Nan's fascinating history. Opposite the museum is **Wat Chang Kham Wora Vihara**, a royal monastery built in 1547.

The base of its pagoda is of interest, being decorated with seven elephant buttresses. Inside the main hall is a standing Buddha image made of solid gold, a fact only discovered by archaeologists in 1955, when the plaster covering of the statue, an earlier precaution against thieves, was broken.

About 100 m on the opposite side of the road from Wat Chang Kham Wora Vihara is **Wat Bhumin**, Nan's most illustrious temple. It has beautifully carved wooden doors, placed the four sides around the main shrine. Inside the shrine are old murals, some of which have been restored, depicting the way of life in Nan's past.

Lampang

About some 100 km along an excellent and scenic road going south from Chiang Mai, is **Lampang**, sitting astride the junction of National Route 1 from Bangkok to Chiang Rai, and Route 11, the Superhighway leading to Chiang Mai. Sitting on the right bank of the Wang River, this bustling provincial capital, 600 km north of Bangkok, is a major train stop on the line to Chiang Mai.

Lampang proudly presents itself to the world as the only Thai town using horse-drawn carriages for urban transport, and the only province in the kingdom with a training school for baby elephants.

Lampang is an old town and has, like all the ancient cities of the north, its fair share of antique temples. **Wat Chedi**

Sao, the Temple of the Twenty *Chedis,* is on the right bank of the Wang River to the north of town, set attractively in the middle of open rice paddies.

Also of note is **Wat Phra That Lampang Luang**, which is located some 20 km south of town. It is rated as one of the north's finest temples.

The *wat's* harmonious proportions plus its exquisite interior decorations make it undoubtedly a masterpiece of northern-style religious architecture. Three more *wats*, all close to the town center, are Wat Sichum, Wat Phra Fang and Wat Sri Rong Muang. **Wat Sichum** is worth a visit because of its excellent state of preservation and its red and gold lacquered window shutters. **Wat Sri Rong Muang** is painted in a mind-numbing array of colors.

54 km east of Lampang, behind Pang La village, is the **Young Elephant Training Camp**. Operated by the Forestry Industry Organization, it was the first center to train elephants for forest work. Presently there are over 100 elephants here,

Above: Funny to watch for tourists – bathing elephants after work. Right: Wat Chamya Thewi near Lamphun.

being trained for five years before graduating to full time work. Training is conducted from June to February (closed during the hot season) with daily schedules from 7:00 to 11:00.

Lamphun

In the lexicon of Thai history, **Lamphun** was formerly known as **Haripunchai**. It is only 26 km south of Chiang Mai and is usually included in one or other round trip from the northern capital. Lying on Route 106, also called the old Chiang Mai Road, Lamphun has gained fame for its beautiful women, its fine hand-woven silk and two very ancient temples.

Founded in 660 as the capital of the old Mon kingdom of Haripunchai, its first ruler was the mythical Queen Chammathevi. For almost 600 years this kingdom flourished until it was conquered by King Mengrai in 1281.

Two of Lamphun's temples are among the finest in the north. **Wat Phrathat Haripunchai** was built in the eleventh century, during the reign of King Athittayarat, the thirty-second ruler of Haripunchai. Its pagoda is 46 m tall and has a nine-tiered umbrella made of 6,498 grams of gold.

Wat Chamya Thewi dates back to around 755 AD and was built by Khmers. The main pagoda is of the square Buddha Gaya style, characteristic of India. On each level of the pagoda's base, 12 standing Buddhas are set in attitudes of blessing. All five levels have Buddhas figures, making a total of 60 statues. The top of the pagoda was once covered with gold but this has since disappeared – hence the temple's popular name *wat ku kut* – the Topless Pagoda.

About 12 km from Lamphun on the road to Lee is **Pa Sang**, a district town, known for its beautiful women, an extensive cotton weaving home industry, batik works and *lamyai*, a fruit not unlike the lychee. Various handicraft workshops along the main road are open to browsers and shoppers.

151

MAE HONG SON
Accommodation
Mae Hong Son Resort, 24 Ban Huai Dua, Tel:611-406; **Siam Hotel**, 23 Khunlum Praphat Rd, Tel:611-139; **Methi**, 55 Khunlum Praphat Rd, Tel:611141; **Mae Hong Son Guest House**, 18 Khunlun Praphat Rd.

Local Festivals
Loy kratong, at the end of October or early November, is celebrated here by flying balloons rather than floating flowered rafts on the waterways, as is customary in the rest of Thailand.

MAE SARIANG
Accommodation
Mit Aree, 158 Mu 2, Mae Sariang Rd, Tel:611-022; **Mae Sariang Resort**, Laeng Phanit Rd.

Chiang Rai
Accommodation
LUXURY: **Dusit Island Resort** (phone Dusit Thani, Bangkok, for reservation); **Wang Come**, 869/90 Pemawiphak Rd, Tel:711-800; **Wiang Inn**, 893 Phahonyothin, Tel:711-533.
MODERATE: **Chiang Rai Island Resort**, 1129 Singhakhlai Rd, Tel:711- 865.
BUDGET: **Ruang Nakhon**, 25 Ruang Nakhon Rd, Tel:711-566; **Rama**, 331/4 Trairat Rd, Tel:711-344.

CHIANG SAEN
Accommodation
Poonsuk, 95 Phahonyothin Rd; **Yonok Lake View**, 109 Chiang Saen Lake, Tel:713-107.

Museum
Chiang Saen Museum, on right hand side of Route 1016 before reaching the city gates. Hours: 8:30 to 12:00, 13:00 to 16:30, Wednesdays to Sundays. Good collection of Chiang Saen Buddhas and influential local art. Admission on Saturdays and Sundays is 2 baht.

MAE CHAN
Accommodation
Mae Salong Resort, Tel:714-047; **Mae Salong Guest House**, Tel:712- 962.

LAMPANG
Accommodation
LUXURY: **Tip Chang**, 54/22 Takrao Rd, Tel:218-078.
MODERATE: **Asia Lampang**, 229 Boonyawat Rd, Tel:217-844.
BUDGET: **Siam**, 260/26-9 Chatchai Rd, Tel:217-472; **Khelang Nakhon**, 719-720 Suandok Rd, Tel:217-137.

Shopping
Lampang is a center for blue and white pottery with some 60 kilns working in and around town. Many are open to visitors, where pieces can be purchased much more cheaply than in Bangkok.

Access and Transport
By Bus – Both regular and air-conditioned buses leave Bangkok's Northern Bus Terminal for the various centers in the north. Buses to Chiang Mai are the most frequent, but up to 10 buses per day leave for centers like Sukhothai and Pitsanulok. The Northern Bus Terminal, locally called Morchit, is located on Paholyothin Rd and schedules and fares can be obtained by calling: 279-4484/7 (air-conditioned) and 271-0101/5 (non air-conditioned).

By Train – Trains to Chiang Mai leave at various times throughout the day from Bangkok's Hualampong Station (Tel:223-7010; 223-7020). Best is the Daily Express, leaving Bangkok in the late afternoon. It stops at Ayutthaya, Lop Buri, Nakhon Sawan, Phichit, Pitsanulok, Uttaradit, Den Chai, Lampang and Lamphun, arriving in Chiang Mai early the next morning. Reservations for tickets are mandatory, especially on weekends and holidays. Check at the Advance Booking counter at Hualampong Station.

By Car – Undoubtedly the most carefree way to travel, private cars allow visitors to leave the beaten track for trips into the back country, where life is still the way it was a hundred years ago. Many car hire firms are operating in Bangkok and most tourist centers.

By Plane – Thai Airways flies to Chiang Mai, Chiang Rai, Lampang, Mae Hongson, Mae Sot, Nan, Phrae, Pitsanulok and Tak. For details and timetable phone: 280-0070 or 280-0080 in Bangkok.

A Word of Caution
Visitors to northern Thailand should be careful to observe local anti-drug laws, as infringements can have dire consequenses. Major tourism centers like Chiang Mai or Chiang Rai pose all sorts of dangers.

The very fact of being in, or near, the infamous Golden Triangle has induced travelers to "try anything once – just for kicks". Don't fall for it. Avoid any drug taking, in whatever form, under any circumstances. Even a friendly pipe of opium in a hilltribe village is taboo. Reject any offer of joining a round of "sharing a joint". It doesn't pay. And never, never agree to carry a parcel, envelope or even a simple letter for starngers, however innocent the article may look.

ISARN, THE NATION'S POORHOUSE

KORAT
SURIN
LOEI
UDORN
ALONG THE MEKONG

Turning onto the Friendship Highway at Saraburi, about 100 km north of Bangkok, the road begins a long, gradual ascent through the rolling countryside, where life seems to take a perceptible leap backwards in time. This is the climb up to the northeast, locally called **Pak Isarn**, a vast plateau where the old ways and traditions of Thailand still endure. Isarn is the region least touched by progress and somewhat misses out on the prosperity experienced by other parts of the kingdom.

The Isarn folk are an independent lot, and in spite of their often grim poverty, they view life with a blend of fatalism and good humor. Most still live in much the same way their forefathers did, eking out a living from the tired soil. Their origins go back to a time when Laos was a vassal state, owing allegiance to the kings of Siam, so the people here speak a dialect of Thai close to the Laotian spoken in Laos today. Many are of Lao descent and often jokingly refer to themselves and their language as Lao, although it is not appreciated if other Thais do so. They rather resent having a reputation as country yokels. In Bangkok they

Preceding page: Thai clothes. Left: The Wat Teppitakpunnaram's giant statue of Buddha welcomes visitors heading north.

can often be recognized by their dark skins, burnt by years of toil in the sun, which set them off from the urban élite, who tend to look down on their darker skinned northeastern cousins.

The northeast has the densest population, the highest level of poverty and the most agriculturally dependent economy of any region in the country. Because there are far more people than jobs, the northeast supplies a greater proportion of migrant labor to Bangkok and the Middle East than other parts of Thailand. It is more likely than not that your taxi or *tuk tuk* driver in Bangkok comes from Isarn, and the thousands of men and women found working on the many construction sites in the capital are almost certainly from the northeast.

Isarn also has the greatest concentration of international volunteers and foreign-funded projects in Thailand. The Thai government has initiated a number of development schemes. It encourages the private sector to locate certain industries in the region and has vastly improved the infrastructure, including the expansion of the road network, telecommunications and the electricity grid.

Although tourism has been slow to come to the region, this is likely to change soon, as Laos has already begun to welcome overland visitors, who have to travel through Isarn and across the Mekong River to get there. Cambodia is expected to open its borders soon, which will bring thousands of tourists to see the famous ruins of Angkor Wat, traveling through Isarn and streaming across the border. Undoubtedly, many of them will stop to see the many attractions Isarn has to offer.

The ancient temples built by the Khmer, like Prasat Hin Pimai in Korat, the recently restored Prasat Hin Khao Phanom Rung in Buriram, the excavations of prehistoric ceramics and bronzes at Ban Chiang in Udon Thani, the natural wonders of Khao Yai and Phu Kradung, and the great temple Phra That Panom at Nakhon Panom, all make the northeast a rich and vibrant destination for visitors who like to get off the usual tourist routes.

In addition, Isarn offers the visitor some colorful festivals, a unique cuisine, which is enjoying growing popularity in Bangkok, handicrafts like its distinctive hand-woven silks and a type of country music all its own.

Getting to the northeast is usually easy, although on major holidays, trains and buses will be packed with Isarn workers from Bangkok. There are regular flights to all the major provincial centers. A railway line runs to Korat, where it branches into the northeastern line, going to Nong Khai, and the eastern route up to Ubon. Buses depart Bangkok's Northern Terminal throughout the day. In Isarn, all district towns have minibuses to carry travelers to the remotest corners.

The first place that normally attracts visitors is on the southern lip of the northeast. **Khao Yai** (Big Mountain) **National Park**, 205 km from Bangkok, is a vast wilderness preserve of 2,168 sq km, spilling into four provinces. It has its own herds of wild elephants, tigers, deer and the rare ox-like gaur. Two rivers run through the park, with a total of 20 waterfalls. There is an 18 hole golf course and

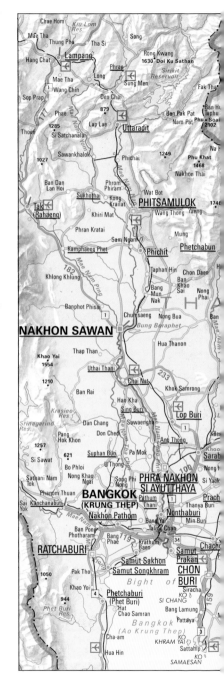

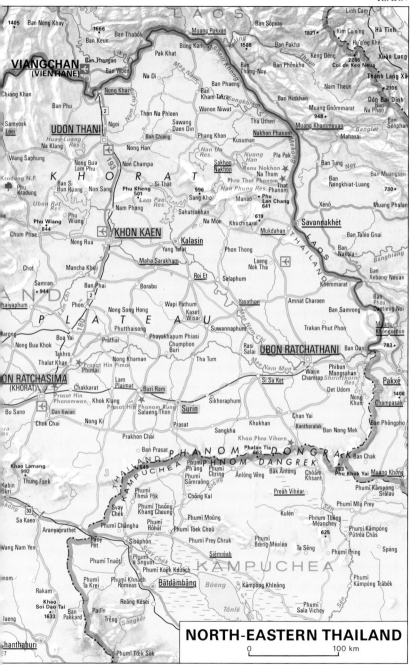

NORTH-EASTERN THAILAND

0   100 km

tennis courts. It is close enough to Bangkok, especially for those with cars, to make the trip in a day. Buses also leave the Northern Terminal in Bangkok for **Khao Yai**. Accommodation, especially on weekends, may be hard to come by, so visitors should inquire at TAT in Bangkok, where reservations may also be made.

KORAT

Leaving Khao Yai, the next stop on the way into the heart of the northeast will be **Nakhon Ratchasima**, commonly known as **Korat**, provincial capital and the gateway to Isarn.

Korat's value is not much more than its strategic location and convenient facilities. It has a number of good hotels with airconditioned rooms. Several good restaurants serve Thai and northeastern dishes and its night market is a lively place to go for a meal. Entertainment facilities tend towards the raucous, with singers crooning popular Thai melodies over squawking microphones. But the town does also have some movie houses and a couple of discos.

Korat's importance for tourists is its proximity to two major historic sites. The first, and closest to town, is **Prasat Hin Phanomwan**. About 14 km northeast on Route 2, this temple supports a few monks who live in the complex. As a result, some of the decorations are of a more recent vintage than the temple itself. But the *wat* does have pervasive tranquility in its isolation 4 km off the highway, and is not visited as often as the more illustrious complex of Pimai.

The other, **Prasat Hin Pimai**, lies about 60 km northeast of Korat, on Route 206, a short distance off the main highway. In style and decoration, Pimai resembles the Khmer ruins of Angkor and,

Right: Even elephants have to be rounded up now and then.

as is generally agreed, was constructed at about the same time, in the thirteenth century. But by whom and for what reason, remains a mystery.

The principal sanctuary is a tower *(prasat)* surrounded by four porches. Throughout this central grouping are elaborate sandstone carvings of *nagas* and *garudas*, the mythical guardians of the temple. The lintel, or carved stone over the main entrance, has attracted much interest because of its unusual figures and their form of dress. Pimai is closed to visitors after 16:30 to prevent looting. On the way to Pimai is an open **museum** which displays historical artifacts and archaeological finds, unearthed in the area.

Another place of interest near Korat is the village of **Dan Kwian**, about 14 km down Route 24. It is noted for producing a unique type of pottery, widely used for ornamental purposes and exported to several countries. Visitors can walk around the village and observe how Dan Kwian clays are molded, turned and then fired into their distinctive forms.

Going east from Korat, the first place of interest will be **Buriram** (150 km), a large province and the site of the recently restored **Prasat Hin Phanom Rung**. This temple, like Pimai, is linked to the Khmer empire centered in Angkor. Prasat Hin Phanom Rung sits at the summit of Phanom Rung Mountain, 12 kms off the highway at a right turn at km 83-84 of Route 24. Another *prasat hin*, or stone pagoda, is located at **Muang Tam** in the Prakon Chai district of Buriram, which has, within its walled-in compound, three ancient brick ponds.

SURIN

Surin, 200 km from Korat, is known for its annual "Elephant Round-up", held the third weekend of November. In the village of Ban Tha Klang, not far from Surin town, a great number of elephants

are kept in trim for the festival. Scattered around Surin, and within a few kilometers of the town, are various ruins of Khmer origin, among them **Prasat Srikhonphum** with its five *prangs* (pagodas). The central one reaches a height of 32 m and is noteworthy for the intricate carvings on its columns.

Thirty kilometers from Surin is the **Prasat Hin Ban Pluang**, recently restored. Although much smaller than the complexes in Korat or Buriram, it is recognized for its beauty. Nearby is **Ban Pluang** village with its many silk weavers, where beautifully hand-woven silk products are for sale.

In 1963, the Province of Sisaket (310 km from Korat) lost a major temple complex to Cambodia, built on a cliff in the hills along the present border. The World Court had decided that the temple, called **Khao Phra Viharn**, belonged to Cambodia. But with the border tension now relaxed, tourists have recently visited the complex from the Thai side by driving down Route 221 to the village of Kan-

tharalak and a little beyond, through dense forest. Inquiries as to the latest border situation should be made at the TAT offices in Bangkok or Ubon Ratchatani (Ubon).

Returning to Korat via Route 24, the National Highway 2 leads to the northern provinces of Isarn and **Khon Kaen**, Isarn's "de facto" capital and a noted university town.

LOEI

This region offers the splendors of one of the very last wilderness areas in Thailand.

Loei Province can be reached via Routes 12 and 201 from Khon Kaen (205 km). Situated between the north and northeast, it combines features of both regions. The province, 520 km from Bangkok, is surrounded by mountains and is the place in Thailand most likely to experience freezing temperatures in winter. Its main attraction, about 70 km south from town on Route 201, is **Phu Kra-**

dung **National Park**, rated as one of Thailand's most beautiful areas.

In the center of the park is one lone mountain with precipitous cliffs rising steeply out of the surrounding country. Phu Kradung or the "Bell Mountain" has featured in many local stories and old legends. It is a table-top mountain with a plateau 60 sq km in area. The size of this sky-high natural table, plus its altitude, make it unique in Thailand.

Its climate, flora and fauna are unlike those in any other part of the kingdom. Several Himalayan tree species, pine, oak, beech, hornbeam and two species of Australasian conifers are found here, and in March/April the plateau is ablaze with rhododendrons in full bloom. Phu Kradung has its own collection of mammals, with characteristics different from their cousins in the lowlands. Mammals found here include wild boar, the Asian wild

*Above: Grasses glowing in the gloaming.
Right: Pottery at an excavation site in Ban Chiang.*

dog, giant black squirrels, the yellow-throated marten, white-handed gibbons, langur and macaque. There are also wild elephants and the Asiatic black bear, sambar deer and serow, but the latter species have become very rare, due to extensive poaching. A number of bird species not native to the rest of Thailand are also found on the mountain.

But these gems of nature, like all gems, come at a price and the price is steep. The trail up the mountain covers 2 km with the last kilometer a rigorous climb. Once on the plateau, it is a further 9 km to the park headquarters with its information center, restaurants, picnic facilities and bungalows. The trail through the forest is filled with flowers and wildlife and at various points small food stalls sell drinks and snacks. They are closed on weekdays, except during the tourist season from November to February.

Temperatures in the hot season easily reach 36 degrees, but in the cool season the average is 14 degrees, often falling to nearfreezing point at night. Located 82

km south of Loei town, the peak time for visitors is from October to January, although weekends are usually crowded throughout the year. The best time to go there is on weekdays or at the beginning of the rainy season in May or June.

UDORN

Udorn Thani (simply called Udorn) was, together with Korat and Ubon, one of the Isarn towns to experience a boom with the establishment of a nearby US military base during the Vietnam conflict. Although these bases were all abandoned in 1976, the remains can still be seen, with tumbleweeds blowing through them like scenes from the New Mexico desert. Today, Udorn offers visitors what's left of those Western-style amenities the GIs left behind: air-conditioned restaurants, fast food shops and fairly good hotels.

In Udorn Province is the village of **Ban Chiang**. In 1966, a young American, Steve Young, was visiting the area, where villagers had long noticed pieces of

human skeleton and broken pottery in the land. Steve Young took several of the pieces to the Fine Arts Department in Bangkok, after which officials came to the site and collected more specimens. These articles were sent to the University of Pennsylvania for a "thermo-luminescence test", which verified that the artifacts at Ban Chiang were from 6,000 to 7,000 years old.

The Fine Arts Department began excavations in earnest, and five years (from 1967 to 1972) of meticulous archaeological digging unearthed a treasure trove of ancient skeletons, animal bones, pottery with elaborate designs, axes, tools, weapons, copper bells, and beads made from glass, ceramic, jade and turquoise.

The Ban Chiang finds have astounded archaeologists worldwide, as similar discoveries were made in North and South America, Turkey and Iraq, suggesting that global trade may have existed over 5,000 years ago. Ban Chiang is 50 km east of Udorn on a large plateau. A small museum has been opened on the site, but

is closed Mondays and Tuesdays. Buses leave Udorn for Ban Chiang throughout the day. A preliminary check at hotels for current fares and departure times is recommended.

ALONG THE MEKONG

In the northern part of Isarn are two provinces, strung along the Mekong-River and overlooking Laos – **Nong Khai** and **Nakhon Phanom**. Nong Khai is the end of the Friendship Highway (Route 2) and also the terminus for the rail line from Bangkok. Across the river, and 20 km to the northwest is the capital of Laos, Vientiane. With the recent improvement in relations between Thailand and Laos, commerce between the two countries is on the upswing and visas are again being issued for travelers wanting to go to Vientiane. Tourists should contact the Laotian embassy on Sathorn Dtai

Above: Trainer and trainee off to the cock-fighting ring.

Road in Bangkok and Phu Kradung National Park before making the journey, as conditions for entry still keep on changing.

Nong Khai is a long narrow province, skirting the south bank of the Mekong for 300 km. It has had a long history of contact with French Laos and this is reflected in its cuisine and local temples. A pleasant few hours can be spent sitting in one of the numerous restaurants along the main street of town, sipping a cold beer and watching the river, which forms the border between Laos and Thailand.

To the east of Nong Khai, 305 km along Highway 212, which parallels the Mekong River, is the city and province of **Nakhon Panom**. Although the town itself holds little to attract tourists, it does have beautiful views of the wide river and the hills of Laos in the distance. Several hotels remain from the days when Americans made reconnaissance flights from a base nearby.

Fifty kilometers down the same highway is **Phra That Phanom**, one of the oldest temples in Thailand, and venerated by Thai and Lao Buddhists alike. The original temple and the base of the present *chedi* go back 1,500 years, but the appearance has been altered frequently over the centuries.

The annual **Phra That Phanom Fair** is celebrated on the full moon of the third lunar month and attracts thousands of visitors from all over the region.

About fifty kilometers from Nakhon Panom town is a small weaving center with another well known temple complex. **Renu Nakhon** is a thriving little place, only about 15 km from Phra That Phanom and wellworth the extra time and effort.

The market has a wide assortment of cotton products, woven and assembled locally, with their own distinctive patterns. Embroidered cotton shirts, silk sarongs and long dresses are displayed in shops along the main street.

NAKORN RATCHASIMA (KORAT)
Accommodation
Muangmai Korat, 191 At-Sadang Rd, Tel:242-444; **Thai Hotel**, 646-50 Mitraphap Rd, Tel:241-613; **Chomsurang**, 2701/2 Mahadthai Rd, Tel:242-940.

KHAO YAI NATIONAL PARK
Accommodation
LUXURY: **Juldis Khao Yai Resort**, Tanarat Rd, Km 17, Tel:255-2480 (Bkk).
MODERATE: **Khao Yai Motor Lodge Bungalow**, TAT, Tel: 282-5209 (Bkk).
Tourist Information
TAT, 2102-2104 Mitraphap Rd, Korat, Tel:243-427, 243-751.
Access and Transport
The shortest route to Nakhon Ratchasima is via National Highway 1, past Don Muang Airport up to the town of Saraburi, where a road turns right, to become Route 2 (Friendship Highway) going to Korat and beyond. The distance from Bangkok is 256 km. Buses, both regular and air-conditioned, leave the **Northern Bus Terminal** (Morchit), on Phaholyothin Road throughout the day. For details phone 271-0101/5 (regularo) or 279-4484/7 (Air-conditioned).

Trains to the northeast leave Bangkok Railway Station (Hualamphong) throughout the day and all pass through Nakhon Ratchasima. For further information call the State Railways of Thailand at 223-7010, 223-7020.

Thai Airways has several daily flights to Korat. For details and reservations contact Tel:280-0070, 280-0080.

In Korat, buses leave for all parts of Isarn and the north, but from different stations. To beat the confusion, contact the TAT office or your hotel counter for accurate information before planning your journey.
Hospitals
Muang Nakhon Ratchasima Hospital, Chang Phuak Rd; St. Mary's Hospital.

BURIRAM
Accommodation
Grand, 137 Niward Rd, Tel:611-559; **Krung Rome**, 78/2 Niward Rd, Tel:611-176; **Niward**, 89/10-2 Niward Rd, Tel:611-640.

KHON KAEN
Accommodation
Rotsukhon, 1/11 Klang Muang Rd, Tel:237-797; **Kaen Inn**, 56 Klang Muang Rd, Tel:237-744; **Khonkaen Hotel**, 43/2 Phimphasut Rd, Tel:237-711; **Roma**, 50/2 Klang Muang Rd, Tel:236-276.

LOEI
Accommodation
Phu Luang, 55 Charoen Rat Rd, Tel:811-532; **Saraithong**, 26/5 Ruamchit Rd, Tel:811-582; **King**, 11/9-12 Chumsai Rd, Tel:811-701.
National Park
For visits to **Phu Kradung** and **Phu Rua Parks** contact the Bangkok Reservation Tel:579-0529 or 5794842; Phu Rua Chalet, Bkk Reserv: Tel:433- 5396; Phu Kradung House (300 bungalows) Bkk Reserv: Tel:271-3737, 270-0488.

SURIN
Accommodation
Phetkasem, 104 Chitbamrung Rd, Tel:511-274; **New Hotel**, 22 Tanasarn Rd, Tel:511-341; **Amarin**, Tesaban 1 Rd, Tel:522-407; **Krung Si**, 15/11-4 Krung Si Nai Rd, Tel:511-037.
Local Festivals
The annual Elephant Round-up in late November. Contact TAT in Bangkok for details and hotel reservations.

UBON RATCHATHANI
Accommodation
Ratchathani Hotel, 229 Kheun Thani Rd; **Pathumrat Hotel**, 173 Chayangkul Rd, Tel:254-547; **Tokyo**, 178 Uparaj Rd; **99 Hotel**, 224/5 Chayangkul Rd; **Racha Hotel**, 149/21 Chayangkul Rd.
Tourist Information
Tourism Authority of Thailand (TAT), Sala Prachakhom, Si Narong Rd, Ubon Ratchathani, Tel:255-603.
Local Festivals
The annual *Ubon Candle Festival* is held in late July and lasts five days. A very spirited festival, but hotels are usually full. Contact TAT Bangkok for further details.
Restaurants
Khao Tom Hong Thong in Kheun Thani Rd is a Chinese restaurant serving as a speciality rice porridge dishes, but also huge selection of Chinese-Thai cuisine; **Sakhon Restaurant**, Pha Daeng Rd, specializes in Isarn food; Garden restaurants outside of town, **Khun Biak**, serve wild curries; **Fern Bakery** (near teacher's college) sells baked goods.

UDON THANI
Accommodation
Charoen, 549 Phosi Rd, Tel:221-331; **Charoen-sri Palace**, 60 Phosi Rd, Tel:222-601; **King**, 57 Phosi Rd, Tel:221-634; **Chaiyphon**, 209-11 Mak Khang Rd, Tel:221-913; **Krung Thong**, 195-9 Phosi Rd, Tel:221-161.

ALONG THE ANDAMAN COAST

PHUKET

PHANG-NGA

KRABI

TRANG

The provinces running along the Andaman coast offer visitors a real South Seas holiday.

From Phuket and Phang-nga in the north to the many islands off the coast of Trang and Satun, including Tarutao National Park in the extreme south, this area holds some of the most popular destinations in Thailand, and at the same time some of the least explored. Here the seas are dotted with small islands, around which coral reefs have been building up for centuries. Today, they are an irresistible lure for scuba divers and snorkelers, tourists in glass-bottomed boats and fishermen.

The Andaman Sea coast is indented by hundreds of bays with long sandy beaches, lined by coconut palms. Sometimes sheer limestone towers rise behind a beach, a natural phenomenon throughout the area, with particularly noteworthy formations in Phang-nga, Krabi and Koh Pi Pi.

A region of intense color – the deep blues of the clear sea, the white sands of the beaches, the iridescent greens of coconut fronds shimmering in the sun – it is not surprising to find also a colorful variety of inhabitants. The large Chinese

Left: Elderly Chinese gentleman in the palm-leaf hut.

community of Phuket has various festivals unique to the island and famous around the country. Sea gypsies live in houses on stilts above the waves and Muslims can be seen on their way to mosques for their evening prayers.

PHUKET

The richest pearl in the Andaman crown is **Phuket**. Shaped like a tear-drop hanging by a thread from the narrow isthmus of Thailand's south, this fabled island has been on the wayfarer's map for centuries. But it was only in the early 1980s when Phuket's backpacking visitors, ambling along empty beaches and wearing nothing more than a smile, began to feel the hot breath of commercialism blowing down their tanned necks.

Phuket has definitly been discovered. Just like Bali in Indonesia, like Boracay in the Philippines and like Goa in India it has arrived. With dizzying speed, its jungled mountains, the coconut-lined bays, its glistening beaches and offshore islands teeming with marine life are attracting the glitterati, the jet-setters. And now, that the smell of money has mingled with the suntan oil, more and more developers are elbowing their way in for a slice of the cake.

165

The Phuket International Airport now welcomes jumbos bringing load after load of pale urban folk, anxious for their square meter of beach and a good dose of sun to burn away their neuroses. In a scant ten years, this former low budget travelers' paradise has been drastically transformed. Today, Phuket is one of the plushest resort islands in Southeast Asia. But the speed of the transition has not necessarily been good for the island or its ecology. Nevertheless, with many world class luxury resorts and five-star beach hotels, and still more to come, Phuket has become firmly entrenched as one of the ritziest tourist meccas in Thailand and Southeast Asia.

In 1974, Phuket, which had been advertised more by "Come to Paradise" slogans on the T-shirts of backpackers than active promotion by the Thai Government, was suddenly thrust into the international limelight. A well-known

Above: The "James Bond rock" in the bay of Phang-nga .

magazine had proclaimed it as one of the world's least discovered beauty spots, and within months dozens of promoters began scouting the area, starting a frenzy that has not stopped to this day.

Hastily built bungalow complexes went up overnight. At Patong Beach, a raucous street of bars, a poor imitation of Pattaya's strip or Patpong in Bangkok, suddenly sprouted. One by one, empty beaches became the sites of rapid development, much of it poorly planned and with little taste. But still the natural beauty of Phuket overwhelmed the ramshackle development. In the meantime, the authorities began to realize that control must be exercised to save the beauty and reputation of what remains intact.

As Thailand's largest island, Phuket is also the kingdom's only island province. Roughly the size of Singapore, Phuket sits in the Indian Ocean about 870 km south of Bangkok. Prior to the tourist boom, the province already enjoyed considerable prosperity from its tin and rubber industries. The island has a long and

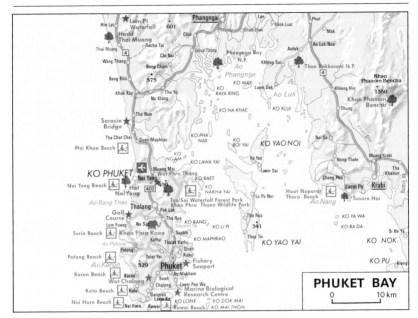

PHUKET BAY
0   10 km

vibrant history, sitting astride the old
trade routes between India and China. In
the log books of ancient mariners, Junk
Ceylon, as Phuket had been named by the
British founder of Penang, attracted thousands of Indian, Arab, Chinese and
European traders.

But not all visitors were interested only
in commerce. Two decades after the fall
of Ayutthaya, the Burmese turned their
covetous eyes on the island. Only the efforts of two women, Thao Thep Kasattri
and Thao Sisunthon, who rallied the islanders in 1785, repelled the Burmese invaders. Today a statue commemorates
their patriotic deed.

The climate of Phuket varies somewhat from the rest of the country. There
are two seasons, the monsoon or rainy
season from May through October, and
the hot season from November through
April. The idea of rain should not deter
visitors though. Tropical showers normally last only an hour or so and leave
the air fresh and the vegetation in-
vigorated. The months most favored by

tourists are November through February,
when temperatures range between 21 and
34 degrees Celsius.

In the southeast corner of the island is
Phuket Town, the province's administrative and commercial center. Dotting the
city are several colonial-era residences,
hidden behind walls and under the shade
of century-old trees. They are the monuments to the tin and rubber barons of
yesteryear.

Overlooking the town is **Rang Hill**
with a good view over the city and its harbor and a fitness park for those in need of
it. The Native Handicrafts Center on
Thepkasattri Road shows artisans working at various items which are offered for
sale. Silk weaving, parasol-making, lacquerware, silverware and jewelry production are all demonstrated at the center. On
the same road is the **Thai Village**, serving a typical Thai lunch. There is a cultural show with the usual range of
dances, Thai-style boxing and sword-
fights. Brochures describing the details
are available at the Tourism Authority of

167

Thailand (TAT) office on Phuket Road in the center of town.

If any one feature of the island is to describe what draws visitors most, it is the marvellously varied coastline. Tiny coves, in which a swatch of white sand has collected, can still be discovered – quiet, empty and untouched. And then, just over the next headland, the surf may roar in and explode in fury against rugged cliffs. The shore facing the Indian Ocean has the finest beaches, while the eastern coastline, shallow and muddy with long stretches of mangroves, is more sheltered.

In the north of the island, Sarasin Bridge connects Phuket with the mainland. Going south, the first beach after crossing the bridge is **Mai Khao**, the island's longest, and 40 km from Phuket town. During the winter months, giant sea turtles, laden with eggs, come here to lay their eggs in the sand up the beach.

Above: At the purifying rite during the Vegetarian Festival in Phuket.

Further south and 34 km from town, is **Nai Yang Beach**, with calm waters, ideal for swimming and snorkeling.

Behind Nai Yang is **Wat Phra Thong**, which houses a partially buried Buddha statue. According to legend, a boy came to this quiet shady spot to take a nap. He tied his buffalo to a post protruding from the ground, after which both he and the animal fell ill. The villagers who came to investigate this strange occurrence, found that the post to which the animal had been tied was actually the top knot on the head of a golden Buddha, long buried in the sand. Only the upper half was uncovered and the present sanctuary was built over it. When the Burmese invaded in 1785, they attempted to steal the statue, but were attacked by a swarm of angry hornets and driven off, or so the story goes.

East of Nai Yang, and 20 km from town, is **Ton Sai Waterfall Forest Park** and **Khao Phra Thaeo Wildlife Park**. Bears, monkeys, gibbons, porcupine and over 100 bird species populate the area.

The main beaches going south along the Indian Ocean are Pansea Bay and Surin, Kamala, Patong, Karon, Kata and finally Nai Harn. At **Surin Beach** the surf is too powerful for swimming and strong rip tides threaten anyone venturing too far into the waves. But there is a rather neglected 9-hole golf course for those desperate for exercise.

A spot in Phuket sometimes compared to Pattaya is **Patong Beach**, south of Kamala. It is the island's most developed area and along its three kilometers of sand are cabins, bungalows, low rise hotels and deluxe resorts. Bars, nightclubs, discotheques, restaurants and shopping arcades line the beach road in a haphazard unplanned manner. Daytime activities include windsurfing, sailing, snorkeling, swimming and sunbathing. Patong is also the magnet for American sailors whenever a US Navy ship anchors in the vicinity.

Across a headland south of Patong are **Karon** and **Kata**, two long stretches of sandy beach, along which numerous luxury properties have been built. The last and most southern beach on the west coast is **Nai Harn**, with the Phuket Yacht Club on one side and Phromthep Cape on the other. **Phromthep Cape** is the island's most southern point and offers good views and spectacular sunsets.

Moving up the east coast from the cape, the first and oldest developed beach is **Rawai**, curving around to Ka Cape. There is a community of sea gypsies living at Rawai, who used to make their living by diving for shells and lobster, but today they have become more or less integrated. Nearby **Chalong Bay**, because of its proximity to Phuket Town (11 km), attracts townsfolk and visitors to its excellent seafood restaurants. **Wat Chalong** enshrines the remains of two of Phuket's most revered monks. The long neck of land sitting to the north of Chalong Bay and forming its northern shore, is Phanwa Cape, with a **Marine**

169

aroma of crab, giant prawns and shrimps being roasted at outdoor barbecues. The island has developed its own unique cuisine, based on Thai, Chinese and Muslim cooking, which, together with exotic cocktails, concocted from a blend of coconuts, pineapple and Thai whisky or rum, are a diner's delight.

PHANG-NGA

Phang-nga, the province north of Phuket, easily reached by bus or rented jeep, has been blessed with some amazing natural attractions, some of which have gained world fame. Remember that scene in *The Man With the Golden Gun*, when 007 speeds over a dazzling bay, dodging countless islands only to beach his craft on an astounding islet, where a dome-shaped pinnacle of rock rises out of the sea? Those spell-binding scenes were filmed around Khao Tapu in Phang-nga Bay. Most visitors to Phang-nga follow the James Bond route, although at a more leisurely pace, by hiring a longtail boat. Package tours also come here from Phuket, and can be easily arranged at any major hotel.

But by far the best way to see the sights in Phang-nga Bay is to hire your own boat at one of the numerous bays or coves. Off the highway to Phang-nga town is the tiny port of **Tha Don**, a customs pier, which has boats for hire. Further on down the road is the turn-off for the Phang-nga Bay Resort, which has a good restaurant and a swimming pool.

Boats can also be hired by inquiring at your hotel's desk, where the price might be higher, but the hotel picks the boatman and the arrangements can be made in English.

Covering an area of 400 sq km, **Phang-nga Bay National Park** is impossible to explore in one day. Its major attractions are the beautiful **Tham Lod Cave**, through which boats can travel while tourists gaze at the amazing lime-

Biological Research Center, **Phuket's Aquarium** and the Cape Phanwa Sheraton Hotel.

Phuket is a sports enthusiast's paradise. Marine sports like windsurfing, sailing, water skiing, deep sea fishing, swimming, snorkeling and scuba diving are all well organized, with equipment and instructors available at all major beaches and resorts. The new **Phuket Country Club**, with its international tournaments, caters to golf addicts and most major hotels have tennis courts. Along with informal volleyball games, which seem to sprout on the beach each evening, jogging along the white sands in the morning is another way visitors keep in trim.

Apart from beaches and marine sports, Phuket is famous for its seafood. Phuket lobster, fresh daily from the island's bountiful waters, is a real delicacy and in the evening the air is laden with the

Above: Fishing boat in Phuket. Right: Mysterious rock formations on the Similan Islands.

stone formations. **Panyi Island** has a sea gypsy village, built entirely on stilts. Out of its center a picturesque domed minaret gleams above the rooftops. **Khao Tapu**, the James Bond island, is a convenient spot to stretch your legs. Here, ladies will be approached by vendors selling pearls from the cultured pearl beds in the bay.

Strung along Phang-nga's indented shore are five other national parks and two forest reserves under the care of the Forestry Department. On the western side, with its own Andaman coast, Phang-nga has access to two more protected areas, the **Similan Islands** and **Surin Island National Parks**. Both can easily be reached by chartered boats. The Similans are 50 km offshore and the Surin Islands another 20 km further south. Boats leave from the port of Kuraburi. Both island groups are visited by several tours from Phuket and have gained a world-wide reputation for easy sightings of whales and dolphins, quite apart from the amazing deep sea coral reefs.

KRABI

Further down the coast from Phang-nga is **Krabi**, a province already eyed impatiently by travel agents. It is still somewhat out of the way and its interior, lush with jungle and astounding mountains, has hardly been touched. But bungalows and better class resorts are starting to develop along its beaches.

Just after crossing the border of the province on National Highway 4, near the town of **Ao Luk** and the bay of the same name, is **Than Bokkoroni National Park**. A tiny oasis nestling among the trees and rocks, this romantic little park has ponds filled with lotus and is fed by waterfalls splashing down from the rocks overhead. Several streams meander through the lush greenery which, on weekends, is filled with laughing groups of Thai picnickers from nearby towns.

Further south on Route 4, 11 km before Krabi town, is a beautiful 2 km long beach called **Haat Noparat Thara**, or "Beach of the Nine-Gemmed Stream",

part of a **National Marine Park**. 7 km from here are **Laem Pho** and **Susarn Hoi**, the Shell Cemetery. On this cape, jutting into the Gulf of Phuket, are flat slabs of rock made up of millions of fossilized shells which are said to be 75 million years old.

Krabi town is about 130 km from Phuket. Like other and similar formations in Phang-nga, three nearby limestone islets are humorously named Bird, Cat and Mouse Islands. Off the coast are over 130 islands, many of which are inhabited and may be visited by chartering boats in Krabi town.

Several companies offer tours to the island group of **Koh Lanta**, of which at least 12 are inhabited. All the islands in the group have beaches on their western sides, facing the Indian Ocean, but the most popular is on Koh Lanta Yai, an hour's boat trip away. There is no accommodation available at present, but bungalows are planned.

Koh Phi Phi is part of the Marine National Park and has two main islands, with Phi Phi Don being the larger. With its two mountains, one at each end and separated by a low land bridge, the island is shaped like a dumb-bell. The cliffs fall steeply into the sea, turning the crystal clear water a deep turquoise. There are bungalows on Koh Phi Phi Don, which can be booked in Phuket through tour agents, but during the high season reservations are advised. The smaller island, Phi Phi Le, is a popular destination for boat tours from Phuket. It is a solid rock with cliffs plummeting into the sea. In its center is a canyon into which the sea has entered, forming an emerald green, saltwater lake.

On this island is a giant cave in which swallows build their nests three times a year. The birds make these nests by threading their own saliva into tiny cups. The saliva congeals into translucent strands and hardens to form the nests.

Above: A breathtaking view of Koh Phi Phi Don. Right: Children from the Andaman Sea coast.

The right to harvest these nests is auctioned off and the workers ascend precarious bamboo scaffolding to collect the precious birdsnests. These nests are then sold to Chinese middlemen, who deliver them to Chinese restaurants throughout the region for the well-known birdsnest soup.

Once the nests are dissolved in chicken broth, they resemble vermicelli noodles. The Chinese regard them as extremely nutritious and almost medicinal in their curative properties.

TRANG

Further south on Route 4 is the province of **Trang** which has the same limestone formations so characteristic of this region. Trang has a history stretching back almost 2,000 years, to the time when Surat Thani and Nakhon Sri Thammarat were major strongholds of the ancient Srivijaya Empire.

Trang served as a west coast harbor for these two centers, with boats coming up from the Malacca Straits and Sumatra. Trang was formerly on the mouth of the Trang River, but was moved because of frequent flooding. It was also the point of disembarkation for the kingdom's earliest European visitors and emissaries, who would either make their way to Ayutthaya overland, or cross the isthmus and take a boat at Nakhon Sri Thammarat, going up the gulf coast to the Chao Phraya River.

Today, Trang is the center of a prosperous rubber growing region. Because of its distance from Bangkok (830 km), it has been largely ignored by travel agents, but its beaches and islands are well worth exploring. Accommodation may be a problem though and visitors must be prepared to accept the most basic of facilities. Camping is the safest bet, especially on the islands.

Twenty kilometers from Trang is the **Ka Chong National Park** with its virgin tropical forest, three waterfalls and comfortable government rest houses. Paths have been laid out through enormous trees, leading to the waterfalls.

173

PHUKET
Accommodation

For reasons of space it is impossible to list the multitude of hotels, guesthouses and resorts found all over Phuket. The following is a sample of the better known and longer established hostelries.

LUXURY: **Amanpuri**, Pansea Beach, Tel:216-545; **Arcadia**, Karon Beach, Tel:214-841; **Club Andaman**, Patong Beach, Tel:321-102; **Club Mediterranee**, Kata Beach, Tel:214-830; **Karon Villa**, Karon Beach, Tel:212-709; **Dusit Laguna**, Cherng Talay, Tel:311-320; **Holiday Inn**, Patong Beach, Tel:236-7245 (Bkk); **Le Meridien**, Relax Bay, Tel:321-480; **Phuket Yacht Club**, Nai Harn Beach, Tel:214-020; **Sheraton**, Cape Panwa, Tel:391-123. *MODERATE:* **Coral Beach** Hotel, Patong Beach, Tel:321-106; **Kata Thani**, Kata Noi Beach, Tel:214-824; **Pansea**, Pansea Beach, Tel:216-137; **Patong Merlin**, Patong Beach, Tel: 321-070; **Pearl**, Montri Rd, Tel: 211-044; **Pearl Village**, Nai Yang Beach, Tel:311-338; **Phuket Island Resort**, Bon Island, Tel:215-950; **Phuket Merlin**, Yawaraj Rd, Tel:212-866; **Thavorn Palm Beach**, Karon Beach, Tel:211-557.

Hospitals

Wachira Hospital, Yaowaraj Rd, Tel:211-114; **Mission Hospital**, Thepkasattri Rd, Tel:212-386; **Phuket Ruam Phaet**, Phuket Rd, Tel:212-950.

Post / Telephone / Telegraph

Overseas Telephone Center, Phang-nga Rd (24 hrs.), Tel:211-199; Domestic Long Distance, Blue Boxes at Telephone Centre. Post and Telegraph Office, at corner of Talang and Suthat Rds.

Tourist Information

TAT Office, 75-77 Phuket Rd, Tel:212-213 (open 7 days a week, 08:30 to 16:30); **Tourist Police** – Tel:212-213, 212-468. Mobile TAT Centers, at Kata, Karon, Patong Beaches and on Rasada Road in town, manned by students.

Access and Transport

By Air: Thai International Airways flies several times daily between Bangkok and Phuket. Domestic connections with Hat Yai and Surat Thani. International flights to Penang, Kuala Lumpur, Singapore and Hong Kong via Thai Inter, Malaysia Air, Singapore Airlines, Dragonair, and Cathay Pacific. For reservations in Phuket phone 211-195, 212-946 (domestic) and 212-400, 212-855 (international). Bangkok Airways flies to Ko Samui, Tel:212-341. **By Bus**: Buses take 14 hours and leave the Southern Bus Terminal at Charansanitwongse Rd, Bangkok frequently. Tel:411-4978 (air- con) or 411-0511 (regular). **Local transport**: Tuk-tuks, or samlors

are available in Phuket Town. Buses to various beaches leave from Ranong Market in town every 30 minutes between 8:00 and 18:00. Inquire at TAT office for fares around the island. Buses to the airport leave from all hotels and the Thai Inter office opposite Ranong Market. Cars may be hired through all major hotels from Hertz or Avis and jeeps and motorcycles are available on most beaches.

Local Festivals

On the first day of the ninth lunar month, (late Sept. early Oct.) the Chinese in Phuket commit themselves to a nine day vegetarian diet to purify body and soul. On the first day, devotees dress in white and perform various acts of atonement, such as walking up sharp-bladed ladders, sticking iron rods through various parts of the body and walking on red-hot coal.

Shopping

Phuket's shops stock various handicrafts, but specialize in southern batiks, coral/shell fashion creations and cultured pearls. Consult TAT office for approved member shops.

Restaurants

Jee Huad, 92 Yaowaraj Rd, Tel:212-802. **Mae Porn**, 50 Phang-nga Rd, in town serves good curries, and for breakfast and various bakery items there is nothing to beat **Kanda Bakery**, 31 Rasada Rd, Tel:213-218, which, by the way, serves the only palatable coffee in town.

Having won the Shell Award (a sign of excellence) a visit to **Kan Eang** at Chalong Bay is in order. Whether you eat at Kan Eang 1 on Viset Rd (Tel:216-726), or Kan Eang 2 on Chao Fah Rd (Tel:216- 288), the seafood is tops.

PHANG-NGA
Accommodation

LUXURY: **Phang-nga Bay Resort**, 20 Tha Dan, Panyee, Tel:411-067. *MODERATE:* **Lak Muang I**, Phetkasem Rd (in town), & **Lak Muang II** on Phuket-Phang-nga Highway, Tel:411-125, 411-288. *BUDGET:* **Tawisuk**, (blue building in center of town).

KRABI
Accommodation

LUXURY: **Phi Phi Island Village**, Phi Phi Don Island, 249 Thalang, Phuket, Tel: 215-014; **Phi Phi Cabana**, Krabi, Tel:611-496; Krabi Resort, Moo 2, Tambon Ao Nang, Tel:612-160.

MODERATE: **Phi Phi Krabi Resort**, Phi Phi Don Island. *BUDGET:* **Kitti Suk**, 9-11 Si Phang-nga Rd, Tel:611-087; **Naowarat**, 403 Utarakit Rd, Tel:611-581; **Wiang Thong**, 155-7 Uttarakit Rd, Tel:611-188; **Jum Island Resort**, Jum Island (35 kms from Krabi), Tel:611-541.

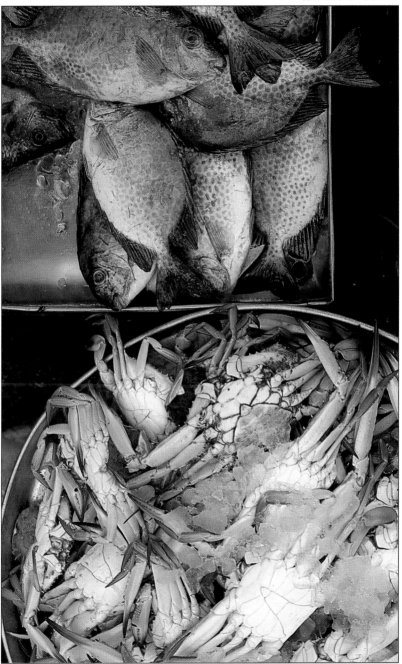

INTO THE DEEP SOUTH

RANONG

KOH SAMUI

THE EASTERN COAST

THE TIP OF THE TRUNK

The shape of Thailand is often compared to the head of an elephant with the elongated southern portion of the kingdom being the trunk. The south is a fascinating part of Thailand for its ethnic diversity, geography, climate and history. It is made up of 14 provinces: Chumphon, Ranong, Surat Thani, Phang-nga, Phuket, Krabi, Nakhon Sri Thammarat, Trang, Phathalung, Songkhla, Satun, Pattani, Yala and Narathiwat.

The southern region is, topographically speaking, remarkably diverse. Although it has few basins suitable for rice cultivation, its wild jungles, spectacularly shaped mountains, beaches, resorts, waterfalls, caves, lakes and gorgeous islands on both coasts make it one of the most interesting regions for the tourist seeking the exotic.

The climate, more similar to that of Malaysia than central Thailand, is determined by the monsoons. The southwest monsoon feeds the west coast on the Andaman Sea with rain from May to September, wheras the northeast monsoon brings heavy rains to the east coast on the Gulf of Thailand from November to late February.

Preceding page: Fish and lobsters for sale. Left: Umbrellas as far as the eye reaches.

Like the north with its hilltribes, the south has some interesting ethnic minorities. The Ngo Sakai are an indigenous people, almost negrito in appearance, with dark skin and kinky hair. They live primarily in Trang and Yala provinces, sometimes coming down from their mountain villages to the town markets to shop. The Chao Leh or "sea gypsies" have lived in their traditional fashion for centuries. Strong-willed, daring fisherfolk, they are totally committed to a life on the sea and resist government attempts to assimilate them. Their villages, built on stilts above the waves, can be found mainly in Phang-nga, Phuket and the islands off Satun. Then there are the "Thai Muslims", who can be found throughout the country, but are concentrated primarily in the four provinces of the "deep south". The provinces of Pattani, Narathiwat, Yala and Satun, for example, are over 80 per cent Muslim.

Culturally, the south's uniqueness is expressed in its cuisine, its handicrafts, festivals and forms of entertainment. Southern food is partly influenced by the Chinese, but is very hot. Malaysian influence can be seen in the many curries, common in all Muslim restaurants. As for handicrafts, mother-of-pearl ornaments are a speciality of Phuket and Ranong. Yan Lipao wicker and rattan ware, niello,

177

Theinkun

Prachuap Khiri Khan

KANMAW I.
(KETTHAYIN I.)

MYANMAR
(BURMA)

Ban Huai Yang

Manoron

876

PAWE-GYI

Lenya

Thap Sakae

SIR J.
MALCOLM I.

Bokpyin

G U L F

OWEN I.

4

Bang Saphan

KAU-YE

582

Karaturi

SIR ROBERT
CAMPBELL

Pathiu

Tha Sae

BUDA I.

Khao
Nam Noi
755

Chumphon

Kra Buri

Ao Sawi

Maliwun

610

Sawi

La-un

KO TAO

HASTINGS
I.

Ulu

Chong Tao

KO
CHANG

282

Ranong

Lang Suan

ISTHMUS

KO
PHAYAM

Pharo

553

OF KRA

KO
PHANGAN

Kapoe

Chong Phangan

KO
PHALUAI

Laem Son N.P.

KO
PHAYAM

Na Khia

1395

Chaiya

635

KO SAMUI

Chong Samui

4

Chiao Lan
Res.

1028

Surat Thani

Kanchanadit

Aó Ban Don

Khanom

Bang O

970

Khlong Mot

Sichon

T H A I L A N D

Khao Nan Mia
1530

(AO THAI)

Thung Birt

Ban
Na San

1366

Tha Sala

Takua
Pa

Phanom

Yan Khian

Huai Yot

Kapong

1050

Phrasaeng

Laem Talumphuk

Thap Put

Thai
Muang

Phang-nga

Ao Luk

NAKHON SI THAMMARAT

Khao
Phanom

Thung Yai

Pak Phanang
Seaside Resort

Takua Thung

1350

Ban Pak Phraek

Khok KO YAO
Kloi NOI

Thung Song
(Cha Mai)

Ron Phibun

Hua Sai

Thalang

343

KO YAO
YAI

Khlong Thom

KO
SI BOYA

Phuket

KO PHI
PHI DON

KO
LANTA

KO PU

Khlong
Phon

Huai Yot

Map Bua

Chai Khlong

KO
PHUKET

Na Wong

Phatthalung

Di Luang

Trang

Khao Ron
1350

Khao Khram Waterfall

Sathing Phra

Khao Chai
Son

Thale
Luang

Yan Ta Khao

KO LI BONG

Palian

261

SONGKHLA

KO SUKON

Rattaphum

Laem Pho

Ban
Khlong Kua

HAT YAI

Chana

Pattani

Panare

Ban Pak Bara

Khlong Ngae

Thepha

Yaring

Tarutao Island N.P.
KO
TERUTAO

Talo Udang

Satun

Khlong Ngae

Na Thawi

Khok Pho

Sai Buri

KO RAWI

Talo Waew

Sadao

Saba
Yoi

1015

Yala

Ban Thop

KO LADANG

Kangar

T
H
A
I

640

Ba La

Ruso

Yi Ngo

Narathiwat

Tg. Chinchin

PERLIS

825

Ban Nang Sata

Sako

841

Rangae

PULAU LANGKAW

Jitra

M
A
L
A
Y
A

Sako

Tak Bai

P. SINGA BESAR

Tg. Pinang

P. DAYANG
BUNTING

Buket Bubat
1145

Sungai
Ko-lok

Pasir
Mas

Alor Setar

KEDAH

1268

1331

1097

Betong

Bt. Ulu Laho
1203

Jeli

SOUTHERN THAILAND

0   100 km

MALAYSIA

silver and lacquerware are the products of the people of Nakhon Sri Thammarat. The south is the source of pearls for the jewelry industry in Bangkok, and beautiful specimens can be purchased in Phuket, Phang-nga and Ranong, streight from the farms where they are cultivated.

Access to the south is traditionally by road or rail, although with the recently upgraded airports in Phuket and Hat Yai, and the new landing strip on Koh Samui, air travel is becoming more common. Thai Airways flies to Surat Thani, Phuket, Trang, Hat Yai, Pattani and Narathiwat and Bangkok Airways has a flight to Hua Hin, and another to Phuket with a stop on Koh Samui. The main route to the south is National Highway 4 (Petchkasem Road), which starts in Thonburi and runs all of a thousand kilometers to Sadao on the border, where it links up with the Malaysian highway system. The railroad runs down the east coast to Hat Yai, from where two branches run to the Malaysian border, connecting with lines going to Butterworth, Kuala Lumpur and Singapore.

The province regarded as the gateway to the south is Chumphon, where a change becomes perceptible as the traveler leaves the central region behind. The air feels more tropical. Plantations of rubber trees come into view, reminding the passerby that rubber is one of the mainstays of the south's economy. Tall fan palms begin to dot the landscape, and fruit orchards run off from the highway.

The town of **Chumphon** sits about 10 km from the coast. It is here that Route 4 makes a right turn to leave the east coast, going to Ranong in the west, before turning south, going all the way down to Trang and Hat Yai. The road running straight south from Chumphon is Route 41, which keeps to the east coast until Phatthalung, where it joins up with Route 4 again.

Chumphon is popular with Thai tourists who travel south in groups visiting the offshore islands. Several of them, including **Lanta Chio**, have good coral reefs sought out by scuba divers and snorkelers. The island is also known for its sea swallow nests, which are collected much like the nests on Koh Phi Phi. In Chumphon, birds' nest soup is more reasonably priced than elsewhere in Thailand, and local tourists are fully aware of this. There are some good hotels on the coast of Chumphon, but those in town, although considerably cheaper, are noisy and crowded, especially on weekends.

RANONG

Going west from Chumphon, Route 4 crosses the **Kra Isthmus**, the site of the often-discussed proposed canal, running along a line presenting the shortest distance between the Andaman Sea and the Gulf of Thailand. The idea is to eliminate the need for going around the Malacca Straits and Singapore, and thus shorten the route for ships from Europe and the Middle East.

On entering Ranong Province, the highway passes through **Kra Buri**, a district famous for the large **Phra Khayang caves** and the impressive **Bokkrai waterfalls**. At La-un the highway goes over a bridge, from which at low tide, the wreck of a Japanese World War II warship can be seen. After 115 km from Chumphon, Route 4 enters **Ranong** town, the provincial capital of the most northerly of the provinces facing the Indian Ocean. It is also the kingdom's least populated province and has the heaviest annual rainfall in Thailand.

Ranong has a thriving trade with Burma via the Burmese town of **Victoria Point**, directly across the estuary of the Kra Buri River. The town is interesting because of its old-style Sino-Portuguese architecture, unique to this region. Similar designs can be found in Phuket and Songkhla, and further south in Penang and Malacca in Malaysia. Ranong also

has one of the few **hot springs** found in Thailand. At **Wat Tapotharam**, 2 km east of town, the waters bubble up at 65 degrees and fill a pool surrounded by dense forest. The public park has changing rooms and rest areas.

Across the La-un River is Victoria Point in Burma. Boats cross the estuary from Ranong for about 200 to 300 baht, but foreigners should make enquiries at their hotel as to the formalities. Burmese souvenirs and food are available in the thriving markets on the other side, but many of the same items can be purchased in Ranong at only slightly higher prices.

Two hours away by boat is **Phayam Island**, which has a pearl oyster farm and a small village of sea gypsies. Further south on the way to Phang-nga is **Laem Son National Park** with its beautiful beaches, islands, coral reefs and some bungalows.

Above: Coconut palms bathing in the evening sun.

Back in Chumphon, Route 41 goes straight south and after 76 km enters **Lang Suan**, a town that owes its prosperity to the vast tracts of fruit orchards, which cover the surrounding hills. Mangosteen, durian, rambutan and coconut plantations are within walking distance of town, which is an attractive collection of bright houses with flower boxes. Lang Suan is also known for its **water festival** held at the end of October. The highpoint of this is a canoe race, with some of the boats large enough to hold 30 rowers.

Surat Thani, 195 km from Chumphon and 645 km from Bangkok, is in terms of area the largest province in the south. Its first town of interest to tourists coming down Route 41 is **Chaiya**, with a history going back to the ninth and tenth centuries, when much of the south was part of the Srivijaya Empire.

This empire, which unified numerous city states in what is today Thailand, Burma and Malaysia, had its capital in Sumatra. Chaiya even predates this empire, since it was a city state in itself until it became part of Srivijaya and one of its major ports.

Many of the artifacts in the National Museum in Bangkok were found in and around Chaiya, with the Srivijaya period figuring strongly in Thailand's impressive art history.

Just outside of town is Chaiya's principal attraction, **Wat Pra Mahathat**, with a recently restored *stupa*. The architecture of this temple, together with **Wat Kaew** not far away, shows ancient Indonesian influences. Chaiya is also the site of **Wat Suanmoke**, a well-known meditation center begun by Buddhadasa Bhikkhu, a monk highly revered all over Thailand. This forest monastery teaches a doctrine blending many other religious beliefs with those of Theravada Buddhism.

Surat Thani, meaning "the city of the good people", but locally called simply Surat, is the next town. About 35 km south of Chaya, Route 41 is intersected by Route 401 which runs from the west coast to the east. Here we turn left, to reach Surat Thani after another 20 km. This administrative and commercial center is also the gateway to Koh Samui, the popular island lying not far offshore. The **TAT office** in Surat is an excellent place to get an overview of the sights in town and its surroundings. One of the more unusual attractions here is the **Monkey School** on the outskirts of town, where a human instructor and two monkey teachers train novice monkeys to climb palm trees and pluck coconuts.

KOH SAMUI

Koh Samui (*koh* means island) lies about 30 km, or two hours by boat, from Surat's port, Ban Don. It was for many years one of the fabled islands on the backpackers' route in search of the ideal tropical nirvana, where prices were low and the living was easy. It still has links to this kind of traveler, easily recognized by the number of restaurants serving

yoghurt shakes, banana pancakes and ganja brownies.

But on Koh Samui, like some other parts of Thailand, the jeans and T-shirt wanderer is being displaced by real estate tycoons and the jet set. Although not yet anywhere near the level of development found on Phuket, Koh Samui is definitely on the way to more sophistication. Already several upmarket resorts with discos, swimming pools and air-conditioned facilities have invaded the tranquility, and even caused a room shortage, aggravated further by the recent opening of the island's brand new airstrip, cut out of the coconut groves.

To understand the attraction of Koh Samui, one merely has to set foot on its shores and let the island atmosphere do the rest. Samui looks and feels like the giant coconut garden that it is, giving its villagers an assured income. All types of coconut known in Thailand are found on the island, only here they happen to be just a little juicier and sweeter than anywhere else. The smell of the fresh fruit

181

drying permeates the air and millions of the nuts and tonnes of several by-products are shipped to Bangkok annually.

Koh Samui, the third largest of Thailand's islands, has an area of about 280 sq km. Roughly the size of Penang, its longest distance from north to south is 25 km and east to west about 22 km. It is one of over 50, mostly uninhabited, islands belonging to the Angthong Marine National Park. The 35,000 native islanders are almost all, in one way or another, connected with either of the island's two industries – coconuts and fishing – and, to a much lesser extend, tourism.

Beaches are found all around the island, reached via a 59 km long hardtopped ringroad, from which lanes lead off to the shore. From **Na Thon**, the main town and port, *songthaews* take the traveler to the main beaches of **Lamai Chaweng**, **Bophut**, **Maenam**, charging 15-20 baht. Chaweng and Lamai are the most developed and crowded. Boput runs in front of a small village which retains a certain rustic charm. To get the feel of the island, the first time visitor may want to settle for a few nights on one beach and then move to another after checking it out by motorcycle.

Rented motorcycles are by far the easiest way to get around and many bungalows or agents in Na Thon rent bikes to tourists. But beware: accidents are quite frequent. When hiring *songthaews* in Na Thon, make sure to ask where they go, as many of the vehicles have an allocated fixed route from which they will not deviate. Others travel around the island highway and can be flagged down on the road.

Besides lolling on the beach, swimming and snorkeling, Samui offers the attraction of two inland waterfalls. The **Hin Lad Falls** are within walking distance of Na Thon, but the first pools are the least interesting. It is worthwhile to hike up the trail through the forest, where several isolated pools are ideal for a cool dip. The more distant falls, **Na Muang** (10 km from Na Thon), are close to a parking area. The water cascades over a sheer wall of ochre rock, before falling into a large pool, are good for swimming.

The weather in Samui is best from February to mid-April, when the sea is calm. From April to September, occasional storms make the sea choppy and from October to February a northeasterly wind brings frequent rains and sometimes violent gales. December has the heaviest rainfall, but, as during the rest of the year, calm clear weather can go on for weeks without interruption.

Several tour operators in Na Thon offer a number of excursions to the islands north of Samui. **Koh Ang Thong**, the center of a **Marine National Park**, is a favorite destination. Boats leave Samui in the morning, so visitors can hike to the highest point on Ang Thong for a spectacular view of islets, an emerald lake and several coral reefs. Further to the east is **Koh Phangan**, still relatively undeveloped with no electricity and only very basic accommodation.

And if you really want to "get away from it all", there is **Koh Tao**, the Turtle Island. This small but gorgeous little jewel is eight hours by fishing boat from Bophut beach. Boats leave several times a week, the excursions being announced a few days in advance in Na Thon. The boats leave when enough passengers have signed up. Koh Tao offers empty beaches, a simple bed in a fisherman's hut and food straight from the sea. There is no electricity, but it has the most extraordinary coral formations in Southeast Asia.

THE EASTERN COAST

The ancient town of **Nakhon Sri Thammarat** is the next stop on Route 401. About 135 km from Surat Thani and 780 km from Bangkok, it is the second largest city in the south and historically

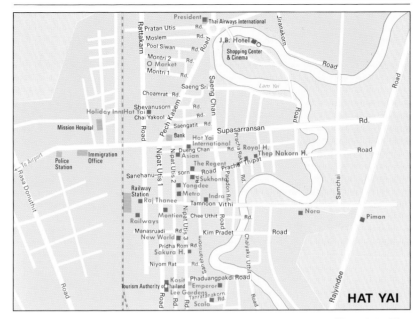

its most important. As the center of Buddhism during the Srivichaya period, it controlled the region for the Sumatra-based empire. Many ancient relics discovered here are now found in museums, here and in Bangkok. Known as *muang phra* or the city of monks, the town is filled with temples, most of which are along the long main avenue.

Wat Phra Mahathat, the more illustrious and one of Thailand's oldest temples, was constructed in 757, during the Srivichaya period. Because of the gradual shift of the city center, this *wat* is now somewhat outside of town. It has a 77 m high *chedi*, the top of which is covered with gold. Next door is **Phra Viharn Luang** with its beautiful roof supported by inward slanting pillars. It is regarded as an architectural gem, built during the Sukhothai period.

The style was much duplicated in Ayutthaya, but is said never to have attained the perfection of the temple in Nakhon Sri Thammarat. Remnants of the old city wall can be seen, especially near Wat

Mahathat. The nearby office of the **Fine Arts Department** houses a sizeable collection of artifacts found in and around the town.

Two aspects of Nakhon Sri Thammarat deserve mention – its renown for the skill of its gold and silversmiths and the ancient art of shadow theater. Many good pieces of incised gold, silver and nielloware can be purchased here at various speciality shops. On festival days, ancient shadow plays and puppet theater performances can be seen. Shadow puppets, made of pounded buffalo hide, can also be purchased here. Several beaches, including Hin Ngam, Khanom and Sa Bua, are within easy reach of town. Pak Phaying beach is 20 km away and the Pak Phanang Seaside Resort, with a long white beach, is a 28 km ride from town.

Continuing south via Route 403 and later 41, the traveler reaches **Phatthalung**, 840 km from Bangkok. Its central landmark, a high limestone hill, is visible on entering town. Phatthalung is also famous for its shadow plays or *nang*

talung, which, as in Nakhon Sri Thammarat, can be seen during temple fairs. Only 8 km from town ist the casuarina-lined Sansuk beach on the northern reaches of **Songkhla Lake**, a large freshwater basin. **Khao Khram waterfall**, about 30 km from Phatthalung, cascades from the mountains, jumping over several levels before reaching a pond, which is large enough for swimming.

Route 41 ends in Phatthalung and we continue on Highway 4 going south to **Hat Yai**, 935 km from Bangkok. Hat Yai is a bustling commercial center and the largest town in Songkhla Province. Sitting at the junction of the south's principal road and rail arteries, and with a new international airport, the town is the most important commercial center between Bangkok and Malaysia. It has developed a thriving entertainment industry, which caters primarily to tourists from Malaysia and Singapore. It also has a busy market

Above: Trained monkeys are the best cocont harvesters.

district, selling a wide range of goods which have been smuggled across the border from Malaysia.

In addition to its well-appointed hotels, cinemas and nightclubs, Hat Yai also stages bull fights, but of a different kind. Instead of confronting a matador, here the animals fight each other. For up-to-date details of this and other events contact the TAT office in Soi 2, Nipat Uthit 3 Road, Tel: 243-747.

Songkhla, the more sedate provincial capital 30 km to the east of Hat Yai, was formerly known as Singora. It sits on a peninsula having on one side the Gulf of Thailand and on the other Songkhla Lake. Samila Beach, with its long lines of casuarina trees, is one of the town's main attractions, although visitors fresh from beaches of Koh Samui or Phuket may not be that impressed. Off the end of the cape are **Koh Maew** and **Koh Nu**, the Cat and Mouse islands.

The old part of town still has many houses built in the Sino-Portuguese style. These picturesque buildings are particularly evident on the inland sea waterfront, which bustles with activity. Near Songkhla bus station is the **National Museum**, housing artifacts and art of the Srivijaya period in a century-old Sino-Portuguese-style building.

Lake cruises are popular, with boats for hire at the Songkhla Market Wharf. They usually go up the lake to Ranot District. The boat trip skirts the islands in the lake, such as **Koh Yo**, which is now connected to town by the newly opened Prem Tinsulanonda Bridge. This island is worth a visit to observe, and perhaps purchase, the cotton being woven on hand-looms around the island.

THE TIP OF THE TRUNK

The four most southerly provinces of Thailand, Satun, Pattani, Yala and Narathiwat, are unique, because, unlike in the rest of the kingdom, the predomi-

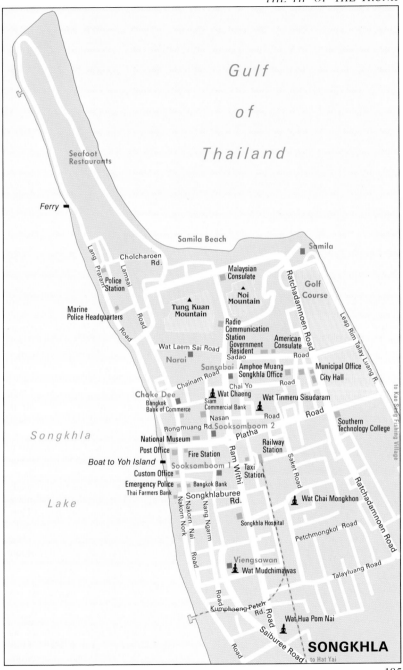

Gulf

of

Thailand

Seafoot Restaurants

Ferry

Samila Beach

Samila

Cholcharoen Rd.

Lang Prarm

Police Station

Lamsai

Malaysian Consulate

Ratchadamnoen Road

Golf Course

Marine Police Headquarters

Road

Tung Kuan Mountain

Noi Mountain

Radio Communication Station Government Resident Sadao

American Consulate

Road

Leap Rim Talay Luang R.

Wat Laem Sai Road

Narai

Sansabai

Amphoe Muang Songkhla Office

Municipal Office City Hall

Chainam Road

Chai Yo

Road

to Kao Seng Fishing Village

Choke Dee

Bangkok Bank of Commerce

Wat Chaeng

Siam Commercial Bank

Wat Tinmeru Sisudaram

Nasan

Road

Songkhla

Rongmuang Rd. Sooksomboom 2

Platha

Southern Technology College

National Museum

Post Office

Boat to Yoh Island

Fire Station

Ram Withi

Railway Station

Saket Road

Custom Office

Sooksomboom 1

Taxi Station

Emergency Police

Bangkok Bank

Thai Farmers Bank

Songkhlaburee Rd.

Nakorn Nai

Nang Ngarm

Wat Chai Mongkhon

Lake

Songkhla Hospital

Nakorn Nork

Road

Petchmongkol Road

Ratchadamnoen Road

Viengsawan

Wat Mudchimawas

Road

Talayluang Road

Kumphaeng Peteh Rd.

Road

Wat Hua Pom Nai

SONGKHLA

Saiburee Road

to Hat Yai

185

nant religion here is Islam and 80 per cent of the inhabitants are Muslims. As a result they have strong associations with Malaysia, and cross-border contacts and trade are thriving.

The small, mountainous province of **Satun** with its multitude of offshore islands is on the west coast, and only a few kilometers from the Malaysian border. Satun town has little of interest to visitors, but **Tarutao Island National Park**, about 30 km offshore, is rapidly becoming another "yet to be discovered paradise". Many tourists, mostly Thai, are visiting the island, enchanted by its untouched beauty, crystal clear waters and coral reefs. For many nature lovers, the lack of modern accommodation and eating facilities are only an added incentive. Tarutao and its neighbors, **Rawi** and **Adang** islands, are truly unspoiled bits of paradise.

Above: Fishing boats at rest in the harbor of Narathiwat. Right: Hauling in the nets.

There are more than 60 islands in the Marine Park, the first to have been established in Thailand. **Tarutao** is the largest in the group and is reached by boat from Pak Bara Wharf, north of Satun town. During the last war, this island was a penal colony for political exiles, and remnants of the old prison can still be visited at Talo Udang and Talo Waew Bay. Because the island is only inhabited by employees of the Royal Forestry Department, visitors may spend days in the dense forest with its spectacular waterfalls and wildlife, without encountering another human being.

The park headquarters are at **Phante Bay**, where some bungalows are available for rent. There are several campsites around the island but you have to bring your tent and camping gear. Reservations for bungalows can be made at the park office at Pak Bara pier.

The other islands, **Adang** and **Rawi**, also have camping facilities with streams running all year round, providing fresh water. For snorkelers and scuba divers,

Rawi is renowned for its long white sand beach and extensive coral reefs with an enormous variety of marine life. Situated 16 km west of Tarutao, some islands, particularly Ko Lee Peh, are home to a community of sea gypsies.

On the east coast, and 105 km from Hat Yai via Route 42, is **Pattani**, with Thailand's largest mosque, a symbol for all Thai Muslims. On the way south to Narathiwat, Patatimaw Beach has a long stretch of sand near the village of **Pase Yawyaw**, famous as a center for wooden boat building. The boats, called *kohlae*, are frequently painted in bright colors and can be seen all along the beaches, especially in Bang Nara fishing village north of town. **Narathiwat** also has some of the most beautiful beaches on the gulf coast.

Phra Buddha Taksin Ming Mongkol is a huge bronze Buddha, sitting at the top of Khao Kong hill, about 6 km south of town. The statue is 25 m high and the largest in Thailand. Further south along Route 4056 is **Sungai Kolok**, where the

road and railway cross the border into Malaysia. A very lively cross-border trade takes place here, with many Malaysians crossing the frontier to sample the seafood in Thailand, which happens to be more reasonably priced than in Malaysia.

Yala province, with its Betong District, runs further south than any other part of Thailand. The provincial capital is a spacious, well-planned town of wide streets, reflecting the prosperity of the area with its large rubber plantations.

About 8 km north of town is **Wat Khuha Phimuk** (also known as **Wat Na Tham**, the cave-front temple). This temple has a huge cave with a large reclining Buddha statue. Believed to date from the eights century, it is Srivijaya in style, and is regarded as one of the major monuments of southern Thailand.

South of town, towards Betong and the Malaysian border, is the **Than To waterfall park**. The falls come down seven spectacular levels, running through a park-like area which is very popular as a picnic ground.

THE SOUTH

Access and Transport

Transportation to the southern provinces of Thailand is fast and convenient, although distances from Bangkok are long and bus journeys can take 14 hours and more to reach Phuket and Krabi, and longer to the deep south. Trains take longer still, but sleepers make the journey more comfortable.

Buses: Several coaches leave Bangkok daily for all major points in the south. For details phone 411-4511, 411-0112 (for regular) and 411-4978/9 (for air-con buses). Private companies also operate various tours to Ranong, Surat Thani, Koh Samui and Krabi. (Tel:281-6939 or 281-2277).

Trains: Rail service to the South passes through Nakhon Pathom, Ratchaburi, Petchaburi, Prachuab Kirikhan, Chumphon, Surat Thani, Thung Song (where it joins lines to Nakhon Si Thammarat and Trang), Phattalung and Hat Yai. At Hat Yai the line intersects with the Padang Besar line, with another branch going to Sungai Kolok.

The distance from Bangkok to Sungai Kolok is 1,159 kms and Bangkok to Padang Besar, 990 kms. For departure times, reservations and fares call Rail Travel Information at Hualampong Station, Tel:223-7010, 223-7020.

Planes: Thai Airways International flies to Surat Thani, Phuket, Trang, Hat Yai, Pattani and Narathiwat. For schedules and fares call 280-0090 Ext. 761. Bangkok Airways, a private company, operates flights to Koh Samui and Phuket. For details phone 253- 4014/6.

Local Festivals

Some of the festivals common to the rest of Thailand, such as *Songkran* in April, and *Loi Krathong* in November, are celebrated with a southern slant. The *Sat Duen Sip*, the Festival of the 10th Lunar Month, is held over 15 days in September. *Chak Phra*, in mid-October celebrates the official end of the Buddhist Rains Retreat *(Phansa)* and, unlike the rest of the country, *Surat Thani* holds a dazzling waterborne procession that attracts many tourists. Also in mid-October is the *Samui* Festival on *Koh Samui*, featuring sporting events, bullfights and football matches between villages. *Lim Ko Nieo*, in Pattani, is usually held in March. The TAT offices in Bangkok, Surat Thani, Phuket, and Hat Yai have details of these and other lesser festivals, the dates of which vary each year, according to the lunar calendar.

CHUMPHON
Accommodation

MODERATE: **Pharadon Inn**, 180/12 Pharadon Rd, Tel:511-500; **Pornsawan Home**, 110 Mu 4, Pharadonshap Beach, Tel:521-521; **Chumphon Cabana**, Thung Wua Laen Beach, Tel:501-990.

Hospitals

General Hospital, Phisit Phayaban Rd, Tel:511-180.

Tourist Information

Chumphon Tourist Service Center, Tel:511-551; Chumphon Tourist Business Center, Pracha Uthit Rd, Tel:511-606.

Post / Telegraph Office

Paraminthara Mankha Rd, Tel:511-013.

RANONG
Accommodation

MODERATE: **Chansom Thara**, 2/10 Phetkasem Rd, Tel:811-511.

BUDGET: **Asia**, 39/9 Ruangrat Rd, Tel:811-113; **Sin Ranong**, 26/23-4 Ruangrat Rd, Tel:811-454; **Laem Son National Park Bungalows**, National Park Division in Bangkok, Tel:579-0529, 579-4842.

SURAT THANI
Accommodation

LUXURY: **Wang Tai**, Talat Mai Rd, Tel:273-410.
MODERATE: **Siam Thani**, Surat Phun Phin Rd, Tel:273-081; **Siam Thara**, Don Nok Rd, Tel:273-740.
BUDGET: **Muang Thong**, Na Muang Rd, Tel:272-960; **Muang Tai**, Talat Mai Rd, Tel:272-599.

Hospitals

Surat Thani, Surat-Phun Phin Rd, Tel:272-231; Taksin, Talat Mai Rd, Tel:273-239; **Bandon**, Na Muang Rd, Tel:271-767.

Restaurants

In Surat the best Thai-Chinese food can be found in eateries near the bus station and in the Chinese restaurants along Talaat Mai road.

Tourist Information

TAT office, 5 Talaat Mai Rd, Tel:281-828; **Songserm Travel**, Talaat Mai Rd, Tel:272-928; **South Wind Tour**, Talat Mai Rd, Tel:272-347.

KOH SAMUI
Accommodation

LUXURY: **The Imperial Samui**, Chaweng Beach, Tel:421-375; **Thong Sai Hotel** & Cottages, Thong Sai Cover, Tel:421-451; **Chaweng Resort**, Chaweng Beach, Tel:421-378; **Samui Pansea**, Chaweng Beach, 421-384.

MODERATE: **Aloha**, Lamai Beach, Tel:421-

418; **Nara Lodge**, Phra Yai Beach, Tel:421-364.
BUDGET: There is cheap accommodation to be found all over the island.

Tourist Information
Best Air Bookings, 88 Na Thon, Tel:421-093; Songserm Travel, 64/1-2 Na Thon, Tel:421-228; World Travel Service, 152/13 Na Thon, Tel:421-475.

NAKHON SI THAMMARAT
Accommodation
MODERATE: **Taksin**, 1584/23 Si Prad Rd, Tel:356-788; **Thai Hotel**, 1373-5 Rachasdamnoen Rd, Tel:356-451.
BUDGET: **New Sithong**, 1547/2-3 Yommarat Rd, Tel:356-357; **Muang Thong**, 1459/7-9 Chamroen Withi Rd, Tel:356-177.

Museums
Nakhon Si Thammarat National Museum, Ratchdamnoen Rd, opposite Wat Thao Khot. Extensive collection of Indian and southern Thai art.

Local Festivals
Chaak Phra Pak Tai is held in Nakhon Sri Thammarat in and around Wat Mahathat and includes shadow puppet theater.

SONGKHLA
Accommodation
LUXURY: **Samila**, 1 Ratchadamnoen Road, Tel:311-310. *MODERATE:* **Pavilion**, 17/1 Pratha Road, Tel:311-355; **Queen**, 20 Saiburi Rd, Tel:311-138.
BUDGET: **Songkhla**, 68-70 Wichianchom Road, Tel: 313-505; **Chokdi**, 14/19 Wichianchom Road, Tel: 311-158; **Wiang Sawan**, 156 Saiburi Road, Tel: 311-607.

HAT YAI
Accommodation
LUXURY: **Royal**, 106 Prachathipat Road, Tel: 232-162; **Regent**, 23 Prachathipat Road, Tel: 245-454; **Sincere**, 33/1 Phasawang 5 Road, Tel: 244-376; **Lee Gardens**, 1 Lee Phatthana Road, Tel: 245-888; **J.B.Hotel**, 99 Chuti-Anuson Road, Tel: 234-300; **Sukhonta**, 26 Sanehanuson Road, Tel: 243-999.
MODERATE: **Sakura**, 185/1 Niphat-Uthit 3 Road, Tel: 243-833; **Scala**, 43/42-3 Tanrattanakorn Road, Tel: 246-983; **Thep Nakhon**, 37 Pracharak Road, Tel: 245-161.
BUDGET: **Hat Yai**, 85/4 Saengsi Rd, Tel: 244-207; **King's**, 199 Niphat-Uthit Road, Tel: 243-966.

Post / Telegraph / Telephone
In Songkhla: Songkhla Telephone Exchange, corner of Tichianchom and Jana Roads.

In Hat Yai: Hat Yai General Post Office, Nipat Songkhro Rd, Tel:243-121; Por Natthapol Branch, Sriphuvanart Rd; Rattakarn Branch, Rattakarn Rd.

Restaurants
Songkhla's best restaurants (Thai and Chinese) are found on Nang Ngam Road, with **Ran Ahaan Tae** rated the best locally. **Black Gold Pub** on Sadao Rd. attracts foreign crews from off shore oil rigs.
In Hat Yai, the better restaurants can be found in the hotels. Muslim cooking is good at the **Muslim-O-Cha** opposite the King's Hotel.

Consulates
Songkhla: American Consulate, Sadao Rd, Tel:311-589; Malaysian General Consulate, 4 Sukhum Rd, Tel: 311-062.

Museums
The **Songkhla National Museum** in Rongmuang Road, houses many rare Thai art objects ranging from prehistoric to modern (open daily except Mon. & Tues. from 9:00 to 12:00 and 13:00 to 16:00).
National Institute of Coastal Aquaculture, 1 km south of Kao Seng, features fish museum & hatchery, Tel:311-895 for admission.
Wat Matchimawat Museum, Saiburi Road, has an interesting collection of ruins and artifacts from throughout the south.

Hospitals
Songkhla Hospital, 161 Ramvithi Road, Songkhla, Tel: 311-494.
Songkhla-Nakarin Hospital, Prince of Songkhla University, Tel: 245-677.
Mission Hospital, 14 Chokesamarn Road, Tel:243-139.
Hat Yai Hospital, Rattakarn Road, Tel:243-016.

Tourist Information
TAT office, Soi 2 Niphat-Uthit Road, Tel:243-747 (open seven days a week and holidays); Hat Yai-Songkhla Hotels Assoc, Laemthong Hotel, Hat Yai, Tammanoonwithi Road, Tel:244-433; Reservation counter at Hat Yai Airport, Tel: 244-145.

Local Transport
Useful numbers: **Hat Yai Railway Station**, Tel: 243-705; **Thai Airways International**, Tel: 245-851; **Bangkok Airways**, Tel: 212-341.
For transport between Songkhla and Hat Yai use the green buses No. 1871, which leave every 30 min. Fare is 7 baht. Taxis carrying 7 passengers are 12 baht but you will have to wait until the taxi is filled.
Within the two towns, *tuk-tuks* or minibuses operate in Hat Yai, while 3-wheeled motor-samlors carry passengers in Songkhla.

A CULINARY ADVENTURE

Bangkok's reputation as one of the world's great eating cities is so well established that many travelers arrive at Don Muang airport, wondering just where to dig in first. As they leave the airport and head into town, the question of where to start sampling the food only gets tougher. At the hotel, elaborate signs and posters sing a siren song about the offerings at the Thai, French, Chinese or Japanese restaurants right on the premises. Then, a quick flip through the newspaper the hotel has provided, turns up a flurry of ads for restaurants featuring food from all over the world.

But most alluring of all is something really food-alert travelers will have noticed from the moment of their arrival in Bangkok: every road and lane seems to have sections lined with noodle stands, curry vendors, Chinese boiled rice shops and other small, informal restaurants of all kinds – and almost all doing a booming business. Are these very basic-looking, but obviously highly popular places, clean? Will those succulent-looking duck noodles, costing 15 per cent of the same dish sold at the hotel, send you straight to the hospital and sabotage your vacation?

Let's start with the hotel restaurants. Bangkok's first-class hotels will rarely disappoint anyone who is not bent on having a ruthlessly authentic Thai-style culinary adventure. All have very good Thai food, but it tends toward standard dishes, prepared in a conservative style. Best of the lot is the Spice Market at the Regent Hotel of Bangkok, expensive but authentic. Still, the elegantly-prepared Thai cuisine served there is special occasion stuff, different from what most Thai people eat every day.

Preceding pages: Soldiers during a religious rite. Colorful life on a floating market. Right: Street markets brim with fresh fruits and vegetables.

Anyone in the mood for Western food is in real luck though, as there are wonders to be had at such legendary places as the Oriental's Normandie, where French cuisine is prepared by visiting superstar chefs, flown in from France. First-class Chinese and Japanese food is also represented at the hotels, by the Dusit Thani Hotel's Mayflower and the Hilton's Genji, just to name two. Needless to say, these places are expensive, even by European standards.

Most visitors, however, will want to get out of their hotels and start sampling the city's independent restaurants, and here the possibilities for exploring are endless. There are many places specializing in fine Western cuisine and in the food of other Asian countries, but the main attraction is, of course, Thai food.

One of the most indestructible myths is the one about all Thai food being unpalatably hot and too spicy for the non-initiated. In fact, most Thai dishes are not peppery at all, and there are many Thais who give the more aggressive preparations a wide berth. The term "Thai cooking" incorporates numerous regional cuisines, the major sub-divisions being central, northern, northeastern and southern. There are also Chinese and Muslim influenced food branches.

Hottest of all are some of the southern dishes, particularly two notorious curries, *kaeng lueang* (yellow curry) and *kaeng tai plaa* (fish kidney curry). Both are thin curries, made without coconut cream (the Thai word for curry, *kaeng*, covers a wide range of dishes, some of which would be called soups in English). When prepared in the authentic southern style, both are so fiery that they should be avoided by any but the most intrepid culinary adventurer. Even diners who have no difficulty getting them down may have problems later from stomachs not prepared to deal with such an onslaught.

Food from the central region is sweeter and less spicy, and many of the most

popular Thai specialities, *kaeng khiao waan* (the thick, grey-green curry made from chicken, beef or shrimp), *tom yam kung* (hot-sour shrimp soup) and the hotter *kai phad bai kraphrao* (chicken stir-fried with hot chillies, garlic and sweet basil), are central region standards.

Northern food includes numerous Burmese-influenced dishes, like the famous noodle-and-curry soup called *khao soi* and the excellent pork curry called *kaeng hangleh*. Northeastern cooking, which comes basically from Laos, is completely different. Formerly considered peasant cuisine, it is now very much in vogue. The hot and sour meat, chicken or fish dish, called *laab*, is a universal favorite, and the nuclear-strength raw papaya salad, *som tam*, has recently even established itself abroad. Any of these regional specialities can most likely be had within a few blocks of wherever you happen to be when you get hungry in Bangkok. Restaurants of all types can be found virtually everywhere.

Fanciest and safest are the beautifully furnished, comparatively expensive Thai restaurants, that offer classical Thai cuisine prepared from old recipes. Dining rooms of this type have proliferated over the past few years, as they have found an enthusiastic clientele.

Although these places are intended primarily for Thai patrons – no concession is made to tender tongues in cooking the spicier dishes – resident foreigners and tourists lucky enough to happen on them are also regular patrons. The Lemon Grass Restaurant on Sukhumvit Soi 24, any one of the Kham Waan restaurants (perhaps the one on Soi Saladaeng) and the Baan Chiang Restaurant off Silom Road's Soi Pramuan are all good examples of this type of place, and all have English-language menus.

But even with fine places like this all over town, many will be unable to resist the thousands of small, open restaurants and food stalls that fill the city. Some of the best food is sold by these sometimes tiny, unprepossessing, shops, and hunting out unusually good ones is something of

a national pastime. Telltale signs that there is a good foodshop nearby include great squadrons of Mercedes Benz, Jaguars and Volvos parked in a side street where they don't seem to belong – this, however, can also signal the presence of a gambling den or worse – or crowds of people filling the tables at a small shop a half hour before lunch hour.

If you decide to try out one of these open restaurants, be sure to take the obvious precautions. Choose a well-scrubbed, well-lit one and you will almost never have to worry about stomach trouble due to insanitary conditions. Thais are extremely fastidious when it comes to the preparation of food, and dirty kitchens are not usual.

Beware of extremely bizarre or gamy ingredients, however taken you may be by the idea of experimenting with insect-based exotica or fermented crabs or fish. Some things that any Thai child can eat

Above: A scrumptious delicacy – fried locusts.

with impunity may lay you out flat for weeks with gastroenteritis. Most restaurant personnel will warn you about foods that will cause you problems.

When ordering beverages, make sure that the ice cubes are clear, with holes running through them. This means that they were made from purified, specially processed water, and not ordinary tap-water. Cold Chinese tea is always safe to drink, but make sure that the plain drinking water served to you comes from a closed bottle. Sweets and snacks bought by the roadside are fine if you can actually see them being prepared, as is most often the case.

Once you have decided on a promising-looking Thai restaurant, make the most of it by ordering your meal in the traditional style, taking a variety of contrasting dishes that complement each other. Such a selection will usually include a hot curry or a spicy soup; a stir-fried dish, a salad-like, hot-sour dish of the *yam* type and, for sure, a *nam phrik* with raw vegetables and fish. *Nam phrik* are pepper sauces and pastes that run the gamut of tastes and textures. They are among the most ancient of Thai foods and show the genius of Thai cuisine in its purest form.

All of the dishes are placed on the table at the same time, and each diner is given a plateful of rice. Each person will then take a spoonful of one dish or another, place it on top of his plate of rice, and eat it. Then, perhaps, he will help himself to another dish, then another so that the various foods are allowed to enhance each other.

Remember that Thai food is not eaten with chopsticks, but with a spoon and fork. The spoon – a large one – is held in the right hand and the fork in the left. The bottom of the fork is used to push food in a direction away from the body and into the spoon, which remains in the right hand when the food is lifted to the mouth. When a diner has finished, he should place spoon and fork in roughly a 4:20 clockface position on his plate to indicates that he has had enough, and no more food will be offered. If the utensils are placed in another position, he may be offered another serving.

Chopsticks are used only for eating Chinese dishes, including the ubiquitous lunchtime favorites belonging to the *kuay tiao* (rice-based) and *mii* (wheat-based) noodle families.

There are a few basic table manners it is wise to observe. Do not allow rice to fall off the side of your plate, and when helping yourself to one of the dishes on the table, use a serving spoon, rather than the one you are eating with. Loud talk or flamboyant behavior is not considered proper at the table. Almost all foods are eaten with fork and spoon, not with the hands.

When scanning Thai menus, there are a few recurrent terms that may cause confusion. Here are some rough definitions:

Kaeng – literally curry, but in reality the term includes a wide variety of liquid and semi-liquid dishes that range from Indian-type curries to clear, mild soups containing vermicelli "glass" noodles and vegetables.

Yam – a hot and sour salad-like dish, which usually contains some form of meat and fish, cut fairly fine and mixed with hot chillies, lime juice, sliced onions, fresh coriander, fish sauce and other seasonings, and served on lettuce.

Tom yam – a hot-sour soup containing shrimp, chicken or fish plus lime juice, chillies, Kaffir lime leaf, lemon grass and other seasonings.

Tom khaa – a thicker soup made from chicken or, less commonly, seafood plus coconut cream, lime juice, lemon grass, mushrooms, Kaffir lime leaf and other seasonings.

Phad bai kraphrao – a potent stir-fried dish in which meat, chicken or seafood is fried with chopped garlic, hot chillies, fresh basil and other seasonings. The chicken version is often served with a fried egg on top.

Phad phed – literally "fried hot" – meat, chicken or seafood fried with chillies and seasonings.

Tawt krathiem phrik Thai – fried with garlic and black pepper. Most common with shrimp and pork.

Yang (pronounced yahng) – broiled *phad khrueang kaeng* – fried with curry paste as seasoning.

Khanom – sweets and desserts (bread is also classed as a *khanom*).

Phrik nam plaa – fish sauce with chopped hot chillies mixed in. The standard Thai table seasoning.

Nam phrik – a class of pepper sauces made from chillies, dried or fresh, and a broad range of other types of ingredients. The textures can range from thin liquids to pastes to coarse, dry concoctions, and the flavors from sweet and aromatic to fiery hot. All are eaten together with vegetables – either raw, steamed or blanched – and perhaps fish that is usually fried.

TOM YAM KUNG

Spicy, sour *tom yam kung* is one Thai soup that has made a name for itself all over the world. Any diner who has tried out a Thai restaurant or two in New York, London, Paris, Düsseldorf or any other large city, has most likely tasted it and visitors to the Land of Smiles will have eaten it on more than one occasion. But defining or even describing this potent dish is far from easy.

Like so many favorite Thai dishes, the preparation of *tom yam kung* is much more a question of culinary intuition and taste than of adherence to any specific recipe. Most good Thai cooks have a fairly personal idea of how it should look and taste, and thus a diner who sets out to sample the versions served at three diffe-rent good Thai restaurants, will find that

Above: Thai cuisine – a blend of carefully chosen flavors and textures. Right: F,ast food in Bangkok.

they differ far more than three different servings of coquilles St Jacques.

Of course, there are "musts". Any bowl of *tom yam kung* must have plenty of whole shrimp in it, plus enough lime juice to make it sour and enough of the tiny, ferociously hot chillies called *phrik kii nuu* to make it hot. This spicy heat, by the way, is one of the variables. Some like their *tom yam kung* to be only a bit nippy. Others want it so hot that unsus-pecting diners who only sample it will still be breathing through their teeth half an hour later.

Besides the shrimp, lime and chillies, there is almost always Kaffir lime leaf and fragrant lemon grass, both intended only to flavor the soup, like bay leaves in a stew, not to be eaten. A well-made *tom yam kung* will also contain a good num-ber of fresh straw mushrooms, cooked only briefly so that they still retain their firm texture. Finally, enough fish sauce is added to salt the soup to taste, and fresh coriander is put in at the last moment as a garnish.

That is what goes into the soup at its most basic and unadorned, but in Thailand a lot of creativity goes into dressing it up. There are many varieties of shrimp and prawns, and some of the costly versions of *tom yam kung* use the large tiger prawns, cut into pieces and with heads included, so the surface of the soup is red with prawn fat, called *man kung* in Thai. Many local foodlovers particularly esteem this version, which is quite a rich soup, somewhat thick from the *man kung* and with many large chunks of white prawn meat, which is reminiscent of lobster.

Other frequent extras are various pepper sauces and pastes of the type known in Thai as *nam phrik*. The chilli paste most frequently used in making *tom yam kung* is called *nam phrik phao*, a sweet and rather mild preparation.

It is made by roasting a great quantity of fresh garlic until it is soft and fairly well burned, then pounding it with large, sweet-hot chillies, which have also been roasted, together with shrimp paste and

various other ingredients. A spoonful of *nam phrik phao* gives *tom yam kung* an appetising color and aroma as well a slight sweetness.

Cooks who want to embellish the basic *tom yam kung* recipe can also do it by adding other types of vegetables – baby corn has been turning up more frequently these days – and varying the seasonings.

Tom yam kung is just one of a whole class of soups called *tom yam*. All have the same sour-hot taste, but instead of shrimp, variants may be based on chicken or various types of fish and fish parts. There is even a vegetarian version which uses just mushrooms. All exist in many varieties, benefiting from the personal approach that is built into Thai cuisine, and which makes every meal a new and unforpettable adventure.

The currently fashionable ready-made *tom yam* cubes, although inexpensive and convenient to use, are just not the real thing. In fact, no real Thai food freak will touch them. So you better ask for their advice.

199

EXPLORING CHINATOWN

To explore Chinatown is by no means a leisurely stroll. For that it would be too crowded and usually too hot. But there is no need to be scared off. This colorful, noisy part is one of Bangkok's major wholesale and retail areas and has much to offer shoppers and browsers alike. Its attractions do not only include endless selection of goods, foodstuffs and eateries, but also the colorful crowds, the lively trading scenes, the old-fashioned buildings and things Chinese in general.

Chinatown, or rather the busiest part of it, is roughly bounded by **Songsawat** in the east, **Charoen Krung** in the north, **Chakraphet** in the west and **Songwat** in the south. Its main arteries are **Charoen Krung, Yaowaraj** and **Sampeng Lane**, intersected by **Chakrawat** and **Ratchawong**. In reality, the Chinese are found everywhere, but this is the biggest concentration and retains much of its ethnic flavor.

The district was, however, not the original Chinese settlement in Bangkok. In 1782, when King Rama I founded the Chakri dynasty and its capital, the Chinese quarter was moved south from its original site, to make way for the construction of the Grand Palace. The new community, known as Sampeng, settled on the waste lands and swamps between Wat Samprueng and Wat Sampeng. Being close to the river and main canals, Sampeng became a bustling trading center, specializing in imported foodstuffs and general merchandise from China. The shopping area later spread inland and, during the construction boom in the reign of Rama V, spilled over into Yaowaraj, Charoen Krung and Songwat.

Even a first-time visitor would recognize Chinatown instantly from the telltale Chinese characters on signboards and advertisements that appear everywhere in the district. **Yaowaraj Road** once boasted the city's highest buildings. A seven-storey hotel and entertainment center, widely known as **Tuek Jed Chan**, used to be the tallest building in the city, and the talk of the town.

Walking with the one-way traffic, coming from **Wat Traimit**, one will find a number of shops selling sunglasses, watches and clocks, old-fashioned drug stores selling traditional Chinese medicines, run-down teahouses and gambling dens. There are Chinese opera buildings, which, their popularity on the wane, have been turned into third-class movie houses. Their former fans have turned to watching videos or wait for overseas troupes, who stage performances once or twice a year.

Grimy-looking old eating houses, offering such Chinese delicacies as shark fin soup, abalone, goose feet and bird nests, are pricing themselves out of the market, the common folk preferring the wide variety of much cheaper noodle and *dim sum* shops in the area.

A walk through Talad Kao on the left, and Talad Mai on the right of Yaowaraj is quite an experience. Built in 1847, **Talad Kao** offers large supplies of fresh and dried fish, shrimp, squid, fish innards etc., while the lane to **Talad Mai** is lined with stalls of fresh produce and strange looking Chinese foodstuffs such as a large selection of pickles and preserved food, assorted fish balls, sea cucumbers, different types of tofu or soybean curds and so forth. Further down the main road, several shops are selling the delicious *Gun Chieng* (Chinese sausage), *Moo Pan* (sweet, sliced, crispy, grilled pork) and *Moo Yong* (dried, shredded pork). Yaowaraj has long been known for its gold shops, where the precious metal is sold in any shape, form, size or weight. Some of these shops are over 100 years old and scrupulously honest. The original **Tang Toh Gang** gold shop has been in a back lane off Yaowaraj longer than anyone can remember. The Roman style building with its barred windows, slow-turning

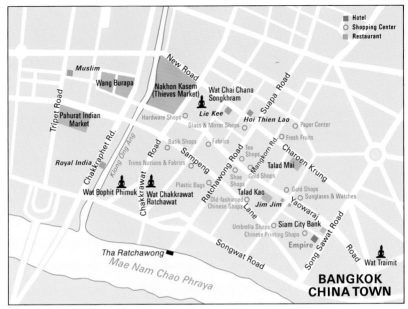

Map legend:
■ Hotel
○ Shopping Center
■ Restaurant

BANGKOK CHINA TOWN

ceiling fans and the large marble-top table, where customers help themselves to fresh green tea, still retains the charm of the old days.

Sampeng Lane runs through a crowded jumble of shops and stalls that sell virtually everything – from junk to the necessary. The most frenetic yet intriguing part of the lane starts at **Thanon Mangkorn**, crosses **Ratchawong** and continues towards **Pahurat**. The section between Mangkorn and Ratchawong specializes in wholesale plastic goods, toys, towels, socks, underwear, stationery and fashion accessories, many of which are sold in the city's fashionable department stores at several times the price.

After the Ratchawong crossing, T-shirts and ready-to-wear items are sold at irresistible prices. But predominating are fabrics sold by the yard or complete bolts. Drapery stores are found at **Sapan Han** with an amazing array of harberdashery goods. Those with a sweet tooth will drool at the heaps of aromatic, mouthwatering Khanom Thai and

candied and glacé fruit. Around the corner of **Chakraphet Road** are shops selling kitchen utensils, baking and confectionery ingredients. Across Chakraphet is **Pahurat**, a wide street with hundreds of Indian shops, selling any imaginable type of cloth and fabric at unbeatable prices.

Klong Ong Ang, between the upper end of Yaowarah and Charoen Krung, is a small canal, lined with cramped, little shops and stalls, selling second hand goods and smuggled stereos, cameras, cassette players and video machines. It is also known for its pet fish stalls, where colorful tropical fish, expensive fancy carp, fighting fish, aquatic plants, live and dry fish food and anything fish-lovers may need, are sold.

A hundred meters from Klong Ong Ang is **Nakhon Kasem**, the former Thieves Market, where you will find brass gongs, drums, ice-cream machines, grinders, lanterns and any musical instrument you can think of. Antiques used to be the main trade here, but only half a

dozen of the old antique dealers are still in business. Some of their shops are over 100 years old.

Klong Thom, one block down from Krung Kasem, is the place to buy electrical appliances. Washing machines, fans, ovens, toasters, microwaves and ice boxes of any type and size are found here. Less serious shoppers mass around the sidewalk stalls like bees, examining or bargaining over tools, mechanical gadgets, car parts and accessories, audiovisual equipment, battery-powered toys, wristwatches and pocket calculators.

Charoen Krung, a road built in 1861, was then Bangkok's largest and longest thoroughfare, and remained so until the 1930s. With the presence of well-established Western companies – the proprietors, unlike the vendors in Sampeng, were wealthy business tycoons – the road became the center of local and international trade. Old buildings in Roman

Above: Chinese festival at the wholesale market.

202

and art deco style can still be found along Charoen Krung Road.

A real curiosity is the shops around **Wat Leng Nei Yi**, selling money, gold lumps, clothes, houses, cars, electrical appliances, housemaids and chauffeurs - all made of paper, mind you – for religious ceremonial use. Further down the road on the right hand side are the shops catering to bridal couples, selling everything needed for a Chinese wedding, and, right across the street, coffin makers display their strangely shaped bulky products. A visit to Wat Leng Nei Yi, known in Thai as **Wat Mangkorn Kamal**, is a fitting finale to a trip through Chinatown. It was the first Chinese temple in Thailand, built by Chinese Buddhists. Regular buses passing through Chinatown are Nos 1, 4, 11, 25, 40, 53, 73, 75 and the airconditioned Nos 1 and 7. Note that the main thoroughfares, Yaowaraj and Charoen Krung, have one-way traffic, but in opposite directions. And don't forget: in Chinatown bargaining is the name of the game.

THE THAI MASSAGE

A couple of hours inside one of Bangkok's numerous massage establishments is for many visitors the most sensuous part of a trip to Thailand. Massage parlors here are unique, many of them being colossal emporia, staffed by hundreds of masseuses. They are multi-million baht businesses with modern, computerized accounting systems and most accept the full range of credit cards.

Their clientele invariably consists of Thai men, starting, or finishing off, an evening out with friends. For them, an hour or two among soap suds, soothing away aches and pains, is just one aspect of the entertainment scene.

Embarking on your first massage in Thailand, you are in for a truly memorable experience. But before venturing inside a massage parlor, one needs to realize that in Bangkok, a "wash and a rub down" can take many forms.

What most newcomers understand as a massage, is the "traditional Thai massage", to be recommended after running a race or a hard game of tennis. It is for the unambitious and falls short of the total Bangkok massage experience. Expect to pay between 150-250 baht an hour for a standard physical massage.

Regular patrons soon learn to ask for a "B-course" massage, involving a wide range of lotions, potions and creams, which the masseuse applies before using every inch of her body to massage yours. Regulars describe the sensation like getting into a bath tub filled with live eels.

A B-course massage, costing between 800 and 1,000 baht for one and a half to two hours, begins with the selection of a masseuse from among hundreds sitting on tiered rows of seats behind one-way mirrors in the lobby.

Each girl wears a numbered badge, and once you have made your choice, the manager will call her out. If you are in the know, or are a frequent customer, a B-course will cost between 500 and 750 baht. In this case you will have to negotiate any extras with the masseuse directly. For this reason, it is perhaps preferable to pay the all-in B-course fee of 800-1,000 baht, just to avoid any misunderstandings.

The bill is then paid at the cashier's counter, before the masseuse and her companion retire to one of the many rooms, invariably equipped with a large bath and a bed, and often decorated with colored lights, television, strategically placed mirrors and wall size posters.

After a hot bath with lots of bubbles (the masseuse will join you in the tub for this) she will ask you to lie down on an inflated rubber mattress. At this point the body massage proper begins. While applying liberal quantities of liquid soap, she proceeds to give a "massage" by using her entire body, rather than just her hands.

If you are in the market for a real top-of-the-range B-course massage, opt for what is known as a "Sandwich". This involves two slippery girls instead of just one, but expect to pay twice as much for the ultimate Bangkok massage.

Well, not quite ultimate. Although many of the larger massage parlors have several hundred girls, they also have a dozen or so "stars". These girls command a fee of 1,200 to 2,000 baht for their services. They have not risen to the top of their profession by coincidence, but are real experts, well worth their fee.

The parlor's stars will be pointed out to you on request, and often sit separately from the rest of the girls. In some establishments, blouses or badges are color-coded, so regular customers can differentiate between the different categories of the masseuses.

There are scores of massage parlors with many of the finer ones situated on Petchburi Road. For a long list, consult the Yellow Pages in the phone book. The rest is up to you.

GETTING ABOUT BY BOAT

To save time and avoid at least some of the pollution, delays and frustration of Bangkok's interminable traffic snarls, it is worth considering travel by boat. It is quick, comfortable and inexpensive.

Whether you merely want a shortcut to the **Grand Palace**, the **Temple of Dawn** *(wat arun)* or the **Royal Barge Museum** from any of the major hotels along the Chao Phraya, or desire to savor the timeless ambience of a bygone age, the River of Kings is the pathway to convenience and some unforgettable sights.

Unmatched is the breathtaking vision from across the river of **Wat Arun** at dawn, as a myriad sparkling reflections from the porcelain insets of King Taksin's soaring monument dazzle the eye in the first rays of the tropical sun. Another memorable sight from a boat is the Grand Palace complex, as the sunset gilds its

Above: A merchant with his boat in the klongs of Thonburi.

whitewashed walls and sets its multitude of majestic spires aglitter.

In addition to enjoying the otherwise hidden views of Bangkok and the jungles, plantations and vegetable farms of outlying Thon Buri, travelers can plot adventures farther afield, to the Summer Palace at Ayutthaya and the famous floating market at Damnoen Saduak.

For centuries, freighters from around the world have sailed up the Chao Phraya as far as the river's depth allowed, and dropped anchor to discharge cargo onto barges, lighters and other local craft for the trip upriver to Ayutthaya, the former capital of Siam.

When King Rama I began building his new capital at Bangkok in 1782, boats were the only means of access to the site, and the many canals, locally known as *klongs*, served as transport lanes for the boatloads of brick, salvaged from the ruins of Ayutthaya, used to build the city's ramparts.

As late as the 1930s, on account of Bangkok's almost total dependence on the river and the city's numberless canals, the capital was internationally known as the "Venice of the East". Regretfully, as land transportation developed, many of the *klongs* were filled in, to become Bangkok's emerging road system. The city's water culture faded back into the shadows of Thai history.

It did not disappear, however, and visitors today can still see more than a reflection of what once was the dominant feature of Bangkok's landscape. It's well worth the small effort, for the majestic Chao Phraya and the countless *klongs* of the area reveal glimpses of Thailand which other modes of transportation can never match.

Local River Buses and Taxis

The red-and-white diesel-powered express boats, holding 30 or more persons, cruise daily at frequent intervals along the river. The fare for short trips varies from 3-5 baht, and for 7 baht only visitors can enjoy a 45-minute cruise through the peaceful and picturesque countryside to Nonthaburi, Bangkok's northern neighbor.

Operating from about 6:00 to 18:00, and stopping at the Oriental Hotel and other points of interest along both banks, they offer an easy and comfortable alternative to taxis, *tuk-tuks* and buses, along with glimpses of the typical riverside life which you should not miss to experience: children playing in the water while their mothers cook or wash clothes nearby, unusual-shaped temples, houses and buildings from another era, and even Thai kick- boxers, working out at the riverside Kittikasem Boxing Camp.

From most landings a fleet of small cross-river ferries carry passengers to the other side for only half a baht a ride. Service is sporadic but adequate and starts at 6:00 and ends at midnight. These boats offer few creature comforts, but the price is right.

For the stout-hearted, nothing beats the thrill of crouching in a gaily painted longtail boat, to escape a drenching from the constant spray, as the slender shallow-draft vessel, with its 2-m propeller shaft, races along the river, bucking wildly as it punches through the mild swells from larger craft. For about 200 baht per hour, these boats, called *rua hang yao*, can be hired at most landings, and will take you along the river or go exploring the many *klongs*.

For a pleasant as well as scenic evening meal, take one of the many restaurant boats which cruise the Chao Phraya and some of the larger *klongs* at sunset, serving drinks and dinner, while Bangkok fades quietly into the twilight. The cooling breezes and the sight of night descending on the city make it an ideal way to unwind, before diving into Bangkok's exciting nightlife.

The top-of-the-line dining experience is the Oriental Hotel's dinner cruise on the Oriental Queen, or some similar service offered by several other companies. Delicious opportunities abound at a number of less expensive restaurants up and down the river, especially in the vicinity of the Grand Palace. Reservations are generally required, and most tour agencies have full particulars on all the popular spots.

The Klongs, a Different World.

Close behind the relatively narrow strip of densely populated land on the Thonburi side of the Chao Phraya River, and along an extensive and tangled network of canals, lies a sequestered world, where time seems to have stopped – a world of lush tropical jungle, coconut plantations, vegetable farms and the life style of another century.

Modestly priced excursions into this old-world charm on some of the larger *klongs* can be arranged easily, by renting one of the clumsy, but comfortable con-

verted rice barges, available near the **Maharaj Landing** behind Wat Mahathat, or just off the veranda of the Oriental Hotel. Since these old boats are too large to enter the smaller *klongs*, especially at low tide, intrepid sightseers may prefer to go by the smaller longtail boats, which run regular routes from terminals near the Grand Palace and Memorial Bridge. It is also possible to hire longtail boats in the vicinity of Maharaj Landing for longer periods and cruise the *klongs* at your leisure.

Bang Pa-in and the Floating Market

Considered a "must" by many visitors to Thailand are river trips to the celebrated Summer Palace of **Bang Pa-in** and the nearby ruins of **Ayutthaya**, as well as to the Floating Market at **Damnoen Saduak** outside Bangkok.

Above: These monks are on an excursion on the Mekong River. Right: A longtail boat with a head of steam on the Chao Phraya.

The most comfortable and convenient way to see Ayutthaya and Bang Pa-in is the approximately 750-baht guided tour from the Oriental Hotel. Early each morning airconditioned buses and the luxurious Oriental Queen cruiser take visitors to Siam's once glorious capital and the enchanting Summer Palace not far away.

Sightseers can choose to go by one means of transport and return by the other. Both ways are delightful, but best is going by bus to see Ayutthaya and Bang Pa-in during the cool morning hours, then returning by the airconditioned cruiser, feasting on the Oriental Queen's lavish buffet.

The cruiser stops briefly at **Bang Sai**, a traditional handicraft center, built with the support of Queen Sirikit, where visitors can watch Thai artisans at work and buy authentic handicraft products. The boat also pauses at the **Wat Pai Lom** sanctuary for a glimpse of the rare, open-billed storks during nesting season. These birds arrive in December and return to

their native Bangladesh in June. Buses and crusier return to the Oriental Hotel by about 18:00.

Also available, and at a cheaper price, is a weekly 140-baht boat trip, leaving at 8:00 on Sundays and most public holidays from **Maharaj Landing**. Be sure to take along some refreshments, for the boat lacks the amenities of the Oriental Queen. The passengers, mostly Thais on holiday, are usually in a festive mood and pass the four-hour upriver cruise in socially congenial activities. After a two-hour stopover at **Bang Pa-in** for lunch and a visit to this uniquely harmonious blend of Chinese, Thai and nineteenth century European architecture, the boat begins its return tour, with a pause at Bang Sai before arriving at Maharaj Landing at about 17:30.

A memorable experience of a different kind is a visit to the early-morning Floating Market at **Damnoen Saduak** outside Bangkok. Be very sure to specify Damnoen Saduak when talking with travel or tour agents, or you may end up at the ves-

tigial "floating market" near Wat Arun. You won't regret the effort to get to Damnoen Saduak. Just at daybreak literally hundreds of tiny boats, paddled by peasant women, meet in an area where numerous small *klongs* intersect, hawking their cargo of flowers, fruit, vegetables and a host of prepared foods and sweets from boat to boat. Bargains abound and there is a holiday air, as vendors and buyers exchange pleasantries. By 10:00, most goods have been sold or traded, and only a few unlucky stragglers remain.

Because market activities start early, and Damnoen Saduak is a two-hour bus trip from Bangkok, it is probably best to visit the Floating Market as part of a full day guided tour, which also includes lunch and visits to such attractions as the **Rose Garden** and the world's tallest *chedi* at **Nakhon Pathom**.

For details of the many sights along the Chao Phraya River, a small book, *Bangkok Waterways* by William Warren, is of great assistance.

PRECIOUS STONES CAPITAL

Bangkok is a gem of a city. It captivates the imagination with dazzling, kaleidoscopic sights. In a more literal sense it is a place for gems. As any visitor with an eye for a bargain quickly discovers, the Thai capital is also a gemstone capital. It is a shopper's paradise for all kinds of precious stones, especially the finest quality rubies and sapphires.

Jewelry shops are the most visible indications of what is now one of Thailand's major foreign exchange earners. In 1987 gems and jewelry exports were valued at 19,695 million baht, while the figure increased to 23,666 million baht the year after. Today the country is the world's second-largest exporter of gems and jewelry, and the industry is now confidently eyeing the number one slot.

The most important gems – and the best buys – are rubies and sapphires which are found in the east coast provinces of Chanthaburi and Trat. Here, close to the Cambodian border some 300 km southeast of Bangkok, miners work between 25 and 30 productive gem fields.

Mining is crude but effective. Mechanical diggers tear up the lush green countryside to expose the gem-bearing gravel, which is then washed out of the ground by high-pressure hoses. The resulting slush is passed over a jig, or vibrating table, which separates the rocks and mud from the gravel and gems. A final washing and sorting by hand reveals – maybe nothing or, hopefully, a scattering of the dull red or blue stones that are rough rubies or sapphires.

Brilliant though Thai stones are, the phenomenal success of the gem and jewelry industry has not depended solely on local production. Increasingly, as Bangkok consolidates its reputation as one of the world's leading colored gem

Left: A ruby miner in Chantaburi province.

centers, rough stones of every kind are being imported for cutting.

In a comparatively short time the Thai cutters have become highly skilled and turn out quality work on a par with that of European and American craftsmen. "Thais are born cutters. They have an amazing eye for the job," comments one American gem dealer.

Developing slightly more slowly has been jewelry manufacture although this, too, is now much more sophisticated than it was only a few years ago. Specifically, designs are today more creative and more in keeping with international styles and tastes. Proof of this is seen in Thai designers winning prizes in international jewelry competitions.

To the delight of the shopper, the growth of the gem business has been paralleled by rapid development of Bangkok's retail facilities. The last few years have seen smart shopping plazas spring up in various quarters of the city, and these have been complemented by an increase in the number of deluxe hotels, where quality shopping arcades are integral features. In all such places jewelry stores are prominent.

You will likely hear of gems being heat treated, a process which can enhance color and clarity. Although controversial, it is not a fraudulent process and merely produces what could have happened in nature. "For all practical purposes," says an established gem dealer, "you should look upon treatments as part of the fashioning of gemstones from their original rough state. They should not be seen in a negative way as long as the treatment process is permanent."

When it comes to shopping, the first thing to remember is to exercise a little common sense in choosing a jewelry store. Indicators of a reliable establishment include location (smart or otherwise); whether or not the shop sells gems and jewelry exclusively is it a member of a trade association; does its staff appear

knowledgeable; is the shop assistant prepared to point out a stone's weakness as well as strengths, or does he or she make an obvious sales pitch.

These and similar common sense considerations will tell you whether a shop has a good reputation to maintain. There are, of course, no guarantees, and if you are doubtful about a particular stone, you can get it independently tested at the Asian Institute of Gemological Sciences on Silom Road.

Above all when you are in a jewelry store, take your time and never, never let a sales assistant pressure you into making a purchase. Don't be afraid to say you need time to consider, to consult your husband, wife or whatever.

To judge prices, it is essential that you shop around and compare (but do not confuse "oranges with apples"). Only in this way can you accurately gauge what

Above: Jeweller selling rubies mined in the village of Bo Rai. Right: Blue ceramics made at Ratpuri.

the standard price levels are. Remember that there are no bargains with gems; "good" and "cheap" just do not go together in the gem world. The big advantage of Bangkok is that prices are more competitive here than elsewhere.

One thing to bear in mind is that ruby prices rise disproportionately to weight because of the greater rarity of large stones. Thus a one-carat ruby will be valued at, say, 1,000 units, while a two-carat stone of comparable quality will be worth 2,000 units per carat, a three-carat stone 4,000 units per carat and so on. Sapphire prices rise less steeply.

When it comes to judging an individual gem, there are no short cuts and no one can become an instant expert – that is why you need to have trust in your jeweler. Nevertheless there is the basic guideline of what is popularly called "the four Cs" – color, clarity, cut and carat weight.

Color consists of three elements: hue, the color itself; intensity, the brightness or vividness of the color; and, thirdly,

tone, the lightness or darkness of the color. As a general rule you should judge color by its distribution – it should be evenly distributed over the entire stone. There should also be high intensity, while the tone should be neither too dark nor too light, the ideal being around 75 to 85 on a scale where zero equals clear and 100 equals black.

Clarity refers to the "purity" or "cleanness" of a stone, the relative lack of surface blemishes and internal inclusions (cracks, foreign particles etc). Some inclusions are inevitable as they are the stone's natural birthmarks, though ideally they should not be visible to the naked eye. When checking clarity, remember SNLTC, which stands for the inclusions' size (the smaller the better); number (the fewer the better); location (away from the face of the stone); type (the least ugly – a crack, for example, is worse than a pinpoint inclusion); and color (no inclusion should be so contrasting as to detract from the stone's overall color).

Cut relates to a stone's proportions and the quality of its cutting. A gem is basically a mirror and its color is assessed by reflected light – the stone's brilliance – which is released by correct proportions and proper cutting. There should be no "windows", areas where light falls right through without being reflected. The ideal proportion is a depth of 60 per cent, plus or minus 10 per cent, of the diameter. The main tip here is to avoid flat stones. They may look more impressive because of the size of the face, but their brilliancy may not be as good as that of a smaller but deeper gem.

Finally there is carat weight and this is obviously dictated by your budget. The best advice is to buy the best you can afford, but if you have to come down in price, go down in carat weight not in quality (ie the other three Cs).

Ultimately, as long as the materials used in a piece of jewelry are as represented, you are the best and final judge. Like a work of art, gems and jewelry should be selected for their aesthetic value, as objects of lasting beauty.

THE THAI MONARCHY

On July 2, 1988, Thailand's present king, His Majesty King Bhumibol Adulyadej, Rama IX, became the longest reigning monarch in Thai history, surpassing the 42 years and 22 days of his grandfather, King Chulalongkorn, Rama V (1868-1910).

The reign is both a personal triumph and an historic milestone. It stands as a remarkable testament to the role of the monarchy, which has guided the nation for more than 700 years since its birth in the thirteenth century.

Thailand, like its immediate neighbors, achieved nationhood through the authority of kingship and the symbol of power emanating from a royal palace. The regal idea was inherited from the ancient In-

Preceding pages: Some kind of magic near the beach. Above: King Chulalongkorn, Rama V. Right: His Majesty King Bhumibol Adulyadej, Rama IX.

dian concept of the god-king, which infiltrated peninsular Southeast Asia during the first centuries AD. Such a form of kingship reached its highest expression among the Khmer of Angkor. From them it was inherited in part by the Thais, when they established their first sovereign state at Sukhothai. The new kingdom did, however, make significant modifications to the Khmer system, notably in relation to the monarch's accessibility and paternalistic stance.

This was clear from the earliest days. A stone inscription accredited to King Ramkamhaeng (c 1279-98), tells how the differences and disputes of nobles and commoners alike were settled at the court of Sukhothai. "At the gateway," reads the inscription, "there is a bell hung up. If any one of the public has a complaint or grievance of body or mind to place before the King, it is not difficult. He goes to sound the bell that is hung up. King Ramkamhaeng hears him call and, on questioning him, makes an upright investigation for him."

Following the founding of Ayutthaya, which eclipsed Sukhothai, and the subsequent Thai victory over Angkor, the Khmer form of kingship became more pronounced. Then the monarchy tended to be more remote and was surrounded by a complex system of court ritual and ceremonial. Nevertheless, the essential idea of a benign power radiating from the royal palace persisted. There were periods when the character of the monarchy changed to meet the needs and pressures of the historical moment, but its role as the most vital cohesive force binding the nation together has remained constant through seven centuries and 55 reigns.

Indeed the strength of the monarchy has been the strength of the nation. In the political realm, this is amply illustrated by such notable kings as Naresuan (1590-1605) and his heroic struggle against the Burmese; Narai (1656-88), under whose rule the power of Ayutthaya reached its glorious zenith, and Taksin (1767-82), who rallied a shattered nation after the destruction of Ayutthaya in 1767.

In the present Ratanakosin era, beginning with King Rama I and the founding of the Chakri dynasty in 1782, the Thai monarchy has successfully steered the country through periods of unprecedented change, as it established itself as a modern, dynamic nation. As an influence on art and culture, the Thai monarchy has had an equal impact. Kings have traditionally been the greatest patrons of the arts and, as upholders of the Buddhist faith, provided a stimulus to achievements in religious architecture, sculpture and painting.

Thailand is today a constitutional monarchy though its particular form is unique and defies comparison. Although absolute powers were dissolved in 1932, the role of the king has not been reduced to that of a figurehead.

When, following a bloodless revolution, the constitutional system was introduced, the political powers of kings were

curtailed, this in no way altered the respect felt for them, nor reduced their role as the single most important unifying force in the state. The concept of nationhood continues to revolve, as in the past, around the three key elements of country, king and religion.

King Bhumibol Adulyadej, the ninth monarch of the Chakri dynasty, was born in 1927 and ascended the throne at the age of 19. Before taking up his duties, the young monarch returned to Switzerland, where he had spent most of his early life, to complete his education at Lausanne University. While in Europe, he met beautiful Mom Rajawongse Sirikit, the daughter of the Thai ambassador to France, and a romance blossomed. The royal couple were married in April 1950, just one week before His Majesty's official coronation ceremony in Bangkok.

King Bhumibol Adulyadej and Queen Sirikit have four children: Princess Ubol Ratana, Crown Prince Maha Vajiralongkorn, Princess Maha Chakri Sirindhorn and Princess Chulabhorn.

There is an almost mystical bond between Thais and their monarch which has no parallel anywhere else in the world. Portraits of Their Majesties are found in virtually every home, office, shop and public building in the land, and the Royal Family draws huge crowds, whether at a state ceremony in Bangkok, or on a tour of some distant farming community or other projects.

Such displays of public devotion are just the more obvious manifestations of the enormous unifying and stabilizing power of the monarchy. As a constitutional monarch, His Majesty the King is above politics, though his status and his place in the hearts of the people is such that without his presence Thailand could not have enjoyed the stability that has made possible its enormous economic and social development. As a modern constitutional monarch, King Bhumibol devotes himself to public service in a practical way, working ceaselessly for the ongoing prosperity of his people. A man of considerable personal accomplishments, he takes a direct hand in initiating and promoting development projects, especially those concerning agriculture, designed to boost national growth. He frequently makes long and tiring journeys to all parts of the country, to inspect personally the implementation of projects and to meet with the people, examining at first hand problems and needs.

This is present-day Thai kingship, a combination of old-fashioned values and adaptation to the needs of a modern society. At the same time, much of the ancient royal ceremonial survives. Numerous events, such as the Annual Ploughing Ceremony, a rite to ensure a good rice crop, and the thrice-yearly changing of the robes of the Emerald Buddha are glorious affairs full of pageantry, serving to preserve vital links with the past, and to exemplify the continuing symbolic role of the Thai monarchy.

Above: The powers that be in the Pantheon.
Right: Full Moon Festival in Lampang.

COLORFUL FESTIVALS

The Thais are a fun-loving people who enjoy their holidays and festivals and love to take part in everyone else's. Thus, times like the Chinese New Year and Christmas, neither of which is on the government's list of holidays, are welcomed. The Thai calender has 12 official holidays, but there are many more festivals, both national and regional, which are celebrated with as much enthusiasm. It is impossible to give accurate dates for most of these events, as they are based on the traditional lunar calender, and differ from year to year. So you will have to inquire when being at the according destination in Thailand.

Folk and Traditional Festivals

The **Flower Festival** is held on the first weekend in February in Chiangmai, when both tropical and temperate flowers are in full bloom. A parade with many imaginative floats and hundreds of northern belles and the obligatory beauty contests are the main attractions.

Chinese New Year is the most important holiday for the Chinese community, and falls in late January/February. Although not an official holiday, the three to four day celebrations completely paralize any commercial activity throughout the country. As the Chinese, combined, employ a large Thai work force, there are probably, apart from civil servants, more Thais on holiday than working.

Songkran, the New Year's day of the traditional Thai lunar calender, is celebrated nation-wide (there are one or two minor regional diviations) on April 13. At this time, people working away from home will return to their villages, filling buses and trains to the roofs. In traditional homes, Buddha images are given a bath and are adorned with fresh flowers, candles and joss sticks. Elders are honored and captive birds and fish are released. And everyone throws water at all and sundry. It is the hottest time of the year and everybody has a grand time.

217

Songkran is perhaps best observed in Chiangmai, where the festivities are just a little more exuberant and last for a whole week. During the day, nobody will escape a drenching or two – or ten. The town is packed with tourists, Thai and foreign, to watch the colorful procession.

For two hours or longer, floats with Buddha images, dancing girls, bands, dancing girls, traditional musicians and sword dancers, dancing girls, Miss Songkran on her throne and, again dancing girls, move (or rather dance) past in slow motion, all soaked to the skin. Every club and association, provincial and municipal office, schools, colleges and many private companies, all take part in the Songkran parade. At night beauty contests, concerts and funfairs draw the crowds, and often one will have to search until late before finding a vacant place in a restaurant for dinner.

Pattaya, Thailand's best known beach resort, celebrates **Pattaya Week** in the heat of April with a non-stop string of events. Beauty contests, parades, unusual floats, international car races, regattas and other sports events attract crowds of visitors from Thailand and abroad.

Raek Nah, the Ploughing Ceremony, is held at Sanam Luang on an auspicious day in May. It is presided over by the King, and marks the beginning of the rice planting season. It involves elaborate Brahmanic rituals to predict the outcome of the annual rice crop. Colorful, traditional costumes are worn by the participants in Yasothon in the northeast, and also, in some parts of the north, villagers built huge rockets, which are fired skywards to assure plentiful rains during the coming monsoons. Usually held before the rains start, in May/June, the **Rocket Festival** is accompanied by lots of drinking, dancing and high-spirited revelry.

Right:Royal barge processions have been performed on rare occasions ever since the 14th century.

For accurate dates it is best to make enquiries at any TAT office.

In Ubon Rachathani in the northeast, Khao Phansa (taking place mostly in July, is celebrated with the **Candle Festival**, when beautifully fashioned beeswax candles, up to 2 m tall, are paraded around town, before being presented to the temples. Merit making, folk theater, beauty contests and funfairs are all part of the action. Similar festivals, but with more elaborate wax creations, are held in several provinces to celebrate the end, not the beginning, of the Rains Retreat in October.

The ten-day **Vegetarian Festival** in Phuket, observed by many of the island's Chinese, starts on the first day of the ninth month of the Chinese calender (usually September/October). For nine days no meat, fish or fowl is consumed, and many of the white-clad devotees will display mind-over-matter feats, such as walking on red-hot coal, stepping on razorsharp swords and sticking steel bars through parts of their bodies.

One of the loveliest of all Thai festivals is **Loy Kratong**, the Festival of Lights, held on the night of the full moon of the twelfth lunar month (usually in November). It is essentially a thanksgiving ceremony, when all waterways are filled after the rains. Fanciful little boats, containing a burning josstick, a flower, a small coin and lit candle are gently sent off on rivers and waterways, to honor the water spirits and wash away one's sins.

Loy Krathong is most impressive in Sukhothai and Chiangmai, the latter featuring a long procession of floats, which are judged before being floated down the Ping River.

Buddhist Festivals

Magha Puja is the calender's first important religious ceremony, held on the full moon of the third lunar month, usually in February. It commemorates the

occasion when 1,250 of the Buddha's disciples gathered spontaneously to listen to his sermon.

Visakha Puja, celebrated in May/June, is the most important of all Buddhist holidays and commemorates the Birth, Enlightenment and Death of Lord Buddha. Merit making and religious ceremonies are the same as on Magha Puja. No alcoholic drinks are sold on this day.

Khao Phansa marks the beginning of the Rains Retreat, when Buddhist monks will stay in their monasteries for about three months to meditate. The day usually falls in July.

Royal Holidays

Chakri Day on April 6 celebrates the founding of the Chakri dynasty (King Bhumibol is the ninth of the Chakri monarchs) in 1782. It is the only day when the Royal Pantheon at the Temple of the Emerald Buddha is open to the public.

Coronation Day falls on May 5, and commemorates the coronation of King Bhumibol in 1950.

Queen Sirikit's Birthday is celebrated nation-wide on August 12, with government buildings decorated and colorfully illuminated at night.

Chulalongkorn Day, held on October 23, honors King Chulalongkorn (Rama V), who reigned from 1868 to 1910.

The King's Birthday is celebrated throughout the country on December 5 as a national holiday, when all public, and many private buildings are decorated and brightly lit at night. A number of religious, official and social functions mark this auspicious day.

Besides the above mentioned events, and the government designated holidays of New Year (January 1), Labor Day (May 1), Constitution Day (December 10) and New Year's Eve (December 31), there are countless additional festivals, fairs, provincial or regional celebrations and sporting and social events. The TAT offices will gladly furnish you with details and information.

219

MINORITIES IN THAILAND

The Thais often consider themselves a homogeneous people, an attitude perhaps reinforced by the fact that over 90 per cent of the population is, at least nominally, Theravada Buddhist. But not even in terms of religion is Thailand homogeneous. There is a sizeable Muslim minority and every major town from north to south has at least one mosque. There are also Christians of different denominations, Hindus, Sikhs and animists.

The Chinese are an ethnic minority, although one with considerable influence and power. They can be found all over Thailand, but are concentrated in Bangkok and the larger provincial towns. With particularly large communities in Chiangmai, Phuket, Hat Yai and Chonburi, they control the economy, running almost

Above: Chinese calligrapher at work. Right: Yao women having a chat.

all shops and most restaurants and light industries. In addition to Muslims and Chinese, a variety of other minorities live in different parts of the kingdom. Indians and Pakistanis, whether Hindu, Muslim or Sikh, are mainly found in Bangkok, but also in most larger provincial capitals, where they control nearly the whole textile market.

In the north are the hilltribes living in villages on the mountain slopes, and along the borders of Cambodia, Laos and Burma are several ethnic minorities who are linked to the countries across the border. Even remnants of the Nationalist Chinese armies, the Kuomintang, established villages in the north after 1949, when China fell to the Communists. In the south, indigenous people of negroid appearance inhabit the mountain jungles and the sea gypsies, with their houses on stilts, are found around Phuket and the islands in the Andaman Sea.

The Chinese in Thailand

Already in the early Ayutthaya period (1350-1767), some Chinese traders had settled in Siam, and it is noteworthy that, while a royal decree prohibited mixed-marriages, the Chinese were allowed to marry native girls.

It was not until the late eighteenth century, when Chinese settlements in Siam started to grow, due to an influx of refugees from China, caused by Manchu oppression, political turmoil and protracted natural disasters. Most of the immigrants were Taechiew, with a sprinkling of Hokkians, Cantonese, Hainanese and Hakkas.

By paying tax to the Siamese Court, the Chinese were free to earn their own living, mainly as vendors, sailors and craftsmen. They were also engaged in fishing, livestock raising and gardening. The less fortunate worked as coolies in the mines, factories and on construction sites.

Eventually, some amassed substantial wealth and became owners of rice, flour and sugar mills, weaving plants and dyeing enterprises. In the Rattanakosin period, Chinese entrepreneurs climbed up the economic hierarchy through their involvement with banking, large-scale trading and small industries, the forerunners of many of today's multi-million undertakings.

Unlike most other countries in the region, Thailand has succeeded in integrating the Chinese into its own society by widespread intermarriage, the compulsory change to Thai names and a voluntary adoption of the Thai lifestyle by the Chinese, who nevertheless managed to keep many of their traditions and customs alive.

Apart from the Chinese descendants found all over the country, there are almost 20,000 Haws from Yunnan, who live in a number of villages in Chiang Mai, Chiang Rai and Mae Hong Son, along the northern border. They are the remnants of the Kuomintang Army's 93rd Division and their families, who fled before the onslaught of Mao's troops some 40 years ago. Until quite recently, most of these Haws earned their living mainly by narcotics trafficking, but with increased suppression by the Thai authorities, they have now largely turned to farming and tourism.

Thai Muslims

This religious minority is divided into several groups: the natives of the southern provinces, those descended from Indian, Pakistani, Indonesian and Malaysian migrants, and the Chinese Haws, mainly found in the north. Combined, they form Thailand's largest religious minority, making up some 5 per cent of the nation's population.

Concentrated primarily in the southernmost provinces of Narathiwat, Yala, Satun and Pattani, where they make up 80 per cent of the population, most Muslims here are ethnically Malay, which led to frequent sectarian distur-

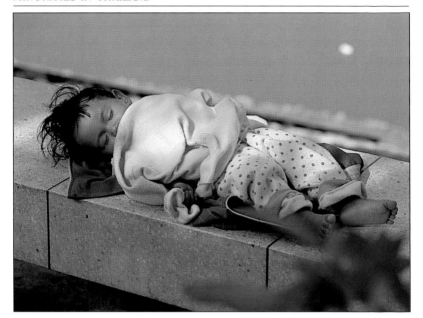

bances after the end of World War II. However, Bangkok's policy of "Friendship with the South", based on increased understanding and minimal interference, has resulted in easing the tension. Great efforts have been made to pacify Muslim feelings on issues ranging from education to Islamic holidays. The most recent problem involved the regulation against women wearing Islamic dress (headdress and veil) to government schools, but after some controversy, local opinion was appeased and the issue died away.

Visitors to these provinces should be aware of the differences from the rest of the country, and should behave the same way as in Islamic countries. Although there is a large and influential Thai and Chinese presence here, it should be understood, for example, that Muslim-run restaurants will frown upon liquor and will not serve pork.

Above: No need to worry she may think.
Right: Siamese Kick Boxing.

The Indian Community

The history of Indian immigration to Thailand goes back to the Ayutthaya period, when trade flourished between India and Siam and some of the Indian traders settled here.

The second influx occurred during the mid nineteenth century. With the rapidly increasing trade between Siam and the British East India Company, a large number of Indians settled in Bangkok.

A third wave arrived here as a direct result of partition, when the sub-continent was carved up and many Hindus and Sikhs from the newly created Pakistan became displaced persons. Even today, a steady stream of Indians, trying to escape job shortage and poverty in their homeland, is arriving in Bangkok. Some come as tourists and many enter illegally, but the great majority are trying, by whatever means, to get a foothold in Thailand.

It is difficult today to estimate the size of the Indian community. Thailand has encouraged assimilation rather than sepa-

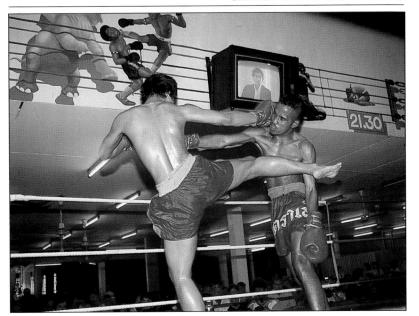

rate communities within its society. Part of the Indian immigrants, who have come to Thailand during the last two hundred years have been absorbed. Their descendants act and speak like Thais, though their features are distinctly Indian. But the great majority, whether Hindu, Sikh or Muslim, resist any form of assimilation, seldom marry outside their caste, religion or language group and rigidly adhere to their own traditions.

Perhaps the highest concentration of Indians in Bangkok is found at Pahurat, adjoining the northern end of Chinatown. Jokingly referred to as "Little India", the area is dominated by Indian textile merchants.

Excellent small Indian eateries serve authentic Indian dishes and several shops specialize in Indian merchandise. Visitors to Thailand will almost certainly encounter Indians if they want to have a suit or dress made, as tailor shops, especially in the top hotels, are almost their exclusive domain, though for the actual tailoring they employ Chinese.

SIAMESE GAMES AND PASTIMES

Thais are a physically active people, who enjoy the excitement of sports and games. They are almost never just spectators and like to participate in the action, if not directly, then as betters, for the Thais are inveterate gamblers. Anything is good enough for a wager, whether the stake is on a horse, a boxer, a beetle or a kite. With a bet on, the action is all the more exciting.

Many Western sports like soccer, volleyball and badminton are very popular in the kingdom, but even more so are the traditional sports and games, which have for many generations amused and entertained the people.

Takraw

Walking around Bangkok, one will often see small circles of young men, passing a hollow, grapefruit-size rattan ball back and forth, using any part of the

body, except the hands. They are practising *Takraw,* an ancient Thai team sport and an amazing test of dexterity and coordination. Two types of *Takraw* games are popular.

One version looks much like volley-ball, with three-man teams on opposite sides of a head-high net. Using feet, knees, elbows, shoulders and head, they bounce the ball back and forth, often spiking it with high scissor kicks that would make even Pelé jealous.

The other game features a six-member team, standing in a circle beneath an odd-looking netted basket, suspended about fife meter overhead.

The team keeps the ball in the air, trying to get it into the net by using all parts of the body, except hands, and so scoring a point. The aim is to score as many hits or points as possible during a fixed period, after which the next team gets its turn.

Above: Cock fights are illegal in Thailand but very popular.

Most *Takraw* facilities are found in temple compounds. Competitions and tournaments are held periodically at various centers around Bangkok, including Sanam Luang.

Siamese Sword and Stick Fighting

During the four centuries of the golden age of Ayutthaya (1350 to 1767), Thai warriors perfected an awesome, combat-effective fighting system, using arms and legs in addition to the traditional sword, spear and pike. To foster this essentially defensive fighting style right from the beginning, Ayutthaya's first king, Ramathipodi I, designated a nearby temple as the royal fighting academy, which for 400 years trained princes, the nobility and outstanding military men, producing peerless warriors to defend the realm.

Many of the succeeding monarchs of Ayutthaya also helped to further fighting skills by patronising the academy. This powerful martial arts tradition helped to keep Siam free through centuries of warfare, regional upheavel and danger. Today, the Thais still practise this fighting art, called *Krabi Krabong,* as part of their cultural heritage.

Krabi Krabong uses different kinds of swords, lances, sticks, staves and blocks of wood as weapons of defense and attack. The art is taught in many high schools, colleges and universities and is a credit course at physical education colleges. Two categories of *Krabi Krabong,* the *daab song mue* (two long-bladed, curved Thai swords with long handles, one in each hand) and the *Krabi* (a fencing weapon not unlike the Western sports sabre), also draw a maximum number of entrants at the annual university games. Although the contest weapons are well padded replicas made of wood or rattan, many competitors leave the arena with bruises, welts, broken thumbs and split skin over their skulls.

A number of private instructors, some well known and highly honored, teach the art in a very traditional manner in their own camps, where the emphasis is, unlike in the student battles, is on ritual and ancient custom. Their very formal and stylized art is beautiful to watch, but too theatrical to be effective in combat. These schools are the main suppliers of performers at tourist demonstrations and cultural shows, but hardly ever enter their students in fighting contests.

Muay Thai:
The Art of Siamese Kick Boxing

Even unarmed Thai warriors of the Ayutthaya era were widely regarded as dangerous adversaries, for they could easily injure or disable opponents with kicks, as well as powerful blows delivered by their knees, elbows and fists.

These techniques of unarmed combat did, in time, develop into a sport, which today occupies more than 12 hours a week of television time. Fights are staged at one or other of several stadia on every day of the week. *Muay Thai* is almost universally regarded as today's most exciting, but also most violent ring sport. The Thais feel that it is superior to all other martial arts, and contests between Muay Thai fighters and students of Karate, Taekwondo and Kung Fu during the last two decades have vindicated this opinion overwhelmingly.

No visit to Thailand would be complete without seeing at least one Muay Thai program. Although matches are televised, attending the live event is an occasion not to be missed. Not all the activity takes place in the ring. While the fighters use fists, feet, knees and elbows to batter each other into submission, spectators all over the stadium frantically wave wads of cash and wager with neighbors, all the while screaming frenetic support for their favorite.

Each bout begins with the boxers performing a ritual, honoring their teacher and invoking mystical help. Bouts are scheduled for five three-minute rounds with a two-minute break between rounds. Despite the formidable arsenal of weapons commanded by the boxers, points decisions far outnumber knockouts, a result of normally matching two opponents with approximately the same degree of competence.

Interested visitors can get information on venues, times and ticket prices at their hotel counter or the TAT. Those interested in the intricacies of this sport may want to obtain a copy of *Muay Thai* by Hardy Stockmann, available in all major book shops.

Fighting
Bulls, Cocks, Fish and Insects

Very popular in the south of Thailand, bull fighting is, unlike the Spanish and Mexican variety, a contest of bull against bull, rather than man against animal. The fighting bulls undergo much the same type of training as boxers, with roadwork

and other exercises to increase stamina and strengthen-neck and back muscles, so necessary to battle and defeat an opponent.

On fight day, handlers lead the bulls into the ring by ropes attached to the animal's nose-ring, jerking the ropes to irritate the beasts and encourage their aggressive instincts. This is often unnecessary, as the bulls seem quite willing to attack each other without provocation. When the ropes are dropped, the bulls charge each other violently, trying to overturn or injure each other. A bull loses if it turns and runs away from its opponent. The crowds are enthusiastic, the action very exciting and betting furious throughout the encounter.

Cock fighting is another popular form of "entertainment", found all over the country. Because it is illegal and thus semi-secret, visitors wanting to watch

Above: The bulls on Koh Samui fight until one of them flees. Right: The colorful kite world on Sanam Luang in Bangkok.

this cruel sport have to make contact through tour agents, Thai friends or taxi drivers, who know where the action is. In Thailand, fighting cocks wear no steel gaffs or razor blades on their natural spurs, so the action is less bloody – but just as vicious – as seen in the Philippines or elsewhere.

Another popular pastime around the kingdom is watching fights between the pugnacious Siamese fighting fish. The gorgeously coloured males fight instinctively whenever they meet, so the only encouragement needed is to place one in a large jar containing another. The fish often fight for hours – until one is dead or too exhausted to continue.

Most such events are confined to small, often private, groups of enthusiasts and the stakes wagered are generally low. Visitors wanting to watch fish fighting can probably satisfy their bloodhust most easily by purchasing the fish, sold cheaply at the weekend market at Chatuchak Park or on Klong Ong Ang in Chinatown.

Also seen occasionally are cricket fights, mostly a game for rural children, but sometimes found in some areas of Bangkok. Handlers "tickle" the insects' tender parts with grass burrs and place them facing each other. The crickets will fight spiritedly for a short while, but one usually runs away soon, thus ending the match.

A variety of this, seen only in the countryside, is the fight between 5-cm long black beetles, placed on the ends of a stick of sugar cane with a hole in the middle. In their effort to get to the juice in the hole, the beetles engage in a fierce battle, encouraged by the shrieks of young gamblers who have not much more to wager than a small coin or another beetle.

Kite Flying

Kite flying is another traditional Thai pastime with a wide and enthusiastic following. Visitors coming to Thailand between the middle of February and the middle of May, the height of the kite season, may witness some spectacular performances.

At Sanam Luang, a collection of colorful kites of all shapes and sizes flutter in the breeze and can be purchased. Individuals and teams of kite flyers often hold kite fighting contests, which are exciting tests of skill.

The most popular battle is to try and snare the line of an opponent's kite with your own, and then pull the enemy kite across a capture line, marked prominently on the ground.

The most popular fights are arranged between the traditional *chula*, a 2-m tall, star-shaped kite, considered to be the male, and the much smaller female, the diamond-shaped *pakpao*, which may seem, to the uninitiated, to be at a great disadvantage. However, it has technically just as much of a chance of winning as its larger adversary – and it often does.

Besides the very popular locally organised events, Thailand has also become a recognized competitor internationally.

RURAL MIGRATION

At the start of 1989, the predicted growth rate of the Thai economy for that year was almost 10 per cent over 1988. Everywhere across Bangkok's skyline construction cranes were at work, some 24 hours a day. Filling the streets of the city are thousands of buses, minibuses, taxis and *samlors* (motorized tricycles) to transport the six million inhabitants of the metropolis that is Bangkok.

At the construction sites you may see hordes of workers, covered from head to toe with grubby cloth as protection against the sun, crawling like ants over the 27 floors of a concrete shell that will be the latest condominium. Factories and production plants sprout at numerous industrial estates, which have mushroomed on the outskirts of the city. And all require labor, specialist and unskilled.

Above: A Karen boy in the north. Right: Carrying wood, by the sweat of one's brow.

Where do all these workers come from? The vast majority are from the rural villages of Isarn, an area which suffers from periodic droughts.

Especially during the dry season when no work is done in the fields, a steady stream of workers is moving south to Bangkok, to other more prosperous provinces, and even overseas. In Bangkok, this influx has resulted in the formation of huge squatter colonies, with one of the city's largest slums located in the district known as Klong Toey.

These shanty towns are scattered across the city alongside railway tracks, under expressways, or on and near the construction sites themselves. And like slums the world over, severe social problems arise: crime, drug addiction, prostitution and disease.

While these labor colonies are an embarassment to the authorities, they not only continue to exist, but are be a dire necessity. Cheap labor is needed to maintain the speed of the urban development boom. The Thai Government has recog-

nized the problem and is now attempting, through investment incentives, to encourage private industries to move into the provinces.

A new policy, the "Greening of Isarn", has generated wide interest and involved the Royal Thai Armed Forces in mobilizing resources to reforest denuded areas and begin planting tree crops in marginal areas.

One persistent economic and social problem is the poor distribution of income. The authorities are aware of the fact that the benefits of strong growth must be passed on to those in the countryside. Alas, as yet much of the wealth that development has brought to the metropolis and its surroundings has made the rich wealthier, while the vast hinterland remains deprived.

Not only does rural migration reflect this continuous economic disparity, but it also highlights the concentration of services and facilities in the city. In villages, television advertises the glitter of the urban world, providing a further lure to migrants to leave the toil of the rice paddies for the glamor of Bangkok.

The newcomers form a permanent under-privileged class in the city, mainly because the work they obtain is so poorly paid. The minimum wage in Bangkok is supposed to be about 100 baht, roughly four US dollars per day, but is hardly ever paid. Yet prices are rising constantly in a city that is overrun with tourists and foreign investors.

The poorly educated villagers, drawn to the Eden called Bangkok, become maids, prostitutes, street sweepers, taxi drivers and food service workers. But the annual rise in the cost of living ensures that their meagre wages buy less and less. In most other social environments this condition would produce volatility, but the Thais are docile and rather fatalistic in their attitudes. While organized labor is growing more restive, strikes are relatively rare.

It would seem that for the foreseeable future the influx of rural migrants to Bangkok will continue.

TRAFFIC AND POLLUTION

It will probably be only minutes after leaving Bangkok International Airport in a limousine or taxi, that new arrivals will notice the least attractive feature of Bangkok – the traffic is simply unbelievable. Whichever way the city-planners may turn, the chaos will persist, and for the next few years the city's traffic problems are definitely not going to get any better.

Visitors to Bangkok should realize that traffic congestion, especially around rush hours, can make any city trip an exercise in futility. Whenever it is necessary to keep an appointment, or to catch a plane, time must be allowed for delays along the route. The normal half hour trip for the 25 km from the city center to the airport, for example, may take as long as two hours or more during the day.

Above: An endless supply of cars wind along Bangkok's avenues. Right: Ablutions at the klongs of Thonburi.

Early morning, late at night or Sundays are generally times of light traffic, but once again nothing can be predicted with any certainty.

Choosing a hotel in the most convenient location for your purpose is the first step in beating the traffic. Next, realize that visitors new to Bangkok are advised against driving themselves. There are many car rental firms in the city, but for only a modest increase in rates, an English-speaking driver can be included in the deal.

Walking is by no means a popular way of moving about in Bangkok, as conditions are simply too hot and humid. Pedestrians should be aware of the traffic flow and one-way lanes going in the opposite direction. It can be very confusing – and dangerous – to suddenly see a bus speeding against the traffic in a one-way street. You should always remember that many drivers in Bangkok do not feel inclined to stop for pedestrians, not even at zebra crossings. So it may become hazardous to cross a street in Bangkok.

Another hazard for the unwary stroller is motorcycles, which, in order to escape having to wait in the heat and filth of an all too frequent traffic jam, simply move from the street onto the sidewalk, completely disregarding not only the comfort, but also the safety of the many pedestrians. So you better carefully watch out for the myriads of roaring motorcycles.

Where there is heavy traffic, there is air pollution. Bangkok's air is anything but clean, and along major thoroughfares, with thousands of cars, trucks and fuming buses idling at intersections, it is downright filthy.

Late afternoon is particularly bad and walking along such roads is a definite health hazard. Avoid going anywhere at such times, but if you have to, go by air-conditioned taxi.

Water pollution is another problem in Bangkok, particularly in the canals and the river. Tap water, in general, is supposed to be safe for human consumption, but the all too frequent repairs to main supply lines or secondary pipes, often allow foreign matter to enter the supply system.

As for beach areas like Pattaya and Phuket, sanitation is becoming a major concern. Local governments, although aware of the problem, are not yet sufficiently alarmed or equipped to deal decisively with controls of effluent discharge from major hotels and condominiums, and in several cases open sewage flowing into the sea has made certain places unsafe for swimmers.

Plastic bags are part of everyday life in Thailand. They are used to hold anything, from soft-drinks and food to gas from the nearest filling station. Unfortunately they all too frequently end up in the ocean, making a dip in the gulf, at certain beach resorts, most unpleasant.

The government is realizing that unless it does something drastic to halt this deterioration in the environment, it may affect the tourism industry. Hopefully, visitors will remember that they can be part of the solution, by placing their own litter in appropriate containers.

THE DRUG PROBLEM

Sandwiched between the converging frontiers of Laos, Burma and Thailand is an area known to the world as the "Golden Triangle". Populated by hilltribes, the region has enjoyed the dubious distinction of being one of the world's major opium growing centers. Politics and economics have contributed to this status. The hilltribes, with few alternatives to the easily grown opium poppy, have traditionally practised slash and burn agriculture, planting their opium fields in the soils of the northern hills.

But the Thai Government, with active UN assistance and help from the United States, has made it a major goal to wean the hilltribes away from their traditional crop. His Majesty the King of Thailand has also, through various projects, introduced the tribal people to crops like

Above: A Lisu woman harvesting opium.
Right: Scenes from the Ramakien on a mural in the Wat Phra Kaew.

coffee, apples, pears, peaches and cut flowers. All these efforts have enjoyed considerable success and Bangkok markets are now filled with a wide variety of the fruits and vegetables grown in the cool valleys of the north.

And yet the unsettled politics and remoteness of the region ensure that some opium is still grown, though not nearly as much as before. Part of this local production serves the needs of local addicts, of whom an estimated 100,000 are heroin users. While trafficking in heroin is an offense with the death penalty as maximum punishment, every year many foreigners are arrested at the airport trying to exit with drugs. Hundreds are presently serving time in Thai prisons, while some have been executed in Malaysia and Singapore, after having been caught coming from Bangkok with heroin.

In addition to heroin, Thailand has a problem with adolescents addicted to sniffing thinner, glue and solvents. The aimless lives of urban youth, many of whom have come from rural areas, contribute to this problem. Hanging around parks and plazas, these young people are a sorry product of the times.

Drug addiction is of course a byproduct of a much bigger problem, part of which is rapid development and urban growth. In parts of Bangkok, and larger centers like Chiang Mai, where the drug trade and tourism often overlap, prostitution and crime are ever-present. Visitors should be aware of the strict laws relating to drug consumption in Thailand. While drug consumption remains a persistent problem, most visitors will never see any evidence of it, unless they actively search for it.

For a metropolis of over six million people, Bangkok is surprisingly free of violence. But there are still areas that visitors should avoid. At night, tourists should stick to well-lit streets and should remember that flashy jewelry, gold chains and watches invite theft.

Nelles Maps ...the maps, that get you going.

Nelles Map Series

- Afghanistan
- Australia
- Burma
- Caribbean Islands 1 / Bermuda, Bahamas, Greater Antilles
- Caribbean Islands 2 / Lesser Antilles
- China 1 / North-Eastern China
- China 2 / Northern China
- Crete
- Hawaiian Islands
- Hawaiian Islands 1 / Kauai
- Hawaiian Islands 2 / Honolulu, Oahu
- Hawaiian Islands 3 / Maui, Molokai, Lanai

- Hawaiian Islands 4 / Hawaii
- Himalaya
- Hong Kong
- Indian Subcontinent
- India 1 / Northern India
- India 2 / Western India
- India 3 / Eastern India
- India 4 / Southern India
- India 5 / North-Eastern India
- Indonesia
- Indonesia 1 / Sumatra
- Indonesia 2 / Java + Nusa Tenggara
- Indonesia 3 / Bali
- Indonesia 4 / Kalimantan
- Indonesia 5 / Java + Bali
- Indonesia 6 / Sulawesi
- Indonesia 7 / Irian Jaya + Maluku

- Jakarta
- Japan
- Kenya
- Korea
- Malaysia
- West Malaysia
- Nepal
- New Zealand
- Pakistan
- Philippines
- Singapore
- South East Asia
- Sri Lanka
- Taiwan
- Thailand
- Vietnam, Laos Kampuchea

TABLE OF CONTENTS

PREPARATION

Geography and Climate

Thailand, a tropical country of some 60 million inhabitants and an area of 514,000 sq km (roughly the size of France), lies between the 5th and 21st parallels north of the equator and the 97th and 106th longitudes east. Bordered by Burma in the west and north, Laos in the northeast, Cambodia in the east and Malaysia in the south, its longest distance from north to south is 1,700, and from east to west 800 km.

The peculiar shape of the country, like an elephant's head with a long trunk, gives it a coastline of some 2,500 km. The country is divided into five regions: central, north, northest, southeast and south. The kingdom's capital, Bangkok, with its six million inhabitants, is located in the central region.

Thailand has three seasons: hot – from March to May, with temperatures in Bangkok reaching 40 degrees C and more; wet – from June to October, when the temperature drops slightly, but humidity may rise to 98 per cent; and cool – from November till February, when it is still hot, but much less humid. The weather in the north is more bearable. In the cool season temperatures may drop to less than 10 degrees at night, and although in April it can get hotter than in Bangkok, it is much less humid.

Beginning around the end of June and lasting until October, the rainy season is probably the most uncomfortable time of the year. Temperatures will reach 32° C during the day and cool down to 24° C at night, but the humidity is so high that one's shirt or blouse is always damp. The monsoon brings moderate to heavy showers at any time of the day, often unexpectedly. Bangkok streets may flood after heavy rain, but the water recedes quickly from most roads.

Clothing

Light, comfortable and easily washed clothes are best to beat the heat. Shorts and short-sleeved shirts or loose dresses are most suitable. Light canvas shoes are recommended for traveling long distances and open shoes or sandals are good around the city. Rubber sandals or boots are useful during the height of the rainy season, when some streets may come in flooded.

Summer clothing is generally adequate, except when going north in the cool season (November/February), when light sweaters or jackets may come in handy. Suits, ties and leather shoes are necessary only when attending formal functions, or dining at some of the top restaurants in first-class hotels.

Light-skinned visitors, not used to local conditions, should use suntan lotion during the hot season, and sun glasses when out during the day.

What Not to Wear

When visiting Buddhist temples, do not wear shorts, tank tops, sleeveless shirts, mini-skirts or any provocative clothing. Thais regard such attire as very disrespectful.

When entering a temple compound, wear shoes, though they must be removed on entering the sanctuary.

Ladies should remember not to wear too revealing clothes when traveling at night, when venturing into the slums of Bangkok or in remote areas. Also never sunbathe nude on a secluded beach on your own. You might get more than you bargained for.

Arrival Formalities

Visa: Three types of visas are available: Transit, Tourist and Non-Immigrant Visas. Generally, each type is good for one entry, and is valid for 90 days from the date of issue. Length of stay for holders of Transit Visas is 30 days, Tourist Visas 60 days and Non-Immigrant

Visas 90 days. Visitors with no entry visa are automatically granted a non-extendable 15-day visa, if they hold valid passports or traveling documents of the following countries:

Algeria, Argentina, Australia, Austria, Bahrain, Belgium, Brazil, Brunei, Burma, Canada, Denmark, Egypt, Fiji, Finland, France, Greece, Iceland, Indonesia, Ireland, Israel, Italy, Japan, Jordan, Kenya, Kuwait, Luxemburg, Malaysia, Mexico, The Netherlands, New Zealand, Nigeria, Norway, Oman, Papua New Guinea, The Philippines, Portugal, Qatar, Saudi Arabia, Senegal, Singapore, South Korea, Spain, Sudan, Sweden, Switzerland, Turkey, Tunisia, UAE, UK, USA, Vanuatu, West Germany, Western Samoa, Yemen and Yugoslavia.

They must enter the kingdom by commercial aircraft or sea vessels of over 500 tonnes and can only apply for extensions in emergencies (illness, aircraft delay etc). Visitors wishing to stay in Thailand for more than 15 days are advised to apply for an entry visa from Thai embassies or consulates, or forward their request to the Immigration Department, Soi Suan Plu, Sathorn Tai Rd, Bangkok 10120. (Tel: 286-9230).

New Zealand passport holders can stay in Thailand for a maximum of three months without a visa. Visitors from 79 additionally specified nations can also obtain 15-day visas upon entry into Thailand, but only at Don Munag Airport's Immigration Office, located inside the airport building.

Should visitors want to leave the kingdom, and return prior to the expiration of their visas, they must obtain a re-entry permit from the Immigration Department in Bangkok, Chiang Mai, Phuket or Hat Yai before their departure. The fee for re-entry permits does not exceed 500 baht.

It is important that travelers check the period of stay stamped on their passports, before leaving the immigration office. If for any reason the holder of a visa fails to travel to Thailand within 90 days of issue, the holder can apply for an extension at any Thai embassy or consulate. Extensions may not be granted for more than six months, nor after expiration of an applicant's passport. Visitors overstaying the period specified in the visa, are subject to pay a fine of 100 baht per day.

Customs

The customs check-points at Bangkok International Airport have a green channel for visitors with nothing to declare and a red channel for dutiable items. Visitors are permitted a reasonable amount of personal belongings without paying duty, but gifts or business samples must be declared.

Customs Regulations

Prohibited items: all narcotics are illegal and traffickers face very harsh penalties. Also prohibited are pornographic and obscene literature and articles. Firearms are prohibited, unless permission is obtained from the Registration Office, Police Department on Rama I Road.

Visitors are permitted, duty free, one still-camera, a movie or video camera, five rolls of still-camera film, three rolls of 8 or 16 mm movie film. As for video tapes, it is recommended to check with Thai diplomatic missions abroad before departure. A maximum of 250 grams of tobacco or cigars, or 200 cigarettes, and one liter of wine or spirits are permitted duty free.

Certain kinds of fresh fruit, vegetables and plants are prohibited. Permission for entry of animals arriving by air, can be obtained at the airport. For those arriving by sea with animals, enquiries should be made at the Disease Control Division in Phya Thai Road.

Currency / Exchange / Banks

The Thai currency unit is the baht with a present exchange value of approximately 25 to the US dollar, 40 to the UK pound and 14 to the DM. There are 100 satang in one baht. Coins come in denominations of 25 stg, 50 stg, 1, 2 and 5 baht. Banknotes come in 10 baht (brown), 20 baht (green), 50 baht (blue), 100 baht (red) and 500 baht (purple) bills.

Thai coins are a constant source of frustration to foreigners, as the same value coin appears in different shapes, sizes and thicknesses. Thus, there are four different 1-baht coins, two sizes of the seldom seen 2-baht coin and four varieties of 5-baht coins. The reason for this is that new coin issues do not replace old designs, but are simply added to existing varieties in use. As some 1- and 5-baht coins look and feel similar, it is advisable to check the number carefully, before spending the coin.

Health

No inoculations or vaccinations are required, unless visitors come from, or have passed through, epidemic areas. Travelers should take precautions against getting bacteriological dysentary. If you are a first-time visitor, you should perhaps stick to bottled water and pass those inviting street-side stalls by. Locals and foreign residents do drink tap water and enjoy the food at these little noodle shops, but some tourists, having eaten here for the first time, have later complained about an upset stomach.

Malaria has been eradicated in Thailand, but when trekking into remote areas, take along the proper medicine. Consult a physician before starting the journey. Visitors should include mosquito repellent in their traveling list.

During the hot season, visitors from temperate climates should beware of heat stroke. Be sure to drink lots of fluid during the day. Salt tablets come in handy when staying in the sun for a long time.

Do not accept food, drinks or candy of any kind from strangers, particularly in buses or trains. They might contain sleeping drugs or worse.

At present, Thailand has a very high standard of medical services. Competent private hospitals and clinics are found throughout the country.

If you are bitten by a stray dog or cat, rabies or tetanus shots are highly recommended. The Thai Red Cross on Rama IV Rd, or any provincial hospital, provides anti-rabies injections.

Departure

An airport tax of 150 baht for international flights, and 20 baht for domestic flights is charged each passenger.

Tax Clearance

Visitors staying in Thailand for 90 days or more are required, on leaving, to produce a tax clearance certificate from the Revenue Department – regardless of whether they have earned income or not. The Revenue Department is on Chakpong Rd, Tel.281-5777 or 280-0140 (open Monday-Friday, 8:30 to 16:30). It is advisable to have a Thai-speaking person to help you with the clearance.

TRAVEL TO THAILAND

By air: There are currently five international airports in Thailand: Bangkok International Airport (known as Don Muang), Chiang Mai, Phuket, Hat Yai and Pattaya/Sattahip. The great majority of visitors arrive at Don Muang, 25 km from the center of Bangkok. Currency exchange, car rentals, hotel bookings and transportation into town can all be arranged in the airport building.

New arrivals at Don Muang are advised to use only authorized transportation services, provided by the Airports Authority of Thailand (AAT) and Thai Airways. The airport bus to the city terminal, near the Asia Hotel, is 60 baht per person. Limousine services to hotels in Bangkok are about 300 baht, depending on destination. Air-conditioned coaches leave the airport for Pattaya at 9:00,

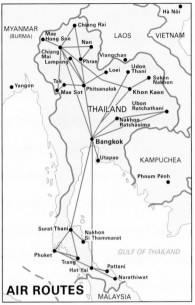

AIR ROUTES

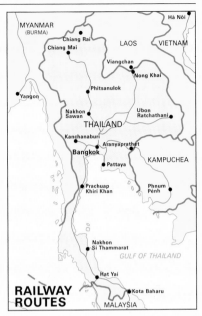

RAILWAY ROUTES

12:00 and 19:00, 180 baht per person. If your flight arrives at night, do not attempt to hire a taxi on your own. A number of innocent tourists have been robbed by drivers of illegal taxis. The safest way to go is by authorised transport. Contact the limousine counter for information.

By road: Travelers can legally enter the kingdom by car or bus only at the Thai-Malaysian border in southern Thailand. The temporary import of vehicles for tourism is permitted. Applications can be made at the customs office of any official border crossing. Road and river border crossings into Burma, Laos and Cambodia are at present closed to non-Thai tourists.

By sea: Visitors coming to Thailand aboard any sea-going vessel are required to go through immigration channels at Klong Toey Port.

TRAVEL IN THAILAND

By air – Thailand's domestic air routes reach many of the most remote outposts, either from Bangkok or airports in Chiangmai, Khon Kaen, Phuket and Hat Yai. For bookings, reservations or information phone Thai Airways International, Domestic Services, at 513-0121. Bangkok Airways operates regular services from Bangkok to Hua Hin, Koh Samui and Phuket. For details Tel:253-4014.

By train – The State Railway of Thailand (SRT) operates probably the safest, though not the fastest, means of travel. It runs trains to Chiangmai in the north; Nong Kai and Ubol Ratchathani in the northeast; to Aranya Prathet on the Cambodian border in the east; to Pattaya and beyond in the southeast; to Kanchanaburi in the west and to Hat Yai and the Malaysian border in the south.

The two types of trains, rapid and express, have three classes, first, second and third. Third class travel, very cheap and ideal for "mixing with the natives", is usually crowded and the wooden benches are not too comfortable. Second class offers a choice of airconditioned sitting or fan-cooled sleeping carriages. First class train travel in Thailand is a treat, with airconditioned two-berth compartments and a fare slightly higher than a plane ticket to the same destination.

Night express trains with sleeper cars are a comfortable way to get to your destination. Leaving Bangkok in the evening, they arrive at the end of the line (Chiangmai, Nong Khai, Ubon, Hat Yai) the next morning. Trains also go from Bangkok to Butterworth (Penang), Kuala Lumpur and Singapore.

Dining cars are usually attached to express trains and serve good basic Thai fare and also some Western dishes, like bacon and eggs for breakfast. Vendors walk the aisles selling soft drinks, beer, Thai whisky and various snacks. English-language books and newspapers can be purchased at Hualampong. Anti-mosquito spray is recommended for night journeys.

The SRT also provides special weekend or holiday excursions to Ayutthaya, Kanchanaburi and the Bridge on the River Kwai, Cha-am, Hua Hin and Pattaya, Khao Yai National Park and Samui Island. They are very popular with Thai holidaymakers and families.

For further information on schedules and fares, there is an English-language information service at Hualampong Station on Rama IV Road, or consult the TAT office at Rajdamnoen Nok Avenue. Advance bookings/reservations can only be made in person, and not more than 20 days before the intended departure date. The advanced booking office at Hualampong is open from 8:30 to 18:00 on weekdays, and 8:30 to 12:00 on weekends and holidays.

By buses – Metropolitan buses: A multitude of bus routes crisscross Bangkok, taking passengers virtually anywhere. Traveling by bus is easy during the day because buses leave the terminals frequently. After 21:00, however, service slows down and you may have to wait 30-45 minutes for a particular bus. Visitors unfamiliar with Bangkok may find a taxi more convenient at night.

Four different kinds of buses operate in Bangkok: the big, blue and airconditioned buses, charging between 5 and 15 baht; blue-and-white public buses charge a flat fare of 2 baht; red-and-white private buses charge a flat 3 baht; and the little green privately-owned mini-buses charge a flat fare of 2 baht.

City maps with bus routes are available at most bookstores and at TAT. It is easier to take a regular bus, since you pay a flat rate, irrespective of the distance you travel. On the more comfortable airconditioned buses, you must buy a ticket on boarding, naming your destination – in Thai.

Sometimes the regular fare is increased by 1 to 1.50 baht if the bus takes the expressway. Tourists are advised to avoid the green mini-buses. They are more often than not driven by impatient and irresponsible even unqualified drivers. Tall foreigners especially should avoid these mini-buses because ceilings are low and seats are very close together, leaving insufficient leg room.

In case of accident, passengers on board public buses with proof of valid tickets can claim insurance from The Bangkok Mass Transit Authority. All buses have large colored signs in the front window, telling if they are regular, express or freeway buses, or if they are going to the depot. Blue signs indicate regular routes, like on the maps. Taking a bus with a red, yellow or white sign may get you lost.

By taxi – Visitors can easily hail taxis or *tuk-tuks* along the streets. Taxis in Bangkok are airconditioned but do not use meters. The fare must be negotiated before boarding. Within the city, fares normally start at 30 baht and can go up to 200/300 baht, depending on the distance.

By tuk-tuk – For adventure-seekers the *tuk-tuk* – a open three-wheel taxi, is a novel way to see the city. They are popular with foreigners, offer more leg room and are cheaper than ordinary taxis. In central Bangkok, the minimum fare starts at 20 baht and can go up to 80 baht. Most taxi and *tuk-tuk* drivers don't speak English. To avoid being cheated, ask somebody you can trust to write down the name and address of your destination, in Thai, and ask for an estimate of the price.

Car and motorcycle rental services are available all over Bangkok and most provincial towns. The largest companies, with branches nation-wide, are Hertz and Avis. Prices range from 1,000 to 1,500 baht per day for automobiles. Hiring a driver with the car is strongly recommended, unless one knows Bangkok well enough to cope with the chaotic traffic.

By upcountry buses – Connecting Bangkok with provinces throughout the kingdom are public and private, regular and airconditioned buses. They are relatively inexpensive and have regular, daily schedules. Airconditioned buses are more comfortable and faster, with fewer stops en route. They also serve drinks and show video movies on board. It should also be noted that the roads in Thailand are very crowded, and frequent accidents occur. Also, bus passengers are cautioned against accepting drinks or snacks from strangers. Incidents have occurred of drugged passengers awakening to find all their valuables stolen.

There are three departure points in Bangkok. The northern Bus Terminal for buses to the North and Northeast is at Morchit on Phaholyothin Road, not far from Chatuchak Park and the Weekend Market (Tel:279-4484/7). The Eastern Terminal, Ekkamai, opposite Soi 63 on Sukhumvit Road serves the southeast – Pattaya, Rayong, Koh Samet (Tel:392-9227), and the Southern Terminal for aircon buses is at Nakorn Chaisri Road in Thonburi, across the river, from where buses leave for Hua Hin, Chumpon, Surat Thani/Koh Samui, Songkhla/Hat Yai and Phuket (Tel:411-4978/9). Information on aircon bus movements and fares may also be obtained from TAT at Tel: 282-1143/7 or Tourist Assistance, Tel:223-2126.

By songthaews-taxis – Operating between small upcountry centers, district towns and villages, are taxis or, more likely, trucks converted for passenger use, called *songthaews*. They are cheap and the easiest way to get to out-of-the-way places. They can be found near bus terminals or markets, waiting for passengers.

By boats – Quite a few tourist attractions in Bangkok can be reached easily by Bangkok's waterways. Besides the regular boat services on the Chao Phraya River, many large and small boats can be rented at Tah Tien pier.

From 6:00 to 18:00 express boats (called *rua duan*) cruise up and down the Chao Phraya River, charging fares of 3 to 7 baht, a rock-bottom price, considering the convenience. The boats make frequent stops at regular landings, including the Oriental Hotel, the Royal Orchid Sheraton, the General Post Office, Tah Chang, Tah Prachan, Tah Rachawong and Tah Sapan Krung Thon.

PRACTICAL TIPS
Accommodation

In Bangkok, every imaginable type of accommodation can be found – from top class luxury hotels to the most economical guest houses. At the top end, all first-class hotels have tastefully decorated rooms, several dining and entertainment facilities, and most have shopping arcades, cocktail lounges, pubs, fitness centers, swimming pools, discotheques and high-class night clubs, business centers and conference facilities.

At the other end of the scale, backpackers may prefer economically priced guest houses, available in large numbers in the Kao Sarn Road area near Sanam Luang. Thailand's climate is hot, so it is recommended to rent a room, equipped with at least an electric fan. And make sure it is working before paying the rent. In Bangkok, apartments are available for rent on a short or long term basis. Some even offer daily rental. Upcountry, deluxe hotels or first-class resorts can be found at Chiangmai, Chiangrai, Pattaya, Rayong, Cha-am, Hua-Hin and Phuket. Other major towns around the country provide second-class standard accommodation, offering clean and comfortable airconditioned or fan-cooled rooms, and coffee shops.

The Guide Posts in the Travel Section list hotels in the different regions, but for completeness sake, we add here a short list of guesthouses and apartments, preferred by many young budget travelers and families:

Guest houses: Apple, 10/1 Phra Arthit Rd, Tel.281-6838; **Bangkok Christian**, 123 Saladaeng Soi 2, Convent Rd, Tel. 233-6303; **Bangkok Inn**, 155/12-13 Sukhumvit 11, Tel.254-4834/7; **Bangkok Youth Hostel**, 25/2 Phitsanulok Rd, Tel. 282-0950; **Ladda**, 21/38-39 Soi Ngam-dupli, Rama IV Rd, Tel.286-2069; **Mermaid's Rest**, 6/1 Sukhumvit 8, Tel. 253-5122; **Scout Hostel**, Physical Education Dept, Rama I Rd, Tel.215-3533; **Sunida**, 7/10 Sukhumvit Road, Tel.252-5565; **Sweety**, 49, Ratchadamnoen Klang Rd, Tel.281-6756. There are also numerous guest houses in the **Kao Sarn** area which charge from 60 to 300 baht per night.

Apartments (Minimum rates 240 B/day, 1,200 B/month): **Amara Court**, 645/44-51 Petchburi Rd, Tel.251-8980/1; **Grand Tower**, 23/1 Sukhumvit 15, Tel. 259-0380; **Krit Thai Mansions**, 931/1 Rama I Rd, Tel.215-0342; **K.T.**, 62-66 Buranasart Rd, Tel.224-4510; **Muang-phon Building**, 931/8-9, Tel.215-0034; **Ruamchit Mansions**, 1-15 Sukhumvit 15, Tel.251-6441/2; **Narai**, 5/7 Sukhumvit 53, Tel.258-7173; **Red Stone Apartments**, 11/1 Soi Thantawan, Surawongse Rd, Tel.236-0108; **S.T. Apartments**, 72/2 Soi Chantima, Nakhon Chaisi Rd, Tel.243-1107.

Banks

Banking services in Thailand, provided by Thai financial institutions and branches of foreign banks, are efficient, reliable and up-to-date. Most are equipped with the latest telecommunication facilities, enabling them to offer a wide range of overseas services. Banking hours are from 8:30 to 15:30, Monday through Friday.

There is no money black market in Thailand, and almost all foreign currencies and traveler checks can be exchanged conveniently at most banks, large hotels and authorized money changers throughout Bangkok. Most large banks, such as Bangkok Bank, Thai Farmers Bank and Krung Thai Bank have booths offering money exchange services after regular banking hours, often until 20:00 and on weekends.

Private authorized money changers display a large "Money Exchange" sign in front of their shops and, depending on the currency, give you a slightly better deal than the banks. Current exchange rates are listed at banks and in the financial section of English language newspapers. Note that exchange rates at hotels and some large restaurants, are usually inflated – in their favor.

There are 15 local and 14 foreign banks operating in Thailand, with 23 more having representative offices in Bangkok. The following is a list of the headoffices of the 20 major banks. Most Thai banks have numerous branches in Bangkok and the provinces. Two money-dispensing machine (ATM) networks operate throughout the country and may be used with international Visa cards.

Bangkok Bank, 333 Silom Road, Tel. 234-3333; **Bangkok Bank of Commerce**, 99 Surasak Rd, Tel. 234-2930; **Bangkok Metropolitan Bank**, 2 Chalermkhet 4, Tel. 223-0561; **Bank of America**, 2 Wittayu Rd, Tel. 251-6333; **Bank of Ayutthaya**, 550 Pleonchit Rd, Tel. 253-8061; **Bank of Tokyo**, Thanya

Bldg, 62 Silom Rd, Tel. 236-0119; **Banque Indosuez**, Kiang Kuan Bldg, 142 Wittayu Rd, Tel. 253-0106; **Chase Manhattan**, Siam Center, Rama I Rd, Tel. 252-1141/50; **Citibank**, 127 Sathorn Tai Road, Tel. 286-3392/4; **Deutsche Bank**, 21 Sathorn Tai Rd, Tel. 240-9401/22; **Hongkong & Shanghai**, Hongkong Bank Bldg, 64 Silom Rd, Tel. 233-1904/16; **Krung Thai Bank**, 35 Sukhumvit Rd, Tel. 255-2222; **Mitsui Bank**, 138 Boonmitr Bldg, Silom Rd, Tel. 234-3841/8; **Nakhornthon Bank**, 90 Sathorn Nua Rd, Tel. 233-2111/9; **Siam Commercial Bank**, 34 Phyathai Rd, Tel. 251-3114; **Standard Chartered Bank**, 946 Rama IV Rd, Tel. 234-0820/9; **Thai Farmers Bank**, 400 Paholyothin Rd, Tel. 270-1122/33; **Thai Military Bank**, 34 Phyathai Rd, Tel. 246-0020; **Union Bank of Bangkok**, New Petchburi Rd, Tel. 253-0488; **United Malayan Bank**, 149 Suapa Rd, Tel. 221-9191/5.

Bookshops

A number of good bookstores in Bangkok offer a comprehensive range of books on any imaginable subject. Books on Thailand, travel literature and maps are also available. Please note that foreign publications imported into Thailand are more expensive than in most other countries. The following stores carry an extensive range of publications:

Asia Books, 221 Sukhumvit Rd, Tel: 252-7277; also branches at Peninsula Plaza and Landmark Plaza; **DK Book House**, 244-6 Siam Sq., Tel: 251-6335/6; DK has many branches throughout town; **Nibondh**, 40-2 Charoen Krung Rd, Tel: 221-2611; **Odeon**, 218/10-2 Siam Sq., Tel: 251-4476.

Business Hours

Government departments and state enterprises are open from 8:30 to 16:30, Monday through Friday. Most private firms are open five days a week, usually from 8:30 to 17:00. Markets, shops and department stores are open every day of the week, some till as late as 21:00.

Business Traveler Information

The best place to obtain investment information is the Board of Investment (BoI) on Vibhavadee Rangsit Road (Tel:270-1400/23), which issues a wide range of informative publications and brochures. The BoI also maintains offices in Frankfurt, New York, Sydney and Tokyo.

Conference Facilities

As a convention center Thailand, has become wellknown throughout the world. A wide range of meeting, seminar and exhibition venues, to suit any requirement, may be booked in Bangkok, Pattaya, Hua Hin, Chiangmai and Phuket. Elegant conference rooms or exhibition halls, full support facilities, including secretarial services, experienced personnel, audio-visual equipment and simultaneous translation systems are readily available.

Most large hotels in Bangkok and up-country also offer business centers with secretarial services.

Credit Cards

Besides a number of only locally valid credit cards, the international issues of Visa, American Express, Master Charge and Diners Club, are widely used and are accepted in many restaurants, department stores, supermarkets and shops in Bangkok and the major tourist centers. Note that some stores and restaurants try to add a service charge when paying by credit card. In such a case, the offending establishment should be reported immediately to the appropriate representative office. Visa cards may be used to draw cash from most ATM machines all over the country.

Visa and **Master Charge**, Thai Farmers Bank, 400 Paholyothin Rd, Tel. 270-1259, 270-1122, ext.3751, (open

8:30-15:30, Mon – Fri); **American Express**, SP Bldg, Paholyothin Rd, Tel. 273-0033, (open 8:30-17:30, Mon – Fri); **Diners Club**, 11th Fl, Dusit Thani Bldg, 946 Rama IV Rd, Tel. 233-2645, (open 8:30 - 17:00, Mon - Fri).

Electricity
Electrical current in Thailand is 220 volt, 50 cycles. Different kinds of plugs and sockets are used throughout the country. In some upcountry areas, round sockets are still in use. Travelers are advised to carry a plug adapter kit. 110 V adaptors are available on request from large hotels.

Fresh batteries in all common sizes, to operate cameras, tape recorders, hearing aids etc., are available at most shops, all department stores and hotel drug stores. Batteries for digital watches and calculators can be purchased at watch shops and department stores.

Etiquette
Thailand may appear in some ways Westernised, but spiritually most Thais – especially the older generation – are conservative, religious and superstitious. Here are some Thai customs and traditions which should be observed, at least when in the company of elders and superiors.

When meeting, Thais don't shake hands. The traditional greeting is the *wai* – pressing the palms together at chest level and bowing the head until the nose touches the index fingers.

Thais usually address one another by first name only. They use the prefix *Khun* (Mr, Mrs or Miss) to show respect and good manners.

Buddha images are highly revered by Thais, so don't ever touch the head of a Buddha image. As a woman, you are not supposed to touch the image at all, unless it is a part of worship.

Women should avoid getting too close to Buddhist monks or novices. If you want to offer alms, let men do it for you.

Thais consider the head the highest and most respected part of the body. Touching or patting anyone on the head is a great insult, except between the very closest friends. Older persons may also touch the head of a small child to show fondness. At the same time, the feet are the lowest part of the body. Pointing at anyone with your foot is considered very rude. Using feet instead of hands to open or shut the door or to move things about is also bad manners.

Thais don't wear shoes inside the house. If you visit a Thai house, be sure to take off your shoes before entering. The same goes for temples.

Export of Art Objects and Antiques
It is prohibited to export Buddha images or fragments thereof for purposes other than worship by Buddhists, or for cultural exchange or study. Where permitted, a licence must be obtained from the Department of Fine Arts. For detailed information contact the National Museum, Tel. 224-1370.

Guides
Tour guides in many languages are available. Contact your hotel counter for details.

Newspapers / Magazines
There are two daily English language morning papers in Thailand, *The Bangkok Post* and the *Nation*, each selling for 10 baht. Both report local and international general, business and sports news. The *Bangkok Post* has about double the circulation of its rival and has twice won the "Best Newspaper in Asia" award.

The *International Tribune* and *Wall Street Journal* are available in the afternoon at better bookstores and hotels. All well-known international magazines are sold and many of the better known dailies in French, German, Italian, Spanish and

Japanese are available at the bigger hotels.

Postal Services

The General Post Office (GPO) offers efficient and reliable postal services at its head office on Charoen Krung Rd and branches throughout the country. Hours are Monday to Friday from 8:30 to 16:30, Saturday from 8.30 to 12:00. Telegraph services are available round-the-clock at the GPO head office.

Mail reaches Europe in four/five days and the US in one week or slightly more. Aerogrammes sell for 8.50 baht. Parcel wrappings are also provided by the GPO. Maximum weight limit for each parcel is 10 kg (22 lb).

Shopping

Thailand is one of the major retail and wholesale centers in Southeast Asia, with a firm reputation for having a dazzling assortment of locally made and imported products at competitive prices. Bangkok has a great many large shopping centers and deparment stores, offering fixed-price Western merchandise, and count-less fashionable boutiques, selling high quality ready-made garments, elegant fashion accessories, leather goods etc.

There are also many bargain-shopping places, the most frequently visited prob-ably being Pratunam on Rajprarob Rd, near the Indra Hotel, where more than 200 garment wholesalers, retailers and exporters are centered. Pahurat is a well-known shopping area for fabrics, fashion ornaments, jewelry and Indian fashion accessories. Adjoining Pahurat is Sam-peng and Chinatown, where just about anything is sold, at negotiable retail and wholesale prices. Another bargain shop-ping area is Banglampoo, not far from Sanam Luang.

Thai arts and crafts products, Thai silk, cotton and ready-made clothes, gems and jewelry, lacquer ware, pottery, ceramics, niello and bronze articles are sold at Naraiphand on Rajdamri Rd, and most shopping centers and hotels. When pur-chasing gems and jewelry, or other valua-ble items, it is safer to buy from outlets displaying the quality sign issued by TAT.

When shopping, never accept the first price quoted. Bargaining is not only com-mon, but expected. The exception is in department stores, supermarkets and those shops where fixed prices are shown on the merchandise. There are many de-partment stores throughout Bangkok, the following being only the better known ones.

Cathay, 263 Yaowaraj, plus four branches; **Central**, 306 Silom Road, plus four branches; **Siam Jusco**, 129 Rach-adapisek, plus two branches; **Sogo**, at Amarin Plaza, Ploenchit Road; **Robin-son**, 2 Silom Road, plus four branches; **Thai Daimaru**, Rajdamri and Phra-kanong; **The Mall**, Rajdamri and Ram-kamhaeng; **Tokyu**, at Mahboonkrong Shopping Center.

Telecommunications

Telephone: The Telephone Organization of Thailand (TOT) and the Communica-tions Authority of Thailand (CAT) pro-vide international telephone services to most countries around the world. Inter-national calls can be made easily, even from smaller hotels. Overseas calls may also be made at the General Post Office on Charoen Krung Road.

Public telephone booths are set up throughout Bangkok and all larger towns. In the metropolitan area, red public phone booths are for local calls and the blue ones for domestic long distance calls. Charges for local calls in Bangkok are 1 baht, with automatic cut-off after three minutes if a new coin is not inserted after the sound of a signal.

Although most public phones are adapted for use with the new, small 1-baht coin, some older ones will accept only medium-size 1-baht coins. To avoid any hassle, be equipped with both sizes.

The minimum charge for a domestic long-distance call is 5 baht. Read instructions on the machine before use.

Telex and fax: All first-class hotels, and many of the smaller ones, provide fax and telex services. Some small companies in most of the tourist centers also offer these facilities.

Television / Radio

Currently, there are five color television channels, broadcasting programs from stations in Bangkok and transmitting programs to all provinces via relays and sub-stations. Channel 3 is semi-private, Channels 5 and 7 are run by the military, Channels 9 and 11 are state-owned. All stations broadcast in Thai, with certain programes, such as international satellite news, Western movies and sport events, having an English soundtrack on FM bands. For programs and soundtrack details check the entertainment page in the Bangkok Post.

At present, there are some 155 radio stations in the country, broadcasting on AM, FM and shortwave. All AM broadcasts are in Thai, but some FM stations feature programs in English. On 97 MHz, Radio Thailand broadcasts local and international news in English from 7:00 - 8:00 and 12:10 - 12:30. Tourist information is broadcast daily at 6:40. Radio Bangkok on 95.5 MHz and Tor Tor Tor on 107 Mhz broadcast exclusively in English. For details, check the entertainment guide in the *Bangkok Post*.

Time

Thailand time zone is GMT plus seven hours.

Tourism

The Tourism Authority of Thailand (TAT) provides a complete range of tourism-related information: brochures on places of interest, Thai festivals, Thai culture, maps, lists of accommodation, etc.

TAT head office is located on Ratchad-amnern Nok Avenue, Tel. 282-1143/7, and is open on weekdays, during government office hours. TAT has eight regional offices: Kanchanaburi, Saeng Chuto Rd, Tel.(034) 511-200; Pattaya, Pattaya Beach Rd, South Pattaya, Tel.(38)418-750; Chiang Mai, 135 Praisanee Rd, Tel.(053)235-334; Phitsanulok, 209/7-8 Surasi Trade Center, Borommtrailokanat Rd, Tel.(055)252-742; Korat, 2101-2104 Mitrapap Rd, Tel.(044)243-427; Phuket, 73-75 Phuket Rd, Tel.(076)212-213; Hat Yai, 1/1 Soi Nipat Uthit 3 Rd, Tel.(074)243-747; Surat Thani, 5 Talat Mai Rd, Ban Don, Tel.(077)281-828.

TAT also maintains overseas branches in Kuala Lumpur, Singapore, Hong Kong, Tokyo, Sydney, Rome, Paris, Frankfurt, London, New York and Los Angeles.

Weights and Measures

Thailand basically uses the metric system, with some traditional terms adapted to decimal usage. Thus a *sok* is 50 cm, a *wah* – 2m, a sq. *wah* – 4 sq m and a *rai* – 400 sq *wah* or 1,600 sq m. Liters and kilograms are in common usage, but gold is measured in baht (15.2 gr). Temperature is expressed in degrees Celsius.

ADDRESSES
Airlines

Aeroflot, 153 Mezzanine, Regent House, Rajdamri Rd, Tel:251-0517/9; **Air France**, Charn Issara Tower, 942/51 Rama IV Rd, Tel:234-1333/9; **Air India**, 16th Fl, Amarin Tower, 500 Ploenchit Rd, Tel:256-9614/8; **Air Lanka**, Charn Issara Tower, 942/34-35, Rama IV Rd, Tel:236-4981; **Alitalia**, 8th Fl, Boonmitr Bldg, 138 Silom Rd, Tel:234-5253; **Biman**, Chongkolnee Bldg, 56 Suriwongse Rd, Tel:235-7643/44; **British Airways**, 2nd Fl, Charn Issara Tower, 942/81 Rama IV Rd, Tel:236-8655/8; **Burma Airways**, 208/1 Surawongse Rd, Tel:233-3052; **CAAC**, 134/1-2 Silom Rd, Tel:235-5250/4; **Canadian Airlines**,

6th Fl, Maneeya Bldg, 518/5 Ploenchit Rd, Tel:251-4521; **Cathay Pacific**, 5th Fl, Charn Issara Tower, 942/136 Rama IV Rd, Tel:233-0051; **Continental**, 5th Fl, Dusit Thani Bldg, Rama IV Rd, Tel:233-0568; **Delta**, 6th Fl, Central Bldg, 306 Silom Rd, Tel:235-0255; **Egypt Air**, 120 Kasemkij Bldg, Silom Rd, Tel:233-7601/3; **Finnair**, Maneeya Bldg, 518/2 Ploenchit Rd, Tel:251-5012; **Garuda**, 944/19 Rama IV Rd, Tel:233-0540; **Gulf Air**, 15th Fl, Maneeya Bldg, 518/5 Ploenchit Rd, Tel:254-8390; **Indian Airlines**, 2/1-2 Dejo Rd, Tel:233-3890/2; **Iraqi Airways**, 325-329 Silom Rd, Tel:233-5950/5; **JAL**, Wall Street Tower, 33/33-34 Surawongse Rd, Tel:234-9111; **KLM**, 2 Patpong Rd, Tel:235-5150/4; **Korean Air**, Rm 306, Dusit Thani Bldg, 946 Rama IV Rd, Tel:234-9288/9; **Kuwait Airways**, Ground Fl, New Bldg, 193 Saint Louis Soi 3, Sathorn Tai Rd, Tel:233-7950; **Lauda-Air**, 14th Fl, 33/67-68 Wall Street Tower, Surawongse Rd, Tel:233-2565/6; **LOT**, 485/11-12 Silom Rd, Tel:235-2223/7; **Lufthansa**, Pilot Bldg, 331/1-3 Silom Rd, Tel:234-1350; **MAS**, 98-102 Surawongse Rd, Tel:236-5871/5; **Northwest**, 4th Fl, Peninsula Plaza, 153 Rajadamri Rd, Tel:253-4423; **PIA**, 52 Surawongse Rd, Tel:234-2961/4; **Philippine Airlines**, 6th Fl, Chong Kolnee Bldg, 56 Surawongse Rd, Tel:233-2350/2; **Qantas**, Charn Issara Tower, 942/51 Rama IV Rd, Tel:236-0306; **Royal Brunei**, 2nd Fl, 942/52 Charn Issara Tower, Rama IV Rd, Tel:234-0007; **Royal Jordanian**, Ground Fl, 56 Yada Bldg, Silom Rd, Tel:236-0030; **Royal Nepal**, 1/4 Convent Rd, Tel:233-3921/4; **SAS**, 412 Rama I Rd, Tel:253-8333; **Sabena**, 11th Fl, CCT Bldg, 109 Surawongse Rd, Tel:233-2020; **Saudia**, Ground Fl, CCT Bldg, 109 Surawongse Rd, Tel:236-9402; **SIA**, 12th Fl, Silom Center, 2 Silom Rd, Tel:236-0303; **Swiss Air**, 1 Silom Rd, Tel:233-2930/4; **THAI**, 89 Vibhavadi Rangsit Rd, Tel:513-0121; TWA, 28/2-3 Sukhumvit 19, Tel:252-0664/7; **United**, 16th Fl, Regent House, Rajdamri Rd, Tel:251-6006.

Churches

Assumption Cathedral (Roman Catholic), 23 Oriental Avenue, Tel: 234-8666; Calvary Baptist Church, Soi 2 Sukhumvit Rd, Tel: 251-8278; Christ Church, (Anglican), 11 Convent Road, Tel: 234-3634, Holy Redeemer Church (RC), 123/19 Soi Ruam Rudee, Tel: 253-0305.

Embassies / Consulates

Argentina, 20/85 Prommitr Villa, Sukhumvit Rd, Tel. 287-2680; **Australia**, 37 Sathorn Tai Rd, Tel. 287-2680; **Austria**, 14 Soi Nantha, Sathorn Tai Rd, Tel. 286-3011; **Bangladesh**, 8 Sukhumvit Soi 63, Tel. 391-8069, **Belgium**, 44 Soi Pipat, Silom Rd, Tel. 236-0150, **Brazil**, 8/1 Sukhumvit 15, Tel. 252-6023, **Brunei**, 25/50 Orakarn Bldg, Chidlom Rd, Tel. 253-9126; **Burma**, 132 Sathorn Nua Rd, Tel. 234-4698; **Canada**, 11th Fl, Boonmitr Bldg, 138 Silom Rd, Tel. 234-1561; **China**, 57 Ratchadapisek Road, Tel. 245-7030-49; **Chile** (Cons), 15 Sukhumvit Soi 61, Tel. 391-4858; **Czechoslovakia**, 7th Fl, Silom Bldg, 197/1 Silom Rd, Tel. 234-1922; **Denmark**, 10 Soi Attakarn Prasit, Sathorn Tai Rd, Tel. 286-3930; **Dominican Republic** (Cons), 96/6 Chakrapaddipong Rd, Tel. 281-2600; **Egypt**, 49 Soi Ruam Rudi, Ploenchit Rd, Tel. 253-0161; **Finland**, 16th Fl, Amarin Plaza Tower, Tel. 256-9306; **France**, 35 Customs Lane, Charoen Krung Rd, Tel. 234-0950; **Germany**, 9 Sathorn Tai Rd, Tel. 213-2332/6; **Greece** (Cons), 412/8-9 Siam Square Soi 6, Tel. 251-5111; **Hungary**, 28 Soi Sukchai, Sukhumvit 42, Tel. 391-2002; **Iceland** (Cons), 59 Soi Nawin, Chuaphloeng Rd, Tel. 249-1300; **India**, 46 Sukhumvit 23, Tel. 258-0300; **Indonesia**, 600-602 Petchaburi Rd, Tel. 252-3135; **Iran**, 602 Sukhumvit Rd, Tel.

259-0611; **Iraq**, 47 Pradipat Rd; Tel. 278-5335/8; **Ireland** (Cons), 11th Fl, 205 United Flour Mill Bldg, Ratchawong Rd, Tel. 223-0876; **Israel**, 31 Soi Luang Suan, Ploenchit Rd, Tel. 252-3131; **Italy**, 399 Nang Lynchii Rd, Tung Mahamek, Tel. 287-2054; **Japan**, 1674/4 New Petchaburi Rd, Tel. 252-6151; **Jordan** (Cons), 47 Sukhumvit 63, Tel. 391-7142; **Korea (North)**, 51 Soi Aree, Paholyothin Rd, Tel. 278-5118; **Korea (South)**, 28/1 Surasak Rd, Tel. 234-0723; **Laos**, 193 Sathorn Tai Rd, Tel. 286-9244; **Malaysia**, 35 Sathorn Tai Rd, Tel. 286-1930; **Mexico** (Cons), 1 Yamaha Bldg, Din Daeng Rd, Tel. 245-1415; **Nepal**, 189 Sukhumvit 71, Tel. 391-7240; **Netherlands**, 106 Wireless Rd, Tel. 254-7701, **New Zealand**, 93 Wireless Rd, Tel. 251-8165; **Norway**, 20th Fl, Chokchai Bldg, 690 Sukhumvit Rd, Tel. 258-0531; **Oman** (Cons), 7th Fl, Asvinvichit Bldg, 134/1-2 Silom Rd, Tel. 236-7385; **Pakistan**, 31 Nana Nua, Sukhumvit Rd, Tel. 253-0288; **Peru** (Cons), Louis T. Leonowens Bldg, 723 Siphya Rd, Tel. 233-5910; **Philippines**, 760 Sukhumvit Rd, Tel. 259-0139; **Poland**, 61 Sukhumvit 23, Tel. 258-4112; **Portugal**, 26 Captain Bush Land, Charoen Krung Rd, Tel. 234-0372; **Saudi Arabia**, 10th Fl, Sathorn Thanee Bldg, 90 Sathorn Nua, Tel. 235-0875; **Singapore**, 129 Sathorn Tai Rd, Tel. 286-2111; **Spain**, 104 Wireless Rd, Tel. 252-6112; **Sri Lanka**, 48/3 Sukhumvit 1, Tel. 251-2788; **Sweden**, 138 Boonmitr Bldg, Silom Rd, Tel. 234-3891; **Switzerland**, 35 Wireless Rd, Tel. 253-0156; **Taiwan** (Cons), 19th Fl, Kian Kuan Bldg, 140 Wireless Rd, Tel. 251-9393; **Turkey**, 153/2 Soi Mahadlek Luang, Rajdamri Rd, Tel. 251-2987; **UK**, 1031 Wireless Rd, Tel. 253-0191l; **USA**, 95 Wireless Rd, Tel. 252-5040; **USSR**, 108 Sathorn Nua Rd; Tel. 234-9824; **Vietnam**, 83/1 Wireless Rd, Tel. 251-5835-6; **Yugoslavia**, 28 Sukhumvit 61, Tel. 391-9090.

Emergency

Police (Emergency), Tel: 191, 123
Tourist Police, Tel: 221-6206/10
Tourist Assistance Center, Tel: 282-8129, 281-5051
Ambulance, Tel: 252-2171/5
Fire Brigade, Tel: 199, 246-0199
Missing Persons Bureau, Tel: 282-3892

General

General Post Office, Charoen Krung Road, Tel: 233-1050, 224-9530
Immigration, 507 Soi Suan Plu, South Sathorn Road, Tel: 286-7013/4, 286-4231
Hua Lampong Railway Station, Rama IV Rd, Tel: 223-0341/8, 222-4171/83
International Airport Information, Tel: 523-6201, 531-0022/59
Domestic Air Terminal, Tel: 235-2081/3
Eastern Bus Terminal, Sukhumvit Rd, opp Soi Ekamai, Tel: 391-2504, 392-2521
North-Northeastern Bus Terminal, Morchit, Phaholyothin Rd, Tel: 279-4484/7
Southern Bus Terminal, Pin Klao Rd, Tel: 434-5557
Southern Aircon Bus Terminal, Charansanitwong Rd, Tel: 411-4978/9
Tourism Authority of Thailand (TAT), Ratchdamnoen Nok Avenue, Tel: 282-1143/7

Hospitals

Bamrungrad, 33 Soi Nana-nua, Sukhumvit Rd, Tel: 253-0250; **Bangkok Adventist**, 430 Phitsanulok Rd, Tel: 281-1422; **Bangkok Christian**, 124 Silom Rd, Tel: 233-6981/9; **Saint Louis Hospital**, 215 Sathorn Tai Rd, Tel: 212-0033/48; **Samitivej Hospital**, 133, Sukhumvit 49, Tel: 392-0011.

Telephone Assistance

Local telephone directory assistance, Tel: 13. Domestic long-distance information, Tel: 101. International directory assistance, Tel: 100. Time (recorded service), Tel: 181. Weather forecast, Tel: 258-2056.

GLOSSARY

ban	village, house
bang	place on the water
-buri	suffix meaning town
chedi	free-standing, mostly round, tapering religious structure, ending in a thin spire, often containing relics
chiang	town, in northern Thailand
doi	mountain, in northern Thailand
khao	hill or mountain
klong	canal
koh	island
mae nam	river
muang	town or city
nakhon	town or city
nam	water
nam tok	waterfall
phra	images of Buddha, also a Buddhist monk
prang	similar to a chedi, but bulkier and of Mahayana origin
sala	an open-sided covered meeting or resting place
sanam	an open piece of groung for meetings, parades etc.
soi	lane
songthaew	truck, small or large, converted to transport passengers
suan	garden, park
talad	market
tha rua	boat landing
thaleh	sea, ocean
tham	cave
tuk tuk	three-wheeled motorized rickshaw
viharn	the largest building in a temple compound
wat	Thai Buddhist temple

USEFUL THAI PHRASES

Thai is a tonal language with five different tones. It is impossible to give the correct pronunciation by using the Roman alphabet without auxiliary signs

I (men)	*pom*
I (women)	*di-chan*
you	*khun*
one	*nueng*
two	*sorng*
three	*saam*
four	*sih*
five	*hah*
six	*hok*
seven	*jed*
eight	*paed*
nine	*kao*
ten	*sib*
eleven	*sib ed*
twelve	*sib sorng*
thirty	*saam sib*
forty	*sih sib*
fifty	*hah sib*
sixty	*hok sib*
seventy	*jed sib*
eighty	*paed sib*
ninety	*kao sib*
one hundred	*nueng roy*
one thousand	*nueng pan*
ten thousend	*nueng muen*
hundred thousand	*nueng saen*
one million	*nueng laan*
Monday	*wan chan*
Tuesday	*wan ang-kan*
Wednesday	*wan pud*
Thursday	*wan prue-had*
Friday	*wan suk*
Saturday	*wan sao*
Sunday	*wan ah-tid*
go to	*pai*
come	*maa*
airport	*sanam-bin*
hotel	*rong-raem*
hospital	*rong-pa-ya-bahn*
road, street	*tanon*
lane	*soi*
restaurant	*ran-ah-haan*
railway station	*satanee rod-fai*
police station	*satanee tam-ruad*
to go shopping	*pai sue khong*
to go by boat	*pai tang ruea*
how much	*tao rai*
what's the name	*chue ah-rai*
slow down	*chaa chaa noi*
stop	*yud*
turn	*liew*

left	*saai*
right	*khwaa*
straight ahead	*trong pai*

Shopping

how much is this?	*an nee tao rai*
too expensive	*paeng pai*
can you lower the price?	*lod dai mai*
color	*see*
bigger	*yai kwa*
smaller	*lek kwa*
this one	*an nee*

Food

pork	*muh*
beef	*neua*
chicken	*kai*
duck	*ped*
fish	*plah*
shrimp	*kung*
crab	*puh*
egg	*khai*
boiled rice	*khao*
fried rice	*khao pad*
sticky rice	*khao niew*
rice noodles	*guay tiew*
wheat noodles	*ba mee*
water	*naam*
ice water	*naam yen*
ice	*naam kheang*
Chinese tea	*cha chin*
black coffee	*kafae dam*
hot tea	*cha dam rawn*
iced coffee	*kafae yen*
iced tea	*cha yen*
iced tea with lemon	*cha yen manao*
beer	*bia*
liquer	*lao*
chopstick	*ta-kiab*
plate	*jaan*
banana	*gluay*
pineapple	*sapparod*
orange	*som*
mango	*ma-muang*
papaya	*malakaw*
watermelon	*taeng moh*
asking for bill	*keb satang*

AUTHORS

Wayne Burns was born in 1946 in Saskatoon, Canada, and was a legal aid lawyer in Vancouver, B.C., for four years, before being posted by the Canadian Government first to Mali, West Africa, and then the Philippines. His writing career began in Japan, where he was a contributor to *The Tokyo Journal*, *Japanalysis* and the *Far Eastern Economic Review*. For the past five years he has lived in Thailand and lectures at Chulalongkorn University.

Mr Burns has traveled extensively within Thailand and writes frequently for several publications, including the *Bangkok Post* and the *Far East Traveler* (Tokyo). He is currently completing his first novel, set in Thailand.

Julius Gorman was born in England in 1962 and graduated from London University's School of African and Oriental Studies, where he studied the politics and geography of Southeast Asia. He first arrived in Thailand at the age of seven with his parents, and has since regarded Bangkok as home, even while away studying in England. Mr Gorman is a journalist working with the *Bangkok Post*.

Robert Halliday was born in New Jersey and received a master's degree in linguistics from Columbia University. He first came to Thailand 21 years ago and has made a name for himself in various fields. He has spent a considerable amount of energy and time in familiarizing himself with Thai food, cuisine and cooking, and anything connected with it. As a recognized authority, he has written extensively on the subject, and writes a weekly food column in the *Bangkok Post*.

John Hoskin was born in southwest England and studied at Birmingham University, where he received a master's degree in cultural studies. He began his career in journalism in London and has subsequently lived and worked in Sydney, Amsterdam and Hong Kong.

He moved to Bangkok in 1979 where he edited a number of travel and cultural magazines, before establishing himself as a freelance writer. He has written several books, including *Ten Contemporary Thai Artists, The Siamese Ruby* and the *Bangkok* and *Burma* titles in the Times Travel Library series.

Priyarat Lovisuth was born in Bangkok in 1957, graduated from Chulalongkorn University in liberal arts and received a master's degree in international relations after an 18 month research stint in Tokyo. She is a staff writer at the *Bangkok Post* and frequently contributes to international publications.

Acharawadi Muangsanit is a Bangkokian with a degree in audio-visual arts and mass communication from Ramkamhaeng University. Besides working as a staff writer and columnist for a popular Thai magazine, she freelances and has had her work published in several national publications.

Hardy Stockmann was born in Düsseldorf, Germany, and worked as a civil engineer in different parts of Africa, during which time he produced photo features for publication as a hobby. After some ten years he switched to a full-time career in photo-journalism. He has traveled in more than 70 countries and has had his work published in in Europe, America and Asia.

Coming to Thailand in 1967, he visited every corner of the kingdom and stayed. He is the author of *Muay Thai*, the most authoritative publication on Thailand's national martial art and has contributed to, revised and edited several publications, including guide books to most Asian countries. Mr Stockmann is an editor at the *Bangkok Post*.

Daniel Webster, a US citizen, was born in Canada 54 years ago. He graduated in journalism from the University of Oklahoma, USA, and received a juris doctor degree at Dallas, Texas, where he practised law for 15 years.

Living in Bangkok since 1984, Mr Webster is a senior staff writer at the *Bangkok Post* and spends his spare time conducting research for a novel.

Shada Bodhisundara was born in Bangkok and received her BA in liberal arts from Thammasat University. She studied journalism at Louisiana State University before returning to Thailand to pursue a writing career. She is working as a sub-editor for the *Bangkok Post* and had the unenviable task of compiling, checking and re-checking the data for the Guidelines section, a job, she handled with meticulous care.

PHOTOGRAPHERS

Beck, Josef — cover, 33, 42, 51, 76, 79, 102, 147, 198, 206, 223, 228, 229
Everingham, John — 16, 23, 34, 48, 82, 84, 107, 108, 120, 128, 149, 153, 161, 173, 192/193, 207, 211, 219, 220, 221
Höbel, Robert — 44, 75
Hörig, Rainer — 20, 60
Kaempf, Bernhard — 8/9, 21, 56/57, 58, 106, 131, 132, 137, 148, 151, 172, 175, backcovers(3)
Klein, Wilhelm — 88, 97, 112, 113
Kunert, Rainer E. — 14, 24, 116, 117, 164, 170, 171, 180, 195, 212/213
Luca Invernizzi Tettoni — 12/13, 37, 52, 61, 70, 85, 134, 140, 142, 159, 168, 176, 184, 186, 187, 190/191, 202, 214, 215, 216, 230
Maiocchi, Angelo — 105
Müller, Kai Ulrich — 1, 66, 81, 233
Nelles, Günter — 144
Radke, Volker W. — 18, 40, 43, 47, 71, 83, 119, 125, 133, 135, 150, 166, 196, 199, 204, 224, 226, 227, 231
Skupy, Hans Horst — 28, 38, 162
Steinhardt, Jochen — 2, 10/11, 25, 26, 27, 30, 31, 32, 36, 45, 49, 54/55, 64, 67, 74, 77, 78, 80, 92, 93, 94, 96, 99, 118, 122, 126, 154, 160, 217, 222
Stockmann, Hardy — 109, 208, 210, 232